ENGLISH THESAURUS FOR STUDENTS

Titles in the series

Companion volumes to this Thesaurus:

English Dictionary for Students	1-901659-06-2
English Workbook for Students	1-901659-11-9

Dictionary of Accounting	0-948549-27-0
Dictionary of Aeronautical English	1-901659-10-0
Dictionary of Agriculture, 2nd ed	0-948549-78-5
Dictionary of American Business	0-948549-11-4
Dictionary of Automobile Engineering	0-948549-66-1
Dictionary of Banking & Finance, 2nd ed	1-901659-30-5
Dictionary of Business, 2nd ed	0-948549-51-3
Dictionary of Computing, 3rd ed	1-901659-04-6
Dictionary of Ecology & Environment, 3rd ed	0-948549-74-2
Dictionary of Government & Politics, 2nd ed	0-948549-89-0
Dictionary of Hotels, Tourism, Catering Management	0-948549-40-8
Dictionary of Human Resources & Personnel, 2nd ed	0-948549-79-3
Dictionary of Information Technology, 2nd ed	0-948549-88-2
Dictionary of Law, 2nd ed	0-948549-33-5
Dictionary of Library & Information Management	0-948549-68-8
Dictionary of Marketing	0-948549-73-4
Dictionary of Medicine, 2nd ed	0-948549-36-X
Dictionary of Military Terms	1-901659-24-0
Dictionary of Printing & Publishing, 2nd ed	0-948549-99-8
Dictionary of Science & Technology	0-948549-67-X

Professional Series

Dictionary of Astronomy	0-948549-43-2
Dictionary of Multimedia, 2nd ed	1-901659-01-1
Dictionary of PC & the Internet, 2nd ed	1-901659-12-7

Workbooks

Check your:

Vocabulary for Banking & Finance	0-948549-96-3
Vocabulary for Business, 2nd ed	1-901659-27-5
Vocabulary for Colloquial English	0-948549-97-1
Vocabulary for Computing, 2nd ed	1-901659-28-3
Vocabulary for Hotels, Tourism	0-948549-75-0
Vocabulary for Law, 2nd ed	1-901659-21-6
Vocabulary for Medicine	0-948549-59-9

Visit our web site for full details of all our books

http://www.pcp.co.uk

ENGLISH THESAURUS FOR STUDENTS

Jim Green

PETER COLLIN PUBLISHING

First published in Great Britain 1999

Published by Peter Collin Publishing Ltd
1 Cambridge Road, Teddington, Middlesex, TW11 8DT

British Library Cataloguing-in-Publication Data

A catalogue record for this book is available from the British Library

ISBN 1-901659-31-3

Text computer typeset by PCP
Printed and bound in Finland by WSOY

PREFACE

This thesaurus is about choosing the right word so that you say or write exactly what you mean to say or write. The first and main part of this book includes words with their definition, example sentences, related and associated words. At the end of the book is an index listing all the words included in the thesaurus, cross-referenced to the main entry.

Entries are arranged alphabetically under main words such as **big**; after each main word we have included the how the word is used (the part of speech) - in this case, *adjective* - its meaning - of a large size - and then at least one example sentence to show how it is used: ***we had a big order from Germany***. If the example is followed by the symbol '⇨', the following words have the same meaning as the main word.

Entries that start with the '◊' symbol are words with associated meanings, similar to the main word. For example, under **big**, there are entries for the associated words ◊ **ample** and ◊ **colossal**.

Some words can have more than one meaning; in this case we indicate the different meanings using (i), (ii), (iii).

This thesaurus is for anyone who wants to use the right words and so write clear and accurate English. If you are not sure about a word, then look it up in the index and it will provide a cross-reference to an alternative word in the main part of the book.

This thesaurus has a companion dictionary for students that provides clear definitions to over 25,000 entries and covers the vocabulary required for all of the major English examinations: *English Dictionary for Students* (ISBN 1-901659-06-2), published by Peter Collin Publishing.

Aa

able

adjective having the force or cleverness to do something; ***he was such an able tennis player he rarely lost a game***; ⇨**competent;** ⇨**efficient**

◊ **capable** able to work well; ***she's an extremely capable secretary***

◊ **clever** intelligent, able to learn quickly; ***he is very clever at spotting bargains***

◊ **expert** good at doing something; ***I'm not very expert at making pastry***

◊ **gifted** with a special talent; ***he was a gifted artist***

◊ **powerful** very strong; ***he was such a powerful speaker he could persuade anyone***

◊ **qualified** with the right qualifications; ***she's a qualified doctor***

◊ **skilful** showing a lot of skill; ***these paintings must have been done by a skilful artist***

◊ **talented** with a lot of ability or skill; ***her playing was wonderful, she's a very talented pianist***

absent

adjective not there; ***the chairman was absent so no meeting was held***; ⇨**away**

◊ **missing** lost, which is not there; ***the police searched everywhere for the missing children***

accept

verb to say 'yes' or to agree to something; ***as you are the expert I accept you must be right***; ***she accepted the offer of a job in Australia***; ⇨**acknowledge;** ⇨**admit;** ⇨**agree**

◊ **abide by** to follow rules or orders; ***you must abide by the rules of the game***

◊ **assume (i)** to suppose something is true; ***let's assume that he is innocent*** **(ii)** to take on; ***he assumed responsibility for fire safety***

◊ **concede** to admit that someone is right; ***she conceded that this time she had been mistaken***

◊ **endorse** to show approval of; ***I heartily endorse what has just been said***

accurate

adjective correct in all details; ***we asked them to make an accurate copy of the plan***; ⇨**exact;** ⇨**precise**

◊ **correct** without fault or mistake; ***'Well done, all your answers were correct'***; ***do you know the correct time?***

adult

adjective fully grown (person or animal); ***adult gorillas can be very large***

◊ **mature** behaving like a grown-up person; ***she's very mature for her age***

adventure

noun new and exciting experience with the possibility of danger; ***I must tell you about our adventure in the Gobi Desert***

◊ **enterprise** plan for something new, often a business, which involves a risk; ***her latest enterprise may make her a great deal of money***

◊ **exploration** travelling and discovering unknown parts of the world; ***he is famous for his exploration of the Himalayas***

◊ **pilgrimage** journey to an important religious place for religious reasons; ***all Muslims should make the pilgrimage to Mecca at least once***

◊ **quest** search with a noble purpose; ***the knight set out on a quest to save the life of his friend***

advertise

verb to make sure that people know about something by display or broadcast; ***there are posters all over town advertising the circus***

◊ **announce** to say officially or in public; ***she announced the results of the competition to the crowd***

◊ **broadcast** to send out on the radio or TV; ***the programme will be broadcast on Monday at 8pm***

◊ **publicize** to attract people's attention to something; ***the advertising campaign was intended to publicize the work of the Tourist Board***

advise

verb to suggest what should be done; ***he advised her to put her money into a deposit account***; ⇨**counsel**

◊ **enlighten** to make someone understand something; ***will someone please enlighten me about what is happening?***

◊ **hint** to say something that makes people guess what you mean; ***she hinted that her sister was pregnant***

◊ **notify** to tell someone something formally; ***the doctor notified the hospital of the case of cholera***

◊ **recommend** to suggest that someone should do something; ***I recommend you see the bank manager about your money problems***

◊ **suggest** to mention an idea to see what other people think of it; ***might I suggest a visit to the museum this afternoon?***

◊ **urge** to advise someone strongly to do something; ***I would urge you to vote for the proposal***

◊ **warn** to inform someone in advance of danger or difficulty; ***the weather forecast warned of storms***

afraid

adjective to be frightened of something; ***I am afraid of snakes***; ⇨**fearful;** ⇨**frightened;** ⇨**scared**

◊ **aghast** amazed and very frightened indeed; ***I was aghast at how terrible the accident had been***

◊ **alarmed** worried and frightened; ***they were alarmed to see that their car was missing***

◊ **anxious** *or* **worried** very nervous and worried about something; ***she was very anxious about the baby's high temperature***

◊ **apprehensive** worried about the future; ***we are apprehensive about our daughter's safety***

◊ **nervous** worried and timid; ***she gets nervous when she is alone in the house at night***

◊ **terrified** very frightened; ***the inhabitants of the island are terrified that the volcano might erupt again***

again

adverb another time, once more; ***he wrote again to say he was ill***; ⇨**afresh;** ⇨**anew;** ⇨**ditto**

◊ **again and again** *or* **repeatedly** over and over, done many times; ***he kept on making the same mistake again and again***

agree

verb to say 'yes', to think the same way as someone; ***he nodded to show that he agreed***; ⇨**assent;** ⇨**concur;** ⇨**consent;** ⇨**have no objection**

◊ **acquiesce** to agree to something without protesting about it; ***the students asked to have the exam postponed and the teacher acquiesced***

◊ **accept** to say 'yes' or to agree to something; ***as you are the expert I accept you must be right***

◊ **approve** *or* **ratify** to agree to something officially; ***the committee approved the scheme***

◊ **comply** to agree to observe a rule or way of doing something; ***it will have to comply with EU regulations***

◊ **confirm** to say that something is certain; ***the dates of the concert have been confirmed by the pop group's manager***

agreement

noun

(a) thinking the same; ***we discussed the plan and they are in agreement***; ⇨**consent**

◊ **consensus** opinion which most people agree on; ***after much discussion the meeting reached a consensus on how to proceed***

◊ **harmony** general peace and agreement; ***they want to live in harmony with their neighbours***

◊ **understanding** private agreement; ***we reached an understanding with the lawyers***

◊ **unison** in total agreement; ***unions and employers must learn to work in unison***

(b) verbal or written arrangement binding on all parties; ***the agreement stipulated that all parties would wait three months before results were published***; ⇨**compact;** ⇨**contract**

◊ **bargain** agreed deal; ***to show we had made a bargain we shook hands***

◊ **pact** special agreement or treaty (often between countries); ***the ministers of the two countries signed the pact that pledged them to economic co-operation***

always

adverb every time, again and again; ***it always seems to rain when we want to go out for a walk***; ⇨**invariably;** ⇨**permanently**

◊ **constantly** *or* **incessantly** all the time; ***the telephone rang constantly all morning***

◊ **continually** almost all the time; ***the photocopier is continually breaking down***

◊ **endlessly** with no apparent end; ***the afternoon seemed to go endlessly, with one boring speech after another***

◊ **eternally** for ever; ***I shall be eternally grateful to you***

◊ **unceasingly** never stopping; ***the waves roared unceasingly through the night as the gale blew***

angry

adjective upset and annoyed, and sometimes wanting to harm someone; ***he is always angry if the post is late***; ⇨**annoyed**

◊ **bitter** angry and resentful; ***she was very bitter that the company had dismissed her***

◊ **cross** angry and annoyed; ***'please don't be cross, the children were only trying to help'***

◊ **displeased** unhappy and annoyed; ***she was most displeased that he had forgotten her birthday***

◊ **hurt** sad and upset; ***he was hurt that she didn't bother to thank him for his present***

◊ **incensed** *or* **irate** *or* **furious** very angry; ***he's furious because someone has scratched his new car***

◊ **indignant** feeling offended or angry; ***the manager came out to speak to the indignant shoppers who had been queuing for hours in the rain***

animal

noun living and moving thing (but usually not people); ***I have a dog and a cat at home - I like animals about the house***

◊ **amphibian** animal that lives both in water and on land; ***frogs, toads and other amphibians***

◊ **insect** small animal with six legs and a body in three parts; ***she was stung by a small flying insect***

◊ **livestock** domesticated farm animals which are reared to produce meat, milk or other products; ***mountain farmers move their livestock from place to place for new grazing***

◊ **mammal** type of animal which gives birth to live young and feeds them with milk; ***human beings, cats, dolphins and bats are all mammals***

◊ **pet** animal kept in or around the home to give pleasure; ***the family has several pets - two cats, a dog and a hamster***

◊ **reptile** cold-blooded animal, with a skin covered with scales, which lays eggs; ***tortoises and lizards are reptiles***

◊ **rodent** animal which chews and gnaws, such as a mouse, rat, etc.; ***the stems of the young trees were damaged by rodents gnawing them***

◊ **vermin** any animal, including insects, which is troublesome or does damage; ***we had to use a strong lotion to get rid of the vermin in his hair***; ***the farmer felt no pity about killing the vermin which killed his chickens***

annoy

verb

(a) to trouble or disturb someone or something; ***the constant noise of the traffic annoyed the man sitting in the park;*** **⇨aggravate; ⇨irritate; ⇨vex**

◊ **exasperate** to make very annoyed; ***the constant noise of the machine exasperates me more than you can imagine***

◊ **upset** to make someone worried or unhappy; ***I was upset by the bad news***

answer

noun reply, letter or conversation after someone has written or spoken to you asking you a question; ***have you had an answer to your letter yet?***; **⇨reply; ⇨response**

◊ **acknowledgement** reply to say that something has been received; ***she sent a letter of acknowledgement***

◊ **explanation** reason given for doing something or for something that has happened; ***the policeman asked for an explanation of why the stolen car was in his garage***

◊ **retort** sharp reply; ***'I don't need your help,' was her retort***

◊ **riposte** quick and funny answer; ***everyone laughed at her wonderful riposte to his silly question***

◊ **solution** the answer to a problem; ***the programmer finally came up with a solution to the computer problem***

answer

verb to reply or respond to a question; ***when he finally answered me I was able to understand what it was all about***; **⇨reply; ⇨respond**

◊ **acknowledge** to reply to say that something has been received; ***I am writing to acknowledge your letter of the 15th***

◊ **echo** to repeat exactly or say straight back; ***the newspaper article echoed the opinions put forward in the minister's speech***

◊ **rebut** to reject an argument or accusation; ***the minister easily rebutted the arguments for a change of policy***

◊ **retort** to reply sharply; ***he retorted angrily to the journalist's question***

appoint

verb to give (a job) to someone; ***he was appointed as manager***; ***she was appointed to the post of chief executive*** (NOTE: appoint to or as); ⇨**designate;** ⇨**engage;** ⇨ **hire**

◊ **assign** to give someone or something a particular function or job; ***the doctor was assigned to a post in the emergency department of the hospital***

◊ **enlist** to get someone to help; ***we enlisted our neighbours' help to cut down the tree***

◊ **recruit** to encourage someone to join (often the armed services) or take a job; ***we are recruiting staff for our new store***

armed forces

noun the military forces of a country; ***all the armed forces were under the control of the government***

◊ **airforce** a country's military air organization; ***American airforce combat planes***

◊ **army** all the soldiers of a country trained for fighting on land; ***he left school at 16 and joined the army***

◊ **guerrillas** soldiers who are not part of a regular national army; ***the guerrillas fought their way to the capital***

◊ **marines** soldiers serving in the navy; ***the ships carrying the marines arrived at the island***

◊ **mercenaries** soldiers paid to fight for foreign countries; ***he was one of a group of mercenaries hired to protect the president***

◊ **militia** emergency police force organized like an army; ***the governor called out the militia to deal with the riots***

◊ **navy** the armed forces of a country which fight on the sea; ***it is the duty of the navy to transport the army to where it is needed***

◊ **paramilitaries** people who are organized like the army but not part of it; ***the government used paramilitaries to put up road blocks in the area***

◊ **troops** soldiers; ***troops loyal to the government opposed the rebel troops outside the town***

arrive

verb to reach a place; ***the train arrived at the station right on time***

◊ **come** to move towards a place; ***come and see us when you are in London***

◊ **dock** *(of a ship)* to arrive in harbour; ***the ship docked at 17.00 hours***

◊ **touch down** *or* **land** *(of a plane or spacecraft)* to arrive by air; ***the plane touched down exactly on time***

artificial

adjective not real; ***she was wearing artificial pearls***

◊ **counterfeit** *or* **fake** not real but made to look real in order to deceive; ***the police have warned shopkeepers that counterfeit £20 notes are in circulation***

◊ **imitation** made to look like the real thing; ***you couldn't tell the difference between the leather shoes and the imitation plastic ones***

◊ **synthetic** man-made, not natural; ***the coat she was wearing was made of synthetic fur***

artist

noun person who paints, draws, etc.; ***he collects paintings by 19th century artists***

◊ **cartoonist** artist who draws humorous pictures; ***I want a cartoonist whose pictures will really make people laugh***

◊ **carver** artist who cuts stone, wood, etc., to create something; ***the carver sharpened his tools carefully before beginning to carve the wood***

◊ **couturier** person who designs expensive, fashionable clothes for women; ***all the Paris couturiers hold shows in the Spring***

◊ **craftsman** highly skilled worker who is expert at making good quality things by hand; ***the chair is beautifully made by a master craftsman***

◊ **designer** artist who plans the shape or appearance of goods, clothes, rooms, etc.; ***we've chosen an interior designer who we think will make the rooms really attractive***

◊ **engraver** craftsman who cuts patterns, letters, etc., on to hard surfaces; ***the engraver had the winner's name on the trophy within ten minutes of the result***

◊ **illustrator** artist who provides the pictures or drawings for books; ***the illustrator made the pictures simple and colourful for the children's book she was working on***

◊ **painter** person who paints pictures; ***he collects pictures by 19th century painters***

◊ **sculptor** person who makes figures or shapes out of wood, metal, stone or other materials; ***we visited the sculptor's studio and looked at his latest statue***

ask

verb to put a question; ***she asked the policeman the way to the hospital***; ⇨**inquire** (NOTE: also enquire); ⇨**request**

◊ **appeal** *or* **entreat** to make a serious request to someone; ***the police appealed for witnesses after the accident***

◊ **beg (i)** to ask for money or charity because of extreme need; ***the homeless man begged for money to get a bed for the night*** **(ii)** to ask someone in an emotional way to do something or to give something; ***his mother begged him not to leave home while he was so upset***; ⇨**beseech**; ⇨**implore**; ⇨**plead**

◊ **demand** to ask firmly for something; ***she demanded a refund***

◊ **invite** to ask someone to do something, especially attend a party or function; ***we invited two hundred people to the dance***

◊ **order (i)** *(usually by someone in authority)* to tell someone to do something; ***they ordered the protesters to leave the parliament building***; ***the doctor ordered him to take complete rest*** **(ii)** *(usually by a customer)* to ask for something to be served or to be sent; ***I have just ordered a new computer for the office***

◊ **persuade** to get someone to do what you want by explaining or asking; ***she managed to persuade the bank manager to give her the loan she needed***

◊ **require** to demand that someone should do something; ***you are required to fill in these forms before I can issue the certificate***

assistant

noun person who helps; ***his assistant prepares his materials next door***

◊ **adjutant** officer specially appointed to assist a commanding officer; ***he was very proud of his appointment as adjutant to the colonel of the regiment***

◊ **aide** assistant to an important person; ***the minister had come with two of his aides***

◊ **collaborator** *or* **co-worker** person who works alongside someone; ***I was her co-worker on that project***

◊ **colleague** person who works in the same company, office, school, etc., as you; ***his colleagues at the office gave him a present when he got married***

◊ **helper** person who helps; ***she works two mornings a week as helper in a playgroup***

◊ **partner** person who works in a business and has a share in it with others; ***she became a partner in the firm of solicitors***

avoid

verb to keep away from something or to try not to do something; ***he always travels early to avoid the traffic jams***; ⇨**eschew;** ⇨**shun**

◊ **abstain (from)** deliberately not to do something (especially not to vote); ***please abstain from smoking during the flight***

◊ **boycott** to refuse to deal with someone; ***so many people boycotted the store it had to close***

◊ **elude** to avoid being taken or captured; ***he eluded the police by wearing a disguise and changing the colour of his hair***

◊ **escape** to get away from prison or an unpleasant situation; ***he escaped from the dull party by claiming he had a headache***

◊ **put off** to arrange for something to take place later; ***we have put off the meeting until next month***

◊ **refrain** not to do something; ***I asked my guests to refrain from smoking while we were eating***

Bb

bad

adjective

(a) not good; ***eating too much and taking no exercise can quickly lead to bad health***

◊ **damaging** *or* **detrimental** which can cause harm; ***the detrimental effects of smoking are well-known to doctors***

◊ **deadly** causing death; ***the level of poisonous fumes in the air made it deadly for anyone without breathing apparatus***

◊ **destructive** which ruins completely; ***the destructive force of the earthquake destroyed most of the buildings***

◊ **dire** very serious indeed (and likely to lead to disaster); ***it was a dire situation for the people trapped by the flood waters***

◊ **dreadful** very bad; ***the wind and rain meant that everyone had a dreadful time on the walk***

◊ **pernicious** harmful; ***the pernicious remarks people repeated might have ruined his career***

◊ **ruinous** so expensive as to be unaffordable; ***the rent of fashionable houses in central London is ruinous***

(b) of poor quality; ***his shoes were so bad they wore out in no time at all***

◊ **awful** very bad; ***the programme was awful so we turned the TV off***

◊ **faulty** with mistakes or imperfections; ***we knew there was a faulty connection because the lights kept on flickering***

◊ **flawed** *or* **imperfect** containing mistakes or imperfections; ***we thought the report was flawed because some of the calculations were wrong***

◊ **shoddy** badly done; ***the workmanship in these shoes is so shoddy, they won't last a week***

◊ **substandard** not up to the usual or required standard; ***the quality control should remove all substandard products before anything is despatched***

◊ **useless** not fit for use, cannot be used; ***these scissors are useless, they won't cut anything***

(c) unpleasant; ***the bad smell from the farm nearly ruined the walk***

◊ **nasty** *or* **ghastly** *or* **horrible** *or* **loathsome** very unpleasant indeed; ***what ghastly wine, it tastes of soap!***

◊ **foul** *or* **obnoxious** offensive and unpleasant; ***his behaviour was so obnoxious we left the party***

◊ **revolting** disgusting, which makes you feel ill; ***I can't eat that revolting food, it makes me ill just to look at it***

◊ **sickening** which makes you sick; ***it's sickening to see so much food being wasted***

(d) *(usually of food)* which has lost freshness to the point of being unusable; ***the meat we bought yesterday has started to go bad***; ⇨**off** *(informal)*

◊ **past its sell-by date** beyond the date attached to food products which is the last date on which the food sold is guaranteed to be of suitable quality; ***don't use that, it's past its sell-by date***

◊ **putrid** *or* **rotten** in the later stages of decay; ***the food thrown onto the rubbish tip was so rotten it had begun to smell***

◊ **rancid** *(usually for dairy products or oils)* with a nasty taste or smell because it has gone bad; ***we knew the butter was rancid as soon as we tasted it***

◊ **stale** *(especially of bakery products)* old and no longer fresh; ***she threw the bread away because it had become stale***

(e) which causes harm or trouble and is regarded as wrong; ***he was a thoroughly bad man who broke the law when it suited him, careless of the harm he did***; ⇨**wicked**

◊ **criminal** referring to illegal acts; ***stealing is a criminal offence***

◊ **evil** very wicked; ***he was such an evil man that he was prepared to kill innocent people to get what he wanted***

◊ **mischievous** *or* **naughty** *(usually of children)* behaving badly or causing a nuisance; ***it was very naughty of you to put glue on your father's chair***

◊ **scandalous** which is shameful and wrong; ***it is scandalous that no one has removed the rubbish left in the school playground***

◊ **unjust** not fair; ***the decision was unjust, it was clear that he was not the winner of the race***

◊ **vicious** wicked and violent; ***the vicious attack left the victim in hospital***

◊ **vile** extremely unpleasant or bad; ***it was a vile evening, drizzly, cold, and with dense fog***

◊ **villainous** of an evil nature; ***the villainous landlord tricked the family so that he could throw them out of the house***

bag

noun container in which you can carry things; ***she put everything in a bag and carried it out of the house***

◊ **briefcase** thin case for carrying papers, documents, etc.; ***he put all the files into his briefcase***

◊ **carrier bag** large paper or plastic bag with handles, for carrying shopping, often given by a shop; ***he put the week's shopping into carrier bags when he went to the supermarket***

◊ **handbag** small bag carried to hold personal items; ***a robber snatched her handbag in the street***

◊ **haversack** *or* **rucksack** strong bag carried over your shoulders or on your back when walking; ***he packed some sandwiches and binoculars in a haversack and went off birdwatching***

◊ **holdall** soft bag for carrying clothes, etc., when travelling; ***he left the bus carrying a small holdall***

◊ **sack** large bag made of strong cloth or paper, used for carrying heavy things; ***he hurt his back trying to lift a sack of potatoes***

◊ **satchel** small leather or canvas bag carried on your shoulders (usually by schoolchildren); ***the schoolboy carried his books in his satchel***

◊ **suitcase** rectangular case with a handle used to carry clothes, etc., on a journey; ***they packed the two suitcases with clothes they would need when they went away for the weekend***

band

noun group of people who play music together; ***the dance band played all night***

◊ **backing group** group which plays music to accompany a singer; ***she sings with an Irish backing group***

◊ **brass band** group of players of mainly brass wind instruments; ***the factory had a brass band formed from a group of workers***

◊ **dance band** band which plays to accompany dancing; ***the hall was full because the dance band playing was so well-known***

◊ **group** people playing music together; ***she plays guitar in a pop group***

◊ **jazz band** band or group which plays jazz; ***there was a jazz band playing on the boat***

◊ **pop group** group of singers and musicians who play pop songs; ***he was lead singer in a 1980s pop group***

bank

noun business which holds money for its clients, which lends money at interest and trades generally in money; ***she took all of her money out of the bank to buy a car***

◊ **building society** organization which pays interest on deposits and lends money to people buying houses or flats; ***he put his savings into the building society***

◊ **credit broker** person who deals in arranging loans; ***they went to a credit broker to see if they could get a loan***

◊ **credit union** non-profit society in which members pay in money in order to be able to get loans; ***a credit union was the only way poor people could afford to borrow money***

◊ **finance house** business which sells loans to people who wish to make expensive purchases; ***he arranged the purchase of his car through a finance house***

◊ **merchant bank** bank which lends money to companies, not to people; ***a merchant bank put up the money to help them buy the business***

◊ **moneylender** person who lends money as a business; ***moneylenders charge a very high rate of interest***

◊ **pawnbroker** person who lends money in exchange for valuables left with him; ***families relied on the pawnbroker to help them through hard times***

beautiful

adjective very nice, especially to look at; ***the spring flowers were beautiful in the garden***; ⇨**attractive**

◊ **elegant** very fashionable and stylish; ***who is that elegant woman in the expensive black dress?***

◊ **exquisite** very finely made; ***the glass vase was of exquisite workmanship and very valuable***

◊ **good-looking** *or* **handsome** well formed, pleasant to look at; ***it wasn't surprising that her boyfriend was so good-looking, he was a film star***

◊ **gorgeous** very beautiful and splendid; ***the palace was a gorgeous piece of architecture***

◊ **lovely** very pleasant; ***it's a lovely warm day***

◊ **ornamental** pretty, decorative but not necessarily useful; ***the ornamental fountain was the central feature of the garden***

◊ **picturesque** *(of scenery, houses, etc.)* attractive, as in a picture; ***the picturesque view of the lake is often photographed by tourists***

◊ **pretty** *(used about girls and women but not men)* quite attractive; ***she looked so pretty in her party dress***

◊ **radiant** brightly attractive; ***the bride came out of the church with a radiant smile***

◊ **stylish** attractive and fashionable; ***she drives a stylish new sports car***

begin

verb to start; ***the referee began the game by blowing his whistle***

◊ **commence** *(formal) or* **establish** *or* **institute** to set up or create; ***the business was established in Scotland in 1823***

◊ **inaugurate** to open, officially, a new building, festival, etc.; ***the minister was invited to inaugurate the new computer system***

◊ **initiate** to start some project or process; ***a new library system has been initiated by the local authority***

◊ **originate** to make for the very first time; ***the character that he originated in his cartoon soon became famous***

◊ **pioneer** to be first to do something; ***the company pioneered developments in electronics***

Bible

noun Christian scriptures in two parts, the Old Testament (Jewish writings) and the New Testament (Christian writings)

◊ **gospel** four books in the New Testament of the Bible which tell the story of Jesus

◊ **New Testament** the second part of the Bible which deals with the life of Jesus, his teachings and the work of his followers

◊ **Old Testament** the first part of the Bible which deals with the origins and history of the Jewish people

big

adjective of a large size; ***their car is bigger than ours***; ***we had a big order from Germany***; ⇨**large**

◊ **ample** more than enough; ***we have ample funds to pay for the development programme***

◊ **bulky** awkwardly large; ***the bulky parcel was difficult for the postman to deliver***

◊ **colossal** *or* **enormous** *or* **gigantic***or* **immense** *or* **mammoth** *or* **massive** very large, huge; ***the company went bankrupt because of massive losses***

◊ **considerable** quite large; ***he was so rich he could afford to lose a considerable amount of money at the race track***

◊ **extensive** *or* **vast** very widespread, huge; ***the vast ranch seemed to go on for ever***

◊ **fat (i)** overweight; ***you'll get fat if you eat too many cakes*** **(ii)** excessive; ***he earned a fat salary for what was an easy job***

◊ **huge** very large indeed; ***huge waves battered the ship***

◊ **infinite** with no end; ***she never gets upset, she seems to have infinite patience***

◊ **king-size** a size much larger than normal; ***the king-size bed only just fitted into the bedroom***

◊ **limitless** without any boundary, which cannot be contained; ***the possibilities of the new drug seemed limitless***

◊ **monumental** very large and impressive; ***the company decided the headquarters must be suitably monumental to impress clients***

◊ **outsize** a larger size than normal; ***because he is so big he has to go to the outsize department for his clothes***

◊ **spacious** very large, with plenty of room; ***the spacious hall can easily accommodate two thousand delegates***

blame

verb to say that someone is responsible for a fault, error or accident; ***she said the accident could be blamed on the icy road surface***; ⇨**censure** *(formal)*

◊ **accuse** to say that someone has done something wrong; ***the police accused him of stealing the money***

◊ **criticize** to give an opinion of something or someone (often unfavourable); ***she criticized the sales assistant for not being polite***

◊ **disapprove** to give or have a poor opinion of someone or something; ***she disapproved of the young man because he looked dirty and untidy***

◊ **deplore** to say that you dislike an action or an attitude or that you are sorry that something has happened; ***the priest deplored the violence that had taken place***

◊ **rebuke** to criticize sharply; ***her attempts to force a vote earned her a quick rebuke from the chairman***

boat

noun small ship; ***they sailed their boat around the lake for the weekend***

(a) *(pleasure or private)*

◊ **canoe** boat that is moved by one or more people paddling; ***he paddled his canoe down the river***

◊ **dinghy** small boat with either oars or sails; ***we spent a day in the harbour sailing the dinghy***

◊ **launch** type of small motor boat; ***he took the launch out on to the lake***

◊ **rowing boat** small boat moved forward by oars; ***we hired a rowing boat and spent the day on the river***

◊ **yacht** **(i)** sailing boat used for pleasure and sport; ***the sails of the yachts as they raced in the channel were a beautiful sight*** **(ii)** large, luxury boat with a motor; ***we were invited to spend some time on her yacht cruising among the Greek Islands***

(b) *(commercial)*

◊ **coaster** ship which sails from port to port along the coast; ***coasters carried local cargo along the coast***

◊ **container ship** ocean-going ship designed to carry cargo already stored in commercial containers; ***the container lorries waited at the port to deliver their loads onto the container ship***

◊ **cruise liner** *or* **cruise ship** large passenger ship providing holidays at sea whilst visiting places of interest on the journey; ***the cruise liner went round the Caribbean***

◊ **factory ship** ship which can process fish caught by trawlers while still at sea; ***the factory ship sailed alongside the trawlers until they were ready to bring in their catches***

◊ **ferry** ship which carries people and vehicles to and fro across a stretch of water; ***the cars and trucks drove on to the ferry while the foot passengers boarded as it got ready to cross the Channel***

◊ **liner** large passenger ship; ***they travelled across the Atlantic by liner because they were not in a hurry and wanted to enjoy the voyage***

◊ **ship** large boat for carrying passengers or cargo on the sea; ***the first time we went to the USA we went by ship***

◊ **tanker** ship for carrying liquids, especially oil; ***only the biggest ports can take the huge oil tankers***

◊ **trawler** fishing boat which uses nets; ***the trawlers all came into the harbour to unload their catches***

◊ **tug** powerful boat which pulls other, bigger boats; ***two tugs helped the liner dock at the port***

(c) *(naval)*

◊ **battleship** *(not usually in service in most navies)* very large ship with banks of high calibre guns; ***the battleship was the biggest ship in the navy other than the carriers***

◊ **carrier** flat decked ship designed to carry aircraft; ***even the rough sea didn't stop the planes taking off from the carrier***

◊ **corvette** small ship usually equipped for escorting convoys or for anti-submarine service; ***the corvette hurried around the convoy carefully watching its progress***

◊ **destroyer** larger class of ship capable of carrying missiles or large guns; ***the destroyer lay outside the harbour beyond the smaller ships***

◊ **frigate** small fast-moving ship; ***he commanded a frigate during the wars against Napoleon***

◊ **minesweeper** ship designed to carry out mine clearance; ***the minesweeper lowered its cutting gear and began its sweep of the area***

◊ **submarine** ship which can travel on or under water; ***soon after the submarine left port it dived and continued under water***

book

noun sheets of printed paper attached together, usually with a stiff cover; ***I'm reading a book on the history of London***

◊ **album** large book usually containing a collection of something; ***we sat and looked through the photographs in the album***

◊ **anthology** collection of stories, poems, etc., usually by different writers; ***she is compiling an anthology of political speeches***

◊ **atlas** book of maps; ***can you find Montserrat in the atlas?***

◊ **biography** the story of someone's life; ***have you read the new biography of Churchill?***

◊ **blockbuster** very successful popular book; ***I read his latest blockbuster while I was on holiday***

◊ **booklet** *or* **pamphlet** small book with not many pages usually giving information; ***you will find booklets about the town at the Tourist Information Office***

◊ **classic** great book which is read by one generation after another; ***books by Dickens are classics of English Literature***

◊ **diary (i)** book in which someone writes their thoughts or records their lives day by day; ***she kept a diary every time she went on holiday and enjoyed reading it when she was at home*** **(ii)** small book in which you write notes or appointments for each day of the week; ***I've made a note of the appointment in my desk diary***

◊ **dictionary** book which lists words in alphabetical order, giving their meanings or translations into other languages; ***look up the word in the dictionary if you don't know what it means***

◊ **encyclopaedia** reference book (sometimes in many volumes) containing articles on all subjects, usually presented in alphabetical order, with an index; ***if you need to know something about planets look up the 'Astronomy' article in the encyclopaedia***

◊ **handbook** *or* **manual** book which gives instructions on how to use or repair something; ***look in the handbook to see if it tells you how to clean the photocopier***

◊ **log** book in which a daily detailed record is kept (as on a ship); ***the ship's log gave details of their position when the fire broke out***

◊ **monograph** specialist treatise on a particular subject; ***the professor's monograph on the results of his experiments caused considerable debate***

◊ **novel** long story with imaginary characters and plot; ***Pickwick Papers was Dickens' first major novel***

◊ **paperback** book, usually cheap, with a thick paper cover; ***the novel is in hardback at the moment but will come out as a paperback in the spring***

◊ **textbook** book used by students to get information or learn about the subject they are studying; ***which is the best maths textbook for the course we are going to do?***

◊ **thesaurus** reference book in which words are grouped, usually around a key word or idea, to help in the selection of the correct or most suitable word; ***don't keep on using the word 'like' - try to find another verb in your thesaurus***

◊ **tome** big book, of considerable length; ***the book she wrote on her family's history was so long it turned into a tome***

◊ **treatise** long piece of formal writing on a specialist subject; ***his treatise on heat is the foundation of our knowledge on the subject***

◊ **volume** one book, often one in a set or series; ***his best arguments are in the third volume of his series on medieval Europe***

◊ **who-dunnit** mystery novel, usually about a crime, which provides the solution to the mystery at the end of the novel; ***he didn't enjoy the who-dunnit because he had worked out who the murderer was long before the final chapter***

border

noun frontier between two countries; ***there was nothing to show they had crossed the border from France into Switzerland***; ⇨**frontier**

◊ **boundary** any line or marking which shows the outermost edge of any area and marks it off from other areas; ***the white fence marks the boundary between our land and his***

◊ **limit** furthest point or points beyond which you cannot go or beyond which things change significantly; ***we reached the limits of the agricultural land and moved on into the desert beyond***

brave

adjective full of courage; ***she was a brave woman to dive into the river and save the little girl***; ⇨**bold;** ⇨**courageous;** ⇨**gallant** *(old-fashioned)*; ⇨**heroic;** ⇨**valiant** *(old-fashioned)*

◊ **daring** taking a chance in a brave way; ***it was a daring thing to run back into the burning house and save the cat***

◊ **fearless** showing or feeling no sign of fear; ***the fearless lion tamer seemed quite calm among the lions***

◊ **indomitable** which cannot be beaten; ***his indomitable will to succeed made him a millionaire***

◊ **intrepid** very brave and fearless; ***she was an intrepid polar explorer who had been to the Arctic many times***

bridge

noun construction built over a road, river, etc., so that you can walk or drive from one side to the other; ***there are a dozen bridges across the Thames in London***

◊ **aqueduct** construction like a high bridge carrying water over a valley, etc.; ***we visited a Roman aqueduct in the south of France***

◊ **flyover** road which passes over another; ***from our car on the flyover we could see the traffic on the motorway below***

◊ **footbridge** small bridge for people to walk across, not for vehicles; ***to avoid accidents the children were told to use the footbridge over the road when they were on their way to school***

◊ **toll bridge** bridge where a charge is made in order to cross; ***the charge to drive across the toll bridge was well worth it because it saved driving all around the estuary***

◊ **viaduct** long bridge carrying a road or railway across a valley; ***the railway viaduct is still under repair and the trains must travel slowly as they travel across the valley***

build

verb to assemble and fit together materials into a structure; ***he built a perfect model of a plane from the materials he bought in the model shop***; ⇨**construct**

◊ **create** to build or make something which has not been made before; ***the scientists finally created a rocket capable of reaching the moon***

◊ **erect** to build something upright such as a mast or tall building; ***they are planning to erect a monument to the princess***

business

noun occupation, trade or commercial organization for making money; ***he's just got a job in an electronics business***

◊ **big business** very large commercial companies seen as a group; ***big business puts a lot of pressure on governments***

◊ **commerce** the buying and selling of goods and services; ***a trade mission went to South America to boost British commerce in the region***

◊ **cottage industry** very small-scale manufacture often carried out in the home; ***the production of local crafts for the tourists was done by just a few people in their homes as a cottage industry***

◊ **enterprise** business venture (sometimes indicating some risk involved); ***his latest enterprise is importing oriental carpets***

◊ **industry** manufacturing business (but can include other types of commercial activity); ***the tourist industry brings in a lot of foreign currency***; ***the country's coal industry is in decline***

busy

adjective occupied in working on something or doing something; ***she was busy repairing the washing machine***

◊ **active** energetic and involved in things; ***my grandmother is still active at the age of 88***

◊ **bustling** very busy and full of energy; ***the marketplace was bustling with the crowds of shoppers***

◊ **engaged** *or* **occupied** involved with a particular task; ***he was occupied in fixing the car when his guests arrived***

◊ **engrossed** totally interested in something; ***she was so engrossed in her book that she didn't hear him come in***

buy

verb to get something by paying money; ***what did you buy your mother for her birthday?***; ⇨**purchase**

◊ **bid (for)** to make an offer at an auction; ***his bid for the painting was too low and it went to another dealer***

◊ **bribe** to give an illegal payment to someone to get something; ***she planned to bribe an official to get her suitcase through customs unexamined***

◊ **hire** to pay money to use a car, boat, piece of equipment or other item for a time; ***he hired a car to get away for the weekend***

◊ **ransom** to pay money so that someone held captive is released; ***her family ransomed her for £1m***

Cc

calm

adjective quiet, not rough or excited; ***the calm sea was almost flat and the boat sat still, hardly moving***; ⇨**placid**

◊ **composed** quiet and settled; ***the accused man sat in the court and his composed manner showed he was not worried about the charges***

◊ **controlled** kept under order; ***she was so controlled she didn't scream when the spider crawled up her leg***

◊ **imperturbable** which cannot be disturbed or upset; ***his imperturbable nature meant he seemed not at all worried when his house burned down***

◊ **sedate** in a calm and dignified manner; ***the procession moved in a sedate way through the centre of the town***

◊ **serene** calm and unworried; ***she sat, serene, in the peace of her garden***

◊ **unruffled** not disturbed by events; ***he remained unruffled by the noise and rush about him***

capture

verb to take someone or something as a prisoner, to catch something in order to keep it; ***four soldiers were captured in the attack***

◊ **ambush** to wait hidden and attack or capture someone by surprise; ***the bandits ambushed the travellers as they went through the forest***

◊ **apprehend** *(formal) or* **arrest** to take someone for breaking the law; ***the police arrested the thieves and took them to the police station***

◊ **catch** to take after preparation or pursuit; ***she was able to catch the mouse by setting a trap in the kitchen***

◊ **seize** to grab something and hold it by force; ***the customs seized the drugs which were hidden in the lorry***

◊ **snare** *or* **trap** to capture or gain what is wanted by means of a device or plan; ***they snared three rabbits in the wood from the six traps they had set***

car

noun small private motor vehicle for carrying people; ***the family all got into their car and drove off on holiday***; ⇨**automobile**

◊ **convertible** car with a roof that folds back; ***it was such a glorious day, we lowered the roof of the convertible and enjoyed driving in the sun***

◊ **coupe** hard-topped two-seater car; ***she chose the coupe because it was safer than the open sports two-seater***

◊ **estate car** *or* **station wagon** *(American English)* car where the interior extends to the end of the car to provide flat carrying space behind the rear seats; ***we bought an estate car so the two dogs could travel with us in the back***

◊ **hatchback** type of car where the back opens up as a door; ***it is so much easier to put bigger things into the back of our hatchback than in the boot of a saloon car***

◊ **hearse** vehicle for carrying a coffin to and from funerals; ***the mourners followed the hearse to the cemetery***

◊ **jalopy** old car in poor condition; ***I bought the jalopy very cheaply but it broke down as soon as I drove it faster than 40 mph***

◊ **limousine** *(sometimes shortened to limo)* large luxurious car; ***when the film star got out of her limousine at the gala the crowds went wild***

◊ **racing car** car specially designed to be used in races; ***the racing car was designed to lap the track at speeds of over 120mph***

◊ **saloon** car with two or four doors designed to carry four or five people and with a boot (US trunk) for luggage at the rear; ***he preferred a saloon car so that anything valuable could be locked in the boot out of sight when the car was parked***

◊ **sports car** car specially designed for high performance on roads, usually for two people and often available as an open model; ***she does a lot of driving and she chose a sports car so she could travel fast and enjoy the speed***

◊ **taxi** *(also cab)* car with a driver which you can hire on the street or by phone; ***he stood by the busy road, waved his hand and a passing taxi pulled in and took him to the station***

◊ **tourer** well-equipped, comfortable car with a good performance designed for long journeys; ***they loved driving about Europe on holiday in their tourer***

careful

adjective with attention and effort so you are sure to get it right; ***we were so careful that no one heard us come in***; ⇨**cautious**

◊ **meticulous** very careful about all the details; ***she was a meticulous accountant and her figures were always correct***

◊ **painstaking** prepared to take great trouble and care in order to get it just right; ***he's such a painstaking worker - he's prepared to spend all the time necessary to restore the painting properly***

◊ **prudent** careful and taking no risks at all; ***it would be prudent to see a good lawyer before you sign the contract***

◊ **scrupulous** very careful and honest; ***she took scrupulous care of the money others gave her to invest and so her clients trusted her completely***

◊ **wary** careful, and on the look out for possible problems or difficulties; ***he had failed so often before that it made people wary of trusting him again***

carry

verb to move something to another place, to move, keeping something with you; ***she carried her handbag home and then threw it onto the chair***; ⇨**convey**; ⇨**transport**

◊ **bring** to move someone or something to this place; ***I will bring the money you want when I come tomorrow***

◊ **collect** to go and pick up something that is waiting; ***he took the car to collect his children from school***

◊ **ferry** to take people or things backwards and forwards between two places; ***they used buses to ferry the workers to the factory from the town and back again***

◊ **move** *or* **shift** to change the place of something; ***move the chairs to the other side of the room please***

◊ **relay** to pass on from one person to another; ***they relayed the message from station to station***

◊ **ship** to send goods (or people) but not always on a ship; ***we ship our products all over the world from our main warehouse***

◊ **transfer** to lift and move something to another place; ***she transferred the papers from the office safe to the bank***

castle

noun large building with strong defensive walls; ***the soldiers felt safe from their enemies as soon as they were in the castle***; ⇨**fortress**

◊ **citadel** fort or castle guarding a city; ***there is a magnificent view over the town harbour from the ramparts of the citadel***

◊ **fort** *or* **stronghold** strong building which can be defended against enemy attacks; ***the soldiers rode out of the fort***

celebration

noun activity which allows people to show and share their enjoyment of some special time or event; ***the party was a celebration of the end of the final exams***

◊ **ball** large formal dance, often to mark a special occasion; ***all the students got dressed up for the annual college ball***

◊ **banquet** formal public dinner for important guests; ***the Lord Mayor's banquet was one of the most important events in the town***

◊ **feast (i)** special religious day or celebration; ***the Patron Saint of Ireland is St Patrick and his feast is kept as a holiday*** **(ii)** very large meal; ***we had a feast in honour of the visiting team***

◊ **festival (i)** religious celebration which comes at the same time each year; ***the tour will visit Hong Kong for the Lantern Festival*** **(ii)** celebration or entertainment which is put on annually, on special occasions or at regular intervals; ***the church looked marvellous with all the displays during the annual flower festival***

◊ **party** private celebration, often in someone's house, to celebrate a special occasion or have a good time; ***we invited some friends to our house for a New Year's Eve party***

change

verb to make something different, to become different; ***London has changed very much since I last lived there***; ⇨**alter**

◊ **adjust** to make a slight change so that something fits or works better; ***if the trousers are too tight we can easily adjust the fitting***

◊ **convert** to change something from one form to another; ***we converted our pounds into Swiss francs***

◊ **disguise** to alter the appearance of someone or something so it is no longer recognised; ***she disguised herself as someone much older in order to leave the country without being stopped***

◊ **distort** to change someone's ideas or words so that they lose their true meaning; ***the newspaper report distorted his speech so much that he decided to sue the paper***

◊ **modify** to change or alter something so as to fit a different use; ***the management modified its wage proposals to fit in with new government guidelines***

◊ **transform** to change the appearance of something or someone completely; ***the new front transformed the shop from being dull and uninteresting to the most spectacular building in the whole street***

cheap

adjective which does not cost a lot of money; ***if you want a really cheap radio you need to shop around***; ⇨**inexpensive**

◊ **economical** which saves money or resources; ***she bought an economical car which didn't use much petrol because she wanted to save money***

cheat

verb to break the rules or act dishonestly in order get what you want or gain an advantage; ***he cheated by taking notes into the exam room with him***

◊ **con** *(informal)* to trick someone, by gaining their trust, in order to cheat them; ***they used false papers when they conned the bank into lending them £25,000***

◊ **deceive** to make someone believe something which is not true; ***he was able to deceive the householders into thinking he was a policeman by wearing a uniform***

◊ **defraud** to use false information or materials in order to steal or cheat; ***he misrepresented himself as an insurance salesman and defrauded the old lady of quite a lot of money***

◊ **fiddle** (informal) to record money transactions in a dishonest way; ***he fiddled his expense account so much that he was finally caught and fired***

◊ **swindle** to get money from somebody by a trick; ***he swindled the old lady out of her savings***

check

verb to make sure by examining; ***did you lock the door? I will go and check***

◊ **audit** to check accounts officially; ***when they audited the accounts they found they were very well kept indeed***

◊ **examine** to inspect something to see if it is healthy or in good order; ***the water samples were examined for traces of pollution***

◊ **inspect** to look at something closely; ***the kitchens are regularly inspected to ensure good hygiene***

◊ **investigate** to study or examine something to solve a problem; ***the detective investigated the case by studying the evidence which had been collected***

◊ **scrutinize** to examine very carefully indeed; ***she was known to be dishonest so the inspectors always scrutinized her accounts fully***

cheque *or US* check

noun note to a bank asking for money to be paid from one account to another; ***I paid for the jacket by cheque***

◊ **credit card** plastic card which allows you to borrow money and to buy goods without paying for them immediately; ***I bought a fridge and put it on my credit card***

◊ **IOU** paper promising that you will pay back money which you have borrowed; ***she gave him an IOU for £10***

◊ **money order** document which can be bought for passing money from one person to another through the post; ***I want a money order for £100 made payable to Mr Smith***

◊ **postal order** order to pay money, which can be bought and cashed at a post office; ***he enclosed a postal order for £10***

◊ **travellers' cheque** *or US* **travelers' check** cheque which you can buy at a bank before you travel and which you can then use in a foreign country; ***the hotel will cash travellers' cheques for you***

choose

verb to pick someone or something you like best or that will do the best job; ***they chose the best player as captain of the team***; ⇨**pick**

◊ **adopt (i)** to take, legally, as a son or daughter; ***they have adopted two boys*** **(ii)** to take, formally, as your own; ***they adopted him as candidate at the coming elections***

◊ **co-opt** to bring in as a member by the votes of those who are already members; ***the committee co-opted the accountant because they needed someone who could sort out the club's finances***

◊ **elect** to choose by voting; ***the Member of Parliament was elected by a very small majority of votes***

◊ **nominate** to name as the preferred choice; ***she nominated her sister for the position but the other members would not accept her choice***

◊ **reserve** to order for use at a later date; ***he reserved two seats at the theatre for the performance the following night***

◊ **select** to choose carefully; ***she selected her smartest outfit for the interview***

◊ **vote for** to show by marking a paper, holding up your hand, etc., which one you choose in an election; ***more people voted for the winning candidate than for all the other candidates put together***

church

noun building where Christians hold religious services and go to pray; ***each Sunday morning there were two services in the village church***; ⇨**kirk** *(Scottish)*

◊ **abbey** religious establishment founded for or used by monks or nuns; ***the ruins of Fountains Abbey in Yorkshire are very beautiful***

◊ **cathedral** large church which is the seat of a bishop; ***the bishop of St David's has his cathedral in the smallest city in the United Kingdom***

◊ **chapel (i)** part of a large church with a separate altar; ***there is a chapel dedicated to St Teresa on the west side of the cathedral*** **(ii)** small church building used by members of the dissenting denominations; ***there are a great number of chapels all over Wales***

◊ **Meeting House** the place used for religious meetings by Quakers; ***Quakers go to the Meeting House for Sunday worship***

◊ **minster** great church of a former monastery, although no monks may be attached to it today; ***you must visit York Minster, it is one of the most beautiful churches in England***

◊ **mosque** building where Muslims meet for prayer; ***the call to prayer at the mosque comes three times a day***

◊ **pagoda** tall tower of several storeys, each with a projecting roof, used as a temple; ***we saw many worshippers at the beautiful pagoda which we visited on our holiday in Korea***

◊ **temple** name of the building used for worship by various religions including Hindus, Sikhs and Buddhists; ***the Hindu temple was in the middle of the city***

city

noun large town; ***the cities of Detroit and Munich are both big car manufacturing centres***

◊ **borough** town or part of a very large city which is run by its own elected councillors; ***the borough council is responsible for the state of the roads***

◊ **capital** the city in which the government of a country is based; ***London is not only England's main city it is also the capital***

◊ **hamlet** settlement of only a few houses or buildings; ***the hamlet was marked on the map but it was so small that we missed it as we drove along the road***

◊ **port** town which has a harbour; ***the port of Liverpool is busier now than it has been for some years***

◊ **suburb** residential area on the outskirts of a town; ***he lives in a quiet suburb of Boston***

◊ **town** place where many people live and work, with industry, commerce, shops, schools, etc.; ***we chose to locate the office in the country town because it was not as big as a city but still had good communications with the capital***

◊ **village** place where people live, smaller than a town; ***the village was quite big but still didn't have good shopping facilities***

clean

verb to make free from dirt or any other unwanted matter; ***remember to clean your teeth each morning***; ⇨**cleanse** *(formal)*

◊ **dry-clean** to clean clothes or other fabric items using chemicals not water; ***when we collected the coat that had been dry-cleaned it filled the car with the smell of chemicals***

◊ **dust** to clean places (especially surfaces) from dust; ***don't forget to dust the china ornaments carefully***

◊ **polish** to rub something to make it shine; ***he polished his shoes until they shone***

◊ **purify** to make free of unwanted substances, to make pure; ***these tablets can be used to purify the water before you drink it***

◊ **rinse** to wash through with water only, especially to remove the soap after washing; ***rinse the soap off the dishes before you put them out to dry***

◊ **scrub** to clean with a hard brush and water, usually also with soap; ***the butcher scrubbed the table to remove all traces of meat or blood***

◊ **spring-clean** to clean a room or house very thoroughly, often after the winter; ***it took me nearly a week to spring-clean the flat***

◊ **sweep** to clean a floor or steps, etc., with a dry brush; ***have you swept the kitchen floor yet?***

◊ **tidy** to make everything neat and in order; ***I want you to help me tidy the house after the party***

◊ **wash** to clean using water; ***cooks should always wash their hands before touching food***

clean

adjective not at all dirty; ***I asked the waiter for a clean glass as the one I had been given had some marks on it***

◊ **hygienic** which is clean and free of germs; ***we decided not to eat at the restaurant as the kitchen didn't look at all hygienic***

◊ **immaculate** perfectly clean and tidy; ***the nurses all wore immaculate white uniforms***

◊ **polished** *or* **shiny** so clean that it is bright and reflective; ***the table top was so highly polished he could see his face reflected in it***

◊ **spotless** very clean, without any marks; ***he cleans his kitchen every day, it is spotless***

◊ **sterile** free from bacteria, microbes or infectious organisms; ***the nurse put a sterile dressing on the wound***

clever

adjective intelligent, able to learn quickly; ***she is very clever at spotting bargains and saving money***; ⇨**brainy;** ⇨**bright;** ⇨**intelligent**

◊ **able** having the force or cleverness to do something; ***he was such an able tennis player he rarely lost a game***

◊ **astute** *or* **shrewd** *or* **smart** clever, especially at spotting an advantage or opportunity; ***it was a smart move to sell those shares before they fell so badly***

◊ **brilliant** extremely clever; ***she is a brilliant student, easily the cleverest in the class***

◊ **capable** able to work well; ***she's an extremely capable secretary***

◊ **discerning** having good judgement; ***he was a discerning collector and had many fine pieces in his collection***

◊ **expert** good at doing something; ***I'm not very expert at making pastry***

◊ **gifted** with a special talent; ***he was a gifted artist***

◊ **skilful** showing a lot of skill; ***these paintings must have been done by a skilful artist***

◊ **talented** with a lot of ability or skill; ***her playing was wonderful, she's a very talented pianist***

◊ **wise** having knowledge and good sense; ***it was a wise decision to cancel the trip when you saw the weather forecast***

close

verb

(a) to shut; ***I had to close the window because it was getting too cold***

◊ **bolt** to close and fasten with a bolt; ***he bolted the door before he went to bed***

◊ **lock** to close a door, safe, box, etc., so that it has to be opened with a key; ***I lock the safe every day before leaving the office***

◊ **seal** to close something tightly; ***the box was carefully sealed with sticky tape***

◊ **secure** to make safe, to attach firmly; ***secure all the doors and windows before the storm comes***

◊ **slam** to shut with force causing a bang; ***the door slammed shut in the high wind***

(b) to make something come to an end; ***he closed the meeting by insisting that a vote be taken***; ⇨**complete**; ⇨**finish**

◊ **conclude** to end, to bring to an end; ***he concluded his speech by thanking everyone who had helped***

◊ **finalize** to put the finishing touches to something; ***we hope to finalize the agreement tomorrow so it can be signed***

◊ **terminate** to bring to an end, to finish; ***the offer terminated yesterday so we can't take advantage of it now***

coast

noun the land by the sea; ***after ten weeks at sea Columbus saw the coast of America***

◊ **beach** area of sand or pebbles by the edge of the sea; ***let's go to the beach today, the weather is fine***

◊ **coastline** the line of a coast; ***the coastline of Cornwall is mostly very rocky***

◊ **seaboard** the country bordering the sea; ***the states of the eastern seaboard of America are among the oldest***

◊ **seashore** the land immediately beside the sea including land covered by tides; ***she walked along the seashore to look at the things the tide had washed up onto the beach***

coat

noun piece of clothing which you wear on top of other clothes when you go outside; ***you will need to put on a coat, there's a cold wind blowing***

◊ **anorak** waterproof jacket with a hood; ***you need a very good anorak for mountain climbing in winter***

◊ **cloak** long loose outer covering which hangs from your shoulders and has no sleeves; ***she wore a long cloak of black velvet over her dress***

◊ **mac** *or* **macintosh** *or* **raincoat** coat which keeps off water, which is worn when it is raining; ***I folded up a plastic mac and put it in my bag in case it started to rain***

◊ **overcoat** thick outdoor coat which you wear over other clothes; ***you need to wear an overcoat, it's starting to snow***

cold

adjective with a low temperature; not hot nor heated; ***you may get cold weather in England at Christmas but it doesn't often snow***

◊ **chilled** made cold; ***he asked for a glass of chilled orange juice because it was a hot day***

◊ **chilly** quite cold; ***even summer evenings can be quite chilly in the mountains***

◊ **cool** without any heat, with the heat gone out of it; ***the evening was pleasantly cool after the heat of the day had gone***

◊ **freezing** *or* **frozen** very cold indeed, below freezing point; ***I was frozen waiting for you at the bus stop***

◊ **icy** covered with frozen water; ***she slipped and fell on the icy pavement***

◊ **raw** cold and damp (usually of weather); ***the raw wind made the day very uncomfortable for anyone outside***

◊ **wintry** cold like winter; ***turn up the heating, they are forecasting more wintry weather tonight***

collect

verb to gather together into a group; ***he collects old golf clubs but he never uses any of them when he is playing golf himself***; ⇨**gather**

◊ **accumulate** to steadily gather together over a period of time; ***her deposit account accumulated interest and eventually grew into quite a good amount***

◊ **amass** to collect in great quantities; ***he amassed a huge pile of information before he started to write the book***

college

noun teaching institution (for adolescents and adults); ***she's studying accountancy at the local college***

◊ **academy** college where specialized subjects are taught; ***she wanted to be a musician so she applied for a place at a music academy***

◊ **school** place where students, usually children, are taught; ***our little boy is four so he will be starting school soon***

◊ **seminary** college (usually Roman Catholic) for the training of priests; ***the seminary in Rome where older Catholic men study for the priesthood is called the Beda***

◊ **staff college** military college which trains officers for staff appointments; ***he was very proud when the senior officer told him he had been selected for staff college***

◊ **theological college** college where people study to be priests; ***she spent four years in a theological college before being sent to a parish in South London***

◊ **university** highest level of educational institution which gives degrees and where a wide range of subjects are taught; ***after he got his first degree he stayed at the university to study for a master's degree***

◊ **university college** college, which with others, makes up a university; ***she got a place at King's College, London, while her older brother was studying at Queen's College, Oxford***

complain

verb to say that something is no good or does not work properly; ***he complained about the very slow service in the restaurant***; ⇨**grumble**

◊ **blame** to say that someone is responsible for a fault, error or accident; ***she said the accident could be blamed on the icy road surface***

◊ **criticize** to give an opinion of something or someone (often unfavourable); ***she criticized the sales assistant for not being polite***

◊ **protest** to take action to show you do not approve of something; ***the crowd had gathered to protest against the increasing price of food***

◊ **whine** to complain in a weak and continuous way; ***he whined on about the poor wages but never looked for another job***

container

noun something in which goods are kept for storage or transport; ***there's a row of containers on the kitchen shelf with all the things I need frequently when cooking***

◊ **bottle** tall plastic or glass container for liquids; ***she bought two bottles of red wine***

◊ **box** container made of wood, plastic, metal, etc., with lid; ***the baker put the cakes into a box***

◊ **carton** container made of cardboard; ***a carton of yoghurt***

◊ **case** large box for goods; ***he bought a case of twelve bottles of wine***

◊ **crate** large rough wooden box; ***the goods arrived safely packed in a crate***

◊ **cylinder** metal tube used to hold gas; ***the divers carried oxygen cylinders on their backs***

◊ **locker** small cupboard for storing personal belongings which you can close with a key; ***she put her clothes in the locker in the changing rooms and went off for a swim***

◊ **safe** strong box with a very secure locking system for keeping valuable things; ***put your valuables in the hotel safe***

◊ **tank** large container for liquids; ***the firemen were very worried that the flames might reach the oil tank***

◊ **trunk** large box for storing or sending clothes, etc.; ***they sent a trunk of clothes in advance to the hotel***

control

verb to keep in order, to direct or restrict; ***the police were out in force to control the crowds***

◊ **administer** *or* **direct** *or* **manage** to be in charge of the running of something; ***we want to appoint someone to manage our operations in Europe***

◊ **govern** **(i)** to rule (usually a country); ***the country is governed by a military ruler*** **(ii)** to influence or have an effect on; ***a person's health is often governed by what they eat***

◊ **limit** *or* **restrict** not to allow something to go beyond a certain point; ***the government has limited the number of new motorways which can be built***

◊ **prohibit** to say that something must not be done; ***the rules prohibit singing in the dining room***

◊ **regulate** to control by using rules or laws; ***speeds are strictly regulated on all classes of roads***

◊ **restrain** to try and stop someone doing something; ***it took six policemen to restrain the man who became violent***

◊ **supervise** to watch carefully to see that work is done well; ***she supervises six trainee receptionists***

◊ **suppress** to not allow to continue; ***all opposition newspapers have been suppressed***

cook

verb to get food ready for eating, especially by heating it; ***I decided to cook a very special meal for our anniversary***

◊ **bake** to cook in an oven, especially bread and cakes; ***mum is baking a special cake for my birthday***

◊ **barbecue** to cook on a metal grill, usually out of doors; ***we weren't able to barbecue the meat because it started to rain and we had to come indoors***

◊ **boil** to cook in boiling water; ***we boiled the small potatoes for about five minutes then served them with some butter***

◊ **fry** to cook in oil or fat in a shallow pan; ***fry the onions on a low heat so they don't burn***

◊ **grill** to cook quickly using direct strong heat; ***if we are having fish I prefer to have it grilled***

◊ **roast** to cook over a fire or in an oven; ***if you want the meat thoroughly cooked, roast it for a longer period at a lower temperature***

◊ **stew** to cook for a long time in liquid; ***stew the apples until they are completely soft***

◊ **stir-fry** to cook vegetables or meat quickly in hot oil while rapidly stirring; ***stir-fry the vegetables separately, not all together***

copy

verb to make something which looks exactly like something else; ***to make the pullover just copy this pattern***; ⇨**duplicate;** ⇨**reproduce**

◊ **forge** to make a copy in order to pass it off as an original; ***he forged the signature on the cheque and presented it at the bank***

◊ **imitate** to try to produce the same style, behaviour or sound, etc., of someone or something; ***he made us all laugh by imitating the teacher's walk***

◊ **photocopy** to copy using a machine which scans the original; ***we were busy photocopying the page from the book when the machine broke down***

◊ **trace** to copy a drawing, etc. by placing a sheet of transparent paper over it and drawing on it; ***she traced the map and put it into her project on the history of the village***

◊ **transcribe (i)** to re-write a piece of music for a different instrument than the one for which it was originally written; ***the piece was originally written for the violin but was transcribed for piano*** **(ii)** to write out the text of something which is heard; ***his speech was transcribed from the radio tape and distributed to the journalists***

copy

noun something made to look the same as something else; ***this is a very good copy of a painting by Picasso***; ⇨**duplicate**

◊ **facsimile** perfect reproduction or a perfect copy; ***he had a framed facsimile of a page from the ancient Book of Kells on his wall***

◊ **replica** copy made to look just like the original; ***this is a replica of a Colt 45 handgun but it doesn't fire bullets***

◊ **reproduction** copy (usually of a painting or drawing); ***the art book had some wonderful reproductions of the paintings of the period***

country

noun

(a) land which is separate and governs itself; ***the African countries voted against the plan***

◊ **nation** land which is separate; ***the member nations of the international organization***

◊ **state** independent country; ***you can travel freely from one member state of the European Union to another***

(b) land which is not part of a town; ***we live in the country and come to town to do our shopping***

crime

noun illegal act or acts; ***the crime he was charged with was breaking and entering***; ⇨**offence**

◊ **capital offence** offence for which the death penalty can be given; ***the crime of treason is still a capital offence in some countries***

◊ **felony** crime classed as serious; ***he was told that felonies usually resulted in a prison sentence***

◊ **misdemeanour** crime classed as a less serious crime; ***as he was only charged with a misdemeanour his case was heard by a magistrate not by a judge and jury***

criminal

noun person who commits a crime (especially someone who lives by committing crime); ***he was a criminal who had been known to the police since he was a young man***

◊ **blackmailer** person who demands money by threatening to reveal a scandal or do some sort of harm; ***the blackmailer demanded £20,000 to keep silent about the man's criminal record***; ***the blackmailer contacted the store, asking for £2m by the following day***

◊ **confidence trickster** *(also conman)* person who tricks people to get money by making them believe something; ***some confidence trickster got her to sign the papers***

◊ **fence** person who receives and sells stolen goods; ***the thief took the jewels to a fence who paid him just a small part of what they were really worth***

◊ **forger** person who copies something in order to pass it off as original; ***the police arrested the forger who had been printing the £20 notes***

◊ **housebreaker** thief who breaks into houses to steal things; ***the police arrested the housebreaker as he came out of the house carrying the owners' money and valuables***

◊ **kidnapper** someone who steals a child, person or animal and makes demands for their return; ***the kidnappers demanded £1m for the return of the little girl***

◊ **mugger** person who attacks and robs someone in the street; ***the muggers were caught sharing out his money in the next street***

◊ **murderer** person who has committed a deliberate, illegal killing; ***the murderer was sentenced to life imprisonment***

◊ **pickpocket** person who steals things from people's pockets; ***racecourses are a favourite place for pickpockets to operate***

◊ **robber** person who attacks and steals from someone; ***the robbers attacked the bank in broad daylight***

◊ **swindler** person who gets money from somebody by a trick; ***the swindler got into the old lady's house and cheated her out of all her savings***

◊ **thief** person who steals; ***the police think they will catch the thief who stole the painting***

cure

verb to make a patient or disease better; ***that medicine is good, it cured my cough very quickly***

◊ **alleviate** to make less painful; ***she was given an injection to alleviate the pain***

◊ **heal** to become healthy again; ***after six weeks the wound finally healed***

◊ **remedy** to correct something, to put something right; ***he had to go on a strict diet to remedy the damage done by years of over-eating***

◊ **revive** to bring back signs of life (to a person); ***the paramedics managed to revive her on the way to hospital***

◊ **treat** to deal with injuries or illnesses in order to cure them; ***the injured people were treated in hospital after the accident***

cure

noun something which makes an illness better; ***doctors are still waiting for a quick cure for the common cold***

◊ **antidote** substance which counteracts the effect of a poison; ***there is no satisfactory antidote to cyanide***

◊ **medicine** drug taken to treat an illness; ***the chemist told me to take the medicine four times a day to cure my cough***

◊ **palliative** something which gives temporary relief from pain or discomfort; ***the drug was just a palliative and the pain soon returned***

◊ **prescription** order written by a doctor to a pharmacist asking for a drug to be prepared and sold to a patient; ***this medicine is only available with a prescription***

◊ **remedy** thing that may cure; ***my grandmother knew an old remedy for hayfever***

◊ **therapy** treatment of a patient to help cure an illness or condition; ***they use heat therapy to treat muscular problems***

◊ **treatment** the way injuries or illnesses are dealt with in order to cure them; ***the treatment for skin cancer is very painful***

cut

verb to separate or open using something with a sharp edge; ***there were six children so she cut the cake into six pieces***

◊ **amputate** to cut off an arm, leg, finger or toe; ***his leg was so badly injured they decided that they would have to amputate***

◊ **carve (i)** to cut up meat into slices or pieces; ***he asked the butcher to carve him six slices from the joint of cooked meat*** **(ii)** to cut stone, wood, etc. to create something; ***he carved a bird out of wood***

◊ **chop down** to cut down a tree, etc. with an axe; ***he was sad to have to chop down the old apple tree but it was almost dead***

◊ **chop up** to cut into small pieces with an axe or knife; ***chop the vegetables up into little pieces***

◊ **gash** to make a deep cut; ***she gashed her foot badly on the broken bottle in the sand***

◊ **hack** to chop roughly; ***he hacked at the bushes and finally cleared a path***

◊ **sever** to cut off; ***the machine severed his arm at the elbow and he was rushed to hospital***

◊ **slash** to make a long quick cut with a knife; ***he slashed the painting with a kitchen knife***

◊ **slice** to cut into thin, flat pieces; ***he sliced the bread to make the sandwiches***

◊ **slit** to cut a narrow opening; ***he slit open the envelope and took out the letter***

Dd

damage

verb to harm something; ***a large number of shops were damaged by the fire***; ⇨**harm**

◊ **break** *or* **smash** to make something come apart by using force; ***she dropped the plate and it broke into pieces on the floor***

◊ **demolish** to knock down completely; ***we demolished the old church and built a new one***

◊ **destroy** to ruin completely; ***the bomb destroyed several buildings***

◊ **disable** to make someone or something unable to function properly; ***a fire in the engine room disabled the ship***

◊ **erode** to wear away gradually; ***the sea has eroded the cliffs so that buildings on top are now in danger***

◊ **hurt** *or* **injure** to cause pain, to damage; ***it hurt him when the book fell on his foot***

◊ **impair** to damage something so that it will not work properly; ***constantly working with a loud machine has impaired his hearing***

◊ **shatter** to break into little pieces; ***he knocked the glass vase onto the floor where it shattered all over the carpet***

◊ **weaken** to lose or take away the strength of something; ***he was very weakened by the disease***

dangerous

adjective which can cause harm, injury or damage; ***be careful, that loose carpet on the stairs is dangerous***; ⇨**hazardous;** ⇨**risky;** ⇨**unsafe**

◊ **insecure** not safe, not firmly fixed; ***be careful, that scaffolding looks insecure, it may fall down***

◊ **menacing** *or* **threatening** behaving in a frightening and dangerous way; ***'give me your money,' said the robber in a threatening voice***

◊ **precarious** not safe, likely to fall off; ***the house is in a precarious position on top of the cliff***

◊ **treacherous** dangerous, but not looking dangerous; ***the sea is treacherous because there are rocks just under the surface***

◊ **unstable** not to be relied upon to hold together; ***we can't use the unstable platform because many of the fastenings are worn and it might give way***

dark

adjective with little or no light; ***the sky turned dark and it started to rain***

◊ **dim** *or* **dull** not bright or distinct; ***the light became dim as the dark clouds filled the sky***

◊ **murky** dark and dirty; ***the police searched the murky waters of the harbour***

◊ **opaque** which you cannot see through clearly but does allow some light to come through; ***the windows were opaque to prevent anyone looking inside***

◊ **overcast** dull and cloudy; ***it has been overcast all afternoon but at least it hasn't rained***

◊ **sombre** dark and gloomy; ***the report gave a sombre picture of the country's economic future***

day

noun period of time lasting 24 hours, period from morning until night, when it is light; ***there are 365 days in a year***; ***he works all day in the office, and then helps his wife with the children in the evening***

◊ **afternoon** time between lunchtime and the evening; ***she always has a little sleep in the afternoon***

◊ **dawn** *or* **daybreak** beginning of a day, when the sun rises; ***we must set off for the Pyramids at dawn, so you will have to get up very early***

◊ **evening** late part of the day, when it is getting dark; ***I saw her yesterday evening***

◊ **midday** *or* **noon** twelve o'clock in the middle of the day; ***we'll stop for lunch at noon***

◊ **midnight** twelve o'clock at night; ***I must go to bed - it's after midnight***

◊ **morning** first part of the day before 12 o'clock; ***every morning he took his briefcase and went to the office***

◊ **night** part of the day when it is dark; ***it's dangerous to walk alone in the streets at night***

dead

adjective not alive any more; ***dead fish were floating on the surface of the water***; ⇨**deceased** *(only people)*

◊ **defunct** *(not people)* no longer functioning; ***the club lost all of its members and became defunct***

◊ **extinct** which has died out completely; ***three kinds of butterfly have become extinct in the last year alone***

◊ **inanimate** without life or having had life; ***he looked at the inanimate rocks and wondered how they had been formed***

◊ **lifeless** not alive; ***her lifeless body was washed up on the shore***

difficult

adjective not easy, which is hard to do; ***the maths examination was very difficult, half the class got low marks***; ⇨**hard**

◊ **arduous** needing a lot of effort or work; ***the work is very arduous so it is not surprising that not many people want to do it***

◊ **awkward** difficult to do or use; ***I couldn't reach the handle because it was in such an awkward position***

◊ **demanding** which takes up much time and energy; ***he may be well paid but that is because it is such a demanding job***

◊ **formidable** frighteningly difficult; ***climbing Mount Everest is a formidable challenge***

◊ **laborious** involving a lot of work; ***it was a laborious job moving the pile of sand round to the back of the house***

◊ **tiring** which makes you tired; ***after a tiring day at the office all I want to do is sit down and rest***

◊ **troublesome** which causes problems or difficulties; ***she still can't get rid of that troublesome cough***

dig

verb to turn over soil (usually for planting) or make a hole in the ground; ***he's been digging in the garden all morning***

◊ **burrow** to dig a tunnel into the ground (usually of animals); ***the rabbits have burrowed under that bank***

◊ **excavate** to dig out or uncover by digging; ***in order to make sure the foundations were strong enough they excavated to a depth of 10m***

◊ **mine** to dig coal, etc. out of the ground; ***they mine for gold in the south of the country***

◊ **plough** to turn over the soil to prepare it for planting crops; ***some farmers still like to plough at least one field using horses instead of tractors***

◊ **tunnel** to dig a long passage underground; ***the prisoners escaped by tunnelling under the wall***

diplomat

noun person who represent their government abroad; ***the diplomats met one another informally at receptions held at different embassies***

◊ **ambassador** the senior representative of one country in another country; ***His Excellency, the French Ambassador***

◊ **chargé d'affaires** diplomat representing the department of foreign affairs of a country's government or holding a representative position on a temporary basis; ***the chargé d'affaires dealt with the tourist who had got into difficulties***

◊ **emissary** person sent with a message or to act on someone's behalf; ***emissaries of the rebel forces had talks with the government representatives***

◊ **envoy** person sent officially by one country to another; ***she was the United Nations envoy to the area***

◊ **High Commissioner** ambassador of a Commonwealth country; ***the Canadian High Commissioner in London***

◊ **nuncio** ambassador from the Vatican; ***the nuncio was the only ambassador who was also an archbishop***

dirty

adjective not clean; ***when he fell in the muddy puddle he got very dirty***

◊ **dusty** covered with dust; ***the dusty old attic had been empty for a very long time***

◊ **filthy** very dirty indeed; ***the filthy rubbish tip gave off an awful smell***

◊ **foul** bad and unpleasant; ***the water had become foul because of the rotting rubbish lying in it***

◊ **grimy** with the dirt well rubbed in; ***the dirty little boy held out a grimy hand and asked for money***

◊ **messy** dirty or disorderly; ***making pottery by hand is a messy business***

◊ **muddy** full of or covered with very wet earth; ***after the heavy rains the rivers were all very muddy***

◊ **polluted** damaged having harmful materials put into it; ***the polluted beaches were covered in oil from the damaged tanker***

◊ **squalid** unpleasant and dirty; ***the refugees were housed in squalid conditions which led to the outbreak of disease***

◊ **tarnished** *(of metal)* discoloured by contact with the air, dirt, water, etc.; ***the tarnished silver shield was cleaned and put on display***

disaster

noun great and sudden misfortune or accident; ***we are insured against natural disasters such as hurricanes and earthquakes***; ⇨**calamity**

◊ **cataclysm** *or* **catastrophe** very great disaster; ***the earthquake was a catastrophe coming, as it did, so soon after the hurricane***

◊ **tragedy** very unhappy event; ***it was a tragedy for the family when the mother was killed in a car accident***

discussion

noun talking about a serious matter or problem; ***the programme included a discussion between environmental experts***

◊ **argument** talk in which people disagree; ***she had an argument with her husband over where to go on holiday***

◊ **debate** formal discussion often following set rules; ***after the lecture a debate had been organized for the students***

◊ **conversation** informal talk between two or more people; ***I had a conversation with my neighbour about the state of the road outside our houses***

◊ **negotiation** talks where two or more sides in a dispute try to find a solution acceptable to everybody; ***the negotiations continued between the government and the rebels but a solution seemed unlikely***

dislike

verb not to like; ***I dislike it when people behind me at the cinema start whispering***

◊ **despise** to think that someone is not worth much; ***I despise people who always agree with the boss even when he is wrong***

◊ **detest** to dislike very much; ***I detest people who say one thing to your face and say something quite different to other people***

◊ **hate** *or* **loathe** to dislike intensely, to dislike with a powerful passion; ***I hate going to the dentist because I always think it will hurt***

◊ **resent** to feel annoyed because of a real or imaginary hurt; ***we resent the idea that the company has tricked its customers into spending more than they needed to***

dismiss

verb to remove someone from a position or job; ***she was dismissed for being late at work so many times***; ⇨**fire**; ⇨**sack**

◊ **disqualify** to make someone no longer able to do or take part in something; ***after being found guilty of two driving offences he was disqualified from driving***

◊ **exclude** to shut someone or something out; ***women were excluded from staying in the monastery***

◊ **expel** **(i)** to send a child away from school for bad behaviour; ***she was expelled from school for having drugs*** **(ii)** to throw someone out; ***as soon as the generals came to power they expelled all their former allies***

◊ **give notice** to inform someone that you intend to terminate their employment; ***the company gave notice to all the employees and the factory was closed***

distant

adjective far away; ***we could hear the sound of distant gunfire***; ⇨**faraway**; ⇨**remote**

◊ **inaccessible** impossible to reach or to get to; ***the valley is inaccessible to motorists***

disturb

verb to break into someone's routine or activity causing a nuisance; ***the loud knock at the study door disturbed him as he was writing***

◊ **agitate** to cause someone worry or upset; ***the bad news about the accident agitated all the people waiting at the airport***

◊ **bother** *or* **pester** to annoy or cause trouble; ***stop bothering me - I'm trying to read***

◊ **harass** to continually bother and worry someone; ***they harassed him with constant phone calls until he finally paid the bill***

◊ **interfere** to become involved in something when you are not wanted; ***her mother is always interfering in her life***

◊ **trouble** to cause a nuisance to someone; ***he was constantly troubled by bad dreams***

◊ **upset** to make someone worried or unhappy; ***I was upset by the bad news***

doctor

noun person qualified to treat people who are ill; ***I have a ten o'clock appointment to see the doctor about my bad toe***; ⇨**physician**

◊ **dentist** person qualified to take care and treat problems with teeth; ***I go to the dentist every six months to have a checkup on my teeth***

◊ **faith healer** person who heals by the power of prayer; ***when she found that the doctors couldn't help her she went to a faith healer***

◊ **GP (General Practitioner)** family doctor who does not specialize in any particular branch of medicine; ***if you feel unwell go to your GP and he will advise you what to do***

◊ **hospital doctor** doctor who works mainly or completely in a hospital; ***he wanted to specialize so he got a job as a hospital doctor***

◊ **psychiatrist** doctor who studies and treats mental illness; ***she seems to have lost all grip on reality, she needs to see a psychiatrist***

◊ **psychologist** person who studies the human mind; ***psychologists have developed a new theory to explain why some people get depressed***

◊ **surgeon** doctor who specializes in performing operations; ***for the surgeon the operation to remove the appendix was just routine***

◊ **vet** someone qualified to treat sick animals; ***the farmer called for the vet as soon as he saw the cow was unwell***

doubt

noun not being sure; ***I try to believe all the government tells me, but sometimes I have doubts about what they say***; ⇨**uncertainty**

◊ **agnosticism** the belief that it is impossible to know whether God exists or not; ***agnosticism sounds easy but a constant state of doubt about God is sometimes very uncomfortable***

◊ **disbelief** surprise at something you find unable to believe; ***she stared at the letter of dismissal in complete disbelief***

◊ **hesitation** pause caused by doubts; ***after a moment's hesitation he dived into the cold swimming pool***

doubtful

adjective not sure; ***I am doubtful about whether we have enough money to pay for such an expensive holiday***; ⇨**dubious;** ⇨**questionable;** ⇨**uncertain**

◊ **ambiguous** which has two meanings, which is unclear; ***as it stands, the phrase is very ambiguous, I would like it made clearer***

◊ **hesitant** in an undecided or unsure way; ***the baby took a few hesitant steps and then sat down***

◊ **problematic** likely to cause problems or difficulties; ***the relationship between the unions and management remained problematic during the dispute***

◊ **sceptical** unwilling to believe something; ***you seem to be sceptical about his new plan***

draw

verb to make a picture with a pen or pencil; ***she drew a picture of the house***

◊ **copy** to make something which looks exactly like something else; ***to make the pullover just copy this pattern***

◊ **design** to draw plans for the shape or appearance of something before it is made or built; ***he designed the new university library***

◊ **doodle** to make drawings without any meaning; ***he doodled on his writing pad all through the boring lecture***

◊ **illustrate** to do the drawings needed for a book; ***he illustrated the children's book with line drawings***

◊ **sketch** to make a quick, rough drawing; ***he sketched out his plan on the back of an envelope***

drink

verb to swallow liquid; ***he drank two glasses of water after his long walk***; ⇨**consume** *(also used for food)*

◊ **gulp** to swallow quickly; ***she gulped her drink and ran to catch her bus***

◊ **sip** to drink, taking only a small amount of liquid at a time; ***the boy sipped his drink as he waited for the girl to arrive***

◊ **suck** to pull liquid into your mouth; ***she sucked the orange juice through a straw***

◊ **swig** to drink in large mouthfuls; ***they stopped walking and swigged large amounts of water from a bottle***

◊ **toast** to take a drink in celebration of someone or something; ***everyone in the room raised their glasses and toasted the guest of honour***

duty

noun the work or behaviour which you feel must be done; ***he felt it was his duty to write a letter to his mother each week***

◊ **allegiance** being loyal; ***she swore an oath of allegiance to the new president***

◊ **liability** legal responsibility; ***make sure you understand what your legal liabilities are before you sign the contract***

◊ **loyalty** the faithfulness and support given to someone or some cause; ***all the staff should show their loyalty by coming to the reception***

◊ **obligation** duty to do something; ***you have an obligation to attend the meeting if you are a good member of the club***

◊ **responsibility** anything which you are in charge of; ***the safety of all the cars in the car park was the responsibility of the security officer***

Ee

eat

verb to chew and swallow food; ***if you eat the right food it will help you to stay healthy***

◊ **consume** *(also used for drink) or* **devour** *(formal)* to eat greedily; ***the lions devoured the pieces of meat***

◊ **dine** *(formal)* to have dinner; ***we normally dine at 8.30***

◊ **feed** to eat or to give food to others or to animals; ***let's go to the park and feed the ducks***

◊ **gobble** to eat greedily; ***he gobbled up his dinner***

◊ **gorge** to eat too much; ***look at her gorging herself on cakes***

◊ **nibble** to take small bites; ***the mice had nibbled into the flour sacks***

◊ **taste** to try something to see if you like it; ***he asked if he could taste the cheese before buying it***

engine

noun machine which powers or drives something; ***the lift engine has broken down - again we will have to use the stairs***

◊ **diesel engine** engine which runs on diesel fuel; ***the train was pulled by a diesel engine locomotive***

◊ **electric motor** engine which is powered by electricity; ***the electric motor in the cleaner is not powerful enough for it to do a satisfactory job***

◊ **jet engine** engine which is propelled by a jet of gas; ***the two jet engines were located on either side of the plane***

◊ **petrol engine** engine which runs on petrol; ***although petrol is more expensive than diesel most people still prefer petrol-engined cars***

◊ **piston** engine which has pistons moving in cylinders; ***pistons are used in car engines***

◊ **rocket motor** motor which uses liquid fuel to drive rockets; ***the rocket motors burst into life and the rocket slowly lifted from the launch pad***

◊ **steam engine** engine which runs on pressure from steam; ***the steam engine was the main engine used in the early development of industry***

◊ **turbine engine** engine where blades are turned by the power of gas or steam; ***the turbine engine followed the piston engine but was followed itself by the jet engine***

enough

adjective as much as is needed; ***have you got enough money to pay your fare?***; ⇨**adequate;** ⇨**sufficient** *(formal)*

◊ **ample** more than just enough; ***we have ample funds to pay for the development programme***

enter

verb to go in, to come in; ***did they stamp your passport when you entered the country?***

◊ **board** to go on to a ship, train, plane, etc.; ***six passengers boarded at Belgrade***

◊ **break in** to use force to get into a building; ***burglars broke into the office during the night***

◊ **call** to visit; ***the doctor called at the house***

◊ **drop in** to call on someone, to visit someone; ***drop in for a cup of tea if you're passing***

◊ **gatecrash** *(informal)* to get into a party, etc. without being invited; ***a group of students tried to gatecrash her party***

◊ **infiltrate** to become, or to make someone become a member of an organization secretly without the officials knowing; ***the local party has been infiltrated by right-wing agitators***

◊ **intrude** to go in or become involved where you are not wanted; ***we condemn TV reporting which intrudes into someone's private life***

◊ **invade (i)** to attack and enter a country with an army; ***William the Conqueror invaded England in 1066*** **(ii)** to disturb someone's private life; ***she complained that the photographers had invaded her privacy by climbing over the wall***

◊ **trespass** to go onto property without the owner's permission; ***the farmer accused him of trespassing on his land***

◊ **visit** to stay a short time with someone, to stay a short time in a town or country; ***I'm on my way to visit my sister in hospital***

entertain

verb to amuse or give pleasure; ***he entertained us with stories of his life in the army***; ⇨**amuse**

◊ **delight** to please and surprise; ***he was delighted with the birthday gift she had chosen***

◊ **divert** to amuse and pass the time; ***while the rain poured down we diverted ourselves by playing cards***

equipment

noun all the tools, arms, machinery, etc., which are needed; ***do you really need all this fire-fighting equipment on a ship?***; ⇨**gear**

◊ **kit** clothes and personal equipment usually packed for carrying; ***did you bring your tennis kit?***

◊ **provisions** food and drink for a journey or a long stay; ***people going on long expeditions need to plan very carefully what provisions they will take***

◊ **rations** amount of food, drink or supplies allowed; ***the prisoners had to survive on meagre rations***

escape

verb to get away from prison or an unpleasant situation; ***he escaped from the dull party by claiming he had a headache***

◊ **abscond** to run away from custody; ***two of the prisoners have absconded***

◊ **avoid** to keep away from something or to try not to do something; ***he always travels early to avoid the traffic jams***

◊ **elope** to run away to get married; ***she eloped with the rich young man and married him without his parents' approval***

◊ **elude** to avoid being taken or captured; ***he eluded the police by wearing a disguise and changing the colour of his hair***

◊ **evade** to avoid or escape something; ***the escaped prisoners tried to evade capture***

◊ **flee** to run away to escape some danger or disaster; ***as the fighting spread the village people fled into the jungle***

expensive

adjective which costs a lot of money; ***fresh vegetables are usually more expensive in winter***; ⇨**dear**

◊ **costly** very expensive; ***it was a costly mistake by the accountant and the company had to pay a lot to fix it***

◊ **exorbitant** *or* **extortionate** priced at beyond the normal, acceptable limits; ***I don't want to pay the exorbitant prices they charge in that restaurant***

◊ **high-priced** priced at a high level; ***the high-priced seats at the theatre sold very well to visiting business people***

◊ **over-priced** something priced at above its value; ***the car was in good condition but it was over-priced for its age***

◊ **prohibitive** so expensive that you cannot afford it; ***the cost of redoing the kitchen is quite prohibitive***

explain

verb to make something clear; ***he tried to explain the new pension scheme to the staff***; ⇨**clarify;** ⇨**elucidate**

◊ **interpret** to translate what someone is saying into another language, so that others can understand it; ***the courier knows Greek so he will interpret for us***

◊ **popularize** to make something understood or liked by a lot of people; ***television has helped to popularize many different kinds of sport***

◊ **simplify** to make something less complicated; ***we're trying to simplify the procedure so that everyone can follow it***

◊ **teach** to show someone how to do something; ***she teaches maths in the local school***

Ff

failure

noun person or thing which does not work satisfactorily; ***his attempts to juggle were a complete failure***; ⇨**flop** *(informal)*

◊ **anticlimax** feeling of disappointment when something does not turn out as expected; ***after weeks of preparation it was something of an anticlimax when we discovered that we couldn't leave because of the weather***

◊ **dud** something which fails to work; ***most of the fireworks we bought were duds and didn't go off***

◊ **fiasco** total failure; ***the exhibition was a fiasco, hardly anybody turned up***

fall

verb to drop down to a lower level; ***she fell down the stairs***; ***the pound has fallen against the dollar***

◊ **cascade** to fall in large quantities; ***pale pink roses were cascading down the garden wall***

◊ **collapse** to fall down suddenly; ***the roof collapsed under the weight of the snow***

◊ **decline** to become less in numbers or amount; ***our sales have declined over the past year***

◊ **descend** to go down (a ladder, stairs, etc.); ***the president seemed to stumble as he descended the steps from the plane***

◊ **dwindle** to get less; ***it seems that the number of butterflies is dwindling***

◊ **plummet** *or* **slump** to fall quickly or sharply; ***share prices plummeted on the news of the devaluation***

◊ **sink** to go down to the bottom (of water, mud, etc.); ***the paper boat floated for a few moments then sank***

◊ **subside (i)** to become less loud or strong; ***he waited for the noise to subside before going on with his speech*** **(ii)** *(of a piece of ground, a building)* to sink, to fall to a lower level; ***the office block is subsiding because it is built on clay***

◊ **tumble** to fall; ***she tumbled down the stairs head first***

family

noun group of people who are related to one another, especially mother, father and children; ***the Jones family are going on holiday to Spain***

◊ **kin** members of your family (normally, next of kin your closest relative); ***after the accident the hospital wanted to find out who was the next of kin of the victim***

◊ **relation** *or* **relative** member of a family; ***all my relations live in Canada***

famous

adjective well-known; ***he's a famous footballer***; ⇨**noted**

◊ **celebrated** very famous; ***the city of Bath gets its name from its celebrated Roman baths***

◊ **distinguished** important and well-known (writer, painter, etc.); ***a concert by a distinguished Czech pianist***

◊ **eminent** very highly respected because of position or work; ***an eminent judge***

◊ **infamous** *or* **notorious** famously bad; ***tourists are warned against the infamous rates charged by backstreet moneychangers***

◊ **notable** which is worth attention; ***the town is notable for its currant cakes***

◊ **renowned** *(formal)* very famous; ***a renowned Italian conductor***

farm

noun land used for growing crops and raising animals; ***she runs a pig farm***

◊ **agribusiness** the business of farming on a very large commercial scale; ***agribusiness is a powerful lobby that the government can't just ignore***

◊ **croft** small Scottish farm in the Highlands or Islands; ***he works on a fishing boat but he has a small croft as well which he works when he's ashore***

◊ **fish farm** farm which specializes in the rearing of fish for commercial markets; ***his fish farm supplies salmon to two main supermarket chains***

◊ **market garden** small farm which grows vegetables or fruit often sold in a local town; ***he specialized in vegetables and fruit in his market garden***

◊ **nursery** place where young plants are grown and sold; ***we bought enough plants from the nursery to fill the front garden***

◊ **ranch** *(N. and S. America)* farm where horses or cattle are reared; *(Australia)* farm where sheep are reared; ***they left the city and bought a ranch in Colorado***

◊ **smallholding** small farm usually run as a family concern; ***they have a smallholding keeping goats and selling cheese***

◊ **vineyard** area planted with vines for making wine; ***there are vineyards in parts of southern England***

farm

verb to grow crops, raise animals, etc., on a farm; ***he farms 250 acres in Devon***

◊ **cultivate** to dig and water the land to grow plants; ***fields are cultivated in early spring ready to grow corn***

◊ **grow** to make plants grow; ***he grows all his own vegetables in his garden***

◊ **harvest** to collect ripe crops; ***the corn will be ready to harvest next week***

◊ **reap** to cut a grain crop; ***in September everyone went to the farm to help reap the corn***

◊ **rear** to breed animals; ***they breed horses on their farm***

◊ **sow** to put seeds into soil so that they germinate and become plants; ***peas and beans should be sown in April***

fashion

noun most admired style at a particular moment; ***it's the fashion today to wear your hair very short***; ⇨**vogue**

◊ **craze** *or* **fad** sudden popular fashion, usually very short lived; ***I don't like the current craze for purple shoes***

◊ **style** elegant and fashionable way of doing things; ***they live in grand style***

◊ **trend** movement towards or away from some fashion; ***the trend in retailing is for bigger and bigger stores***

fashionable

adjective being of the most admired style at a particular moment; ***she lives in the fashionable West End of London***

◊ **chic** elegant and fashionable; ***it's very chic these days to have an all-white sports car***

◊ **classy** *(informal)* chic and expensive-looking; ***this is a very classy restaurant and the food is too expensive for most people***

◊ **posh** very smart, belonging to a high social class; ***after the wedding they all went to a posh restaurant***

◊ **smart** well dressed or elegant; ***a smart young man asked to use my mobile phone***

◊ **stylish** attractive and fashionable; ***he drives a stylish sports car***

◊ **tasteful** showing an appreciation for things of good quality; ***the decoration was tasteful but not expensive***

◊ **well-dressed** dressed in good clothes, in the latest fashion; ***what is the well-dressed businesswoman wearing these days?***

fast

adjective quick; ***this is the fast train to London***; ⇨**quick;** ⇨**rapid;** ⇨**swift**

◊ **hasty** carelessly fast; ***it was a hasty decision which he regretted afterwards***

◊ **hurried** *or* **rushed** done in a rush, too quickly; ***we just had time to snatch a hurried lunch before catching the train***

◊ **lively** very active; ***the boss is very lively at the age of 85***

◊ **prompt** done immediately; ***thank you for your prompt reply***

◊ **speedy** very fast; ***we all wished her a speedy recovery***

fat

adjective **(i)** overweight; ***you'll get fat if you eat too many cakes*** **(ii)** excessive; ***he earned a fat salary for what was an easy job***; ⇨**corpulent**

◊ **buxom** plump and attractive; ***we were served by a buxom waitress***

◊ **chubby** *or* **plump** *(of a child)* pleasantly fat; ***she tickled the chubby little baby***

◊ **obese** much too fat or too heavy; ***she's not just overweight, she's obese***

◊ **overweight** too heavy; ***the doctor says I'm overweight and must go on a diet***

◊ **plump** fat and tender (of something to be eaten); ***we had a plump chicken for dinner***

◊ **portly** fat but dignified; ***her father was a portly old gentleman***

◊ **stout** quite fat; ***she has become much stouter and has difficulty going up stairs***

favourite

adjective which you like best; ***which is your favourite TV programme?***

◊ **best** very good, better than anything else; ***what is the best way of getting to London from here?***

◊ **chosen** the one which someone picks as the best; ***the chosen candidate was everyone's first choice***

◊ **preferable** which you would like rather than any other; ***any exercise is preferable to sitting around and doing nothing***

fear

noun feeling of being afraid; ***fear of the dark is common in small children***; ⇨**fright**

◊ **alarm** being afraid; ***the expression on his face increased her alarm***

◊ **cowardice** being afraid and not behaving bravely; ***his cowardice was well-known so no one would trust him in a dangerous situation***

◊ **dismay** horror, great disappointment; ***to her great dismay she found she had lost her passport***

◊ **dread** great fear; ***she has a dread of being touched***

◊ **horror** feeling of being very frightened; ***he couldn't hide his horror at hearing the awful news***

◊ **panic** sudden great fear; ***the forecast of flooding caused panic in the riverside town***

◊ **phobia** extreme fear; ***fear of snakes is one of the commonest phobias***

◊ **stage fright** nervousness which actors feel before going onto the stage; ***she overcame her stage fright and gave a wonderful performance on the first night of the play***

◊ **terror** great fear; ***they live in constant terror of racist attacks***

fear

verb to be afraid of something; ***what do you fear most?***

◊ **cower** to sink down through fear; ***she cowered in front of the police chief who accused her of the terrible crime***

◊ **panic** to become suddenly frightened; ***they told us not to panic, the fire engine was on its way***

◊ **stampede** to rush madly; ***when the fire alarm went off the people stampeded for the exits***

◊ **take flight** to run away; ***they took flight in front of the invading army***

feeling

noun something which you sense with your mind; ***I had a feeling that the stranger knew who I was***

◊ **craving** strong desire; ***he has a craving for chocolates***

◊ **desire** something you want very much; ***she had a sudden desire to lie down and go to sleep***

◊ **emotion** strong feeling; ***hatred and love are two of the most powerful emotions***

◊ **instinct** feeling rather than a reason for deciding or doing something; ***his instinct told him that the building was dangerous so he got out quickly***

◊ **intuition** thinking of or knowing something naturally, without it being explained; ***she had an intuition the interview would go badly before she opened the door of the room***

◊ **passion** very strong emotion or enthusiasm; ***he has a passion for motor racing***

few

adjective not many; ***she has very few friends at work***

◊ **infrequent** not happening very often; ***my parent's visits became more and more infrequent as they got older***

◊ **scanty** small, not big enough; ***we only had very scanty information about where they lived***

◊ **scarce** not enough for the amount needed; ***this happened at a period when food was scarce and people were hungry***

◊ **sparse** thinly spread over a wide area; ***the plain is covered with sparse vegetation***

field

noun piece of ground on a farm with a fence, wall or hedge around it; ***the sheep were moved from field to field to graze***

◊ **grazing land** *or* **pasture** grassy area where animals such as horses, cows and sheep can feed on grass; ***every summer the cows are taken up to the mountain pastures***

◊ **Green Belt** area of farming land or woods or parks, which surrounds a town, and on which building is restricted or completely banned; ***they can't put houses in Old Oak Wood, it's Green Belt***

◊ **meadow** large field of grass; ***the cows stared at us as we crossed the meadow where they were grazing***

◊ **orchard** field of fruit trees; ***the apple orchard was overgrown because nobody bothered to prune the trees***

◊ **paddock** small enclosed field, usually near farm buildings, where horses can run; ***she keeps her pony in a paddock***

◊ **park** open space with grass and trees mainly for leisure; ***the park near the centre of town is a favourite place for people to walk especially at lunchtime***

fight

noun struggle against someone or something; ***fights broke out between the demonstrators and the police***

◊ **affray** fight in a public place usually involving a number of people; ***an affray broke out between rival groups of fans in the street outside the football ground***

◊ **battle** important fight between armed forces; ***many soldiers were killed and wounded in the battle***

◊ **combat** fighting in a war; ***these young soldiers have no experience of combat***

◊ **duel** arranged fight between two people with swords, guns, etc. usually to settle an affair of honour; ***he challenged the man who had insulted him to a duel***

◊ **feud** bitter long-lasting quarrel; ***I don't want to get involved in their family feud***

◊ **row** serious argument; ***they had a row about who was responsible for the accident***

◊ **scuffle** small fight; ***scuffles broke out in the crowd***

◊ **skirmish** minor fight between opposite sides; ***there were several skirmishes between rival fans, but no serious fighting***

◊ **war** fighting between countries; ***in 1914 a war broke out in Europe***

fight

verb to struggle against someone or something using force; ***two boys were fighting over a comic***

◊ **attack** to try to hurt someone or something; ***three men attacked him and stole his watch***

◊ **box** to fight with your fists as a sport; ***he learned to box at a gym in the East End of London***

◊ **resist** to fight against something, not to give in to something; ***he resisted all attempts to make him sell the house***

◊ **spar** to practise boxing with someone; ***if you spar with someone you don't mean to hurt them***

◊ **struggle** to fight with an attacker; ***she struggled with the man who had tried to snatch her handbag***

◊ **wage war on** to conduct an all-out fight against something or some country; ***the government is waging war on the problem of homelessness***

fill

verb to make something full; ***he filled the bottle with water***

◊ **cram** to squeeze into a small space; ***he crammed all his clothes into a small suitcase***

◊ **fill in** *or* **fill up** to put into or onto something until all the space is occupied; ***he filled in the application form and sent it off***

◊ **replenish** *(formal)* to fill up again; ***the waiter replenished their glasses with wine***

◊ **saturate** to fill something with the maximum amount of a liquid or substance which can be absorbed; ***the rain was so heavy that the ground was saturated for several days***

◊ **stuff** to push something into something to fill it; ***he stuffed the bank notes into a small plastic wallet***

find

verb to discover (something hidden or lost); ***did she find the book she was looking for?***

◊ **detect** to discover, to notice; ***the smoke alarm detected the smoke from the fire***

◊ **discover** to find something new; ***in the year 1492 Columbus discovered America***

◊ **ferret out** to find by endless searching; ***the journalist ferreted out some surprising facts about the murderer's family***

◊ **find out** to discover information; ***the police are trying to find out why he went to Scotland***

◊ **locate** to find the position of something; ***divers are trying to locate the remains of the Spanish galleon***

◊ **unearth** to dig up, to discover; ***where did you unearth this document from? - everyone said it was lost***

finish

noun end of a race, film, enterprise, etc.; ***the runners came in close together at the finish***; ⇨**end**; ⇨**conclusion**

◊ **closure** the closing down of something; ***the number of factory closures has increased this year***

◊ **completion** act of finishing; ***the project to build the bridge is nearing completion***

◊ **finale** the last part of a piece of music, of a show; ***after the finale the audience applauded enthusiastically***

finish

verb to come to an end; ***the game will finish at about four o'clock***; ⇨ **close**; ⇨**complete**; ⇨**end**

◊ **conclude** to end, to bring to an end; ***he concluded his speech by thanking everyone who had helped***

◊ **die out** to disappear gradually; ***tigers are likely to die out unless measures are taken to protect them***

◊ **expire** to come to an end because the time allowed has run out; ***her passport expired and she needed to get a new one***

◊ **finalize** to put the finishing touches to something; ***we hope to finalize the agreement tomorrow so it can be signed quickly***

◊ **terminate** to bring to an end, to finish; ***the offer terminated yesterday so we can't take advantage of it now***

fire

noun something which is burning; ***they burnt the dead leaves on a fire in the garden***

◊ **blaze** large bright fire; ***five fire engines were called to the blaze***

◊ **bonfire** outdoor fire; ***he put the dead leaves on the bonfire in the garden***

◊ **conflagration** *(formal)* enormous fire; ***two whole blocks of flats were destroyed in the conflagration***

◊ **flame** bright tongue of fire; ***flames could be seen coming out of the upstairs window of the burning building***

first

adjective before all others; ***the bank is the first building you come to in the street***; ⇨**initial**

◊ **maiden** the first journey or occasion; ***the Titanic sank on her maiden voyage***; ***it was the politician's maiden speech after he was elected***

◊ **original** new and different, made for the first time; ***they solved the problem by using a very original method***

◊ **unprecedented** which has never happened before; ***the heavy rain led to unprecedented flooding***

fix

verb to make something work again; ***we need someone to come and fix the telephone***; ⇨**mend;** ⇨**put right;** ⇨**repair**

◊ **amend** to change for the better; ***the Prime Minister amended his speech after taking advice on the latest situation***

◊ **correct** to take away mistakes in something; ***you must try to correct the mistakes in your driving or you will never pass your driving test***

◊ **rectify** to correct something, to make something right; ***he has been asked to rectify the incorrect entry in the catalogue***

◊ **rehabilitate** to train someone to lead a normal life again after disablement, illness or imprisonment; ***prisoners need to be rehabilitated to make sure they do not re-offend***

◊ **rejuvenate** to give something new vigour and strength; ***he hopes to rejuvenate the club by attracting younger members***

◊ **remedy** to correct something, to make something better; ***tell me what's wrong and I'll try to remedy it straight away***

◊ **renovate** to make a building like new again; ***we plan to renovate the offices this year***

◊ **restore** to repair, to make something like new again; ***he spent many hours restoring the old car to its original condition***

◊ **revive (i)** to bring back signs of life (to a person, animal or plant); ***the paramedics managed to revive her on the way to hospital***; ***when she came back from holiday she needed to revive all her house plants with a***

good watering **(ii)** to make something popular again; ***they decided to revive the old musical show and put it on in a modern setting***

flag

noun piece of material with the design or emblem of a country, club, regiment, etc., on it; ***the French flag has blue, red and white stripes***

◊ **banner** long flag or long piece of cloth with a slogan on it; ***the banner was carried between two poles at the head of the procession***

◊ **ensign** national flag flown by a ship; ***the ensign showed that the ship was part of the US navy***

◊ **pennant** long thin triangular flag; ***the pennant was flying from the top of the mast***

◊ **standard** large official flag; ***the Royal Standard flies over Buckingham Palace***

flat

adjective level, not sloping or curved; ***you can have a flat roof on a building but the water will not run off so quickly as on a sloping roof***; ⇨**even**; ⇨**level**

◊ **flush (with)** perfectly level with; ***the two surfaces were flush so there was no hint of a join between them***

◊ **smooth** with no uneven surface; ***the marble top of the table was very smooth***

follow

verb

(a) to come after, to come next; ***the letter B follows the letter A in the alphabet***; ⇨**ensue**

◊ **succeed** to follow in order, especially in office, title or possession; ***Mrs Smith was succeeded as chairman by Mr Jones***

(b) to go after someone or something to keep in touch with it or catch it; ***the dog followed the man across the field***

◊ **chase** *or* **pursue** to run after someone to try to catch him; ***the policeman chased the burglars down the street***

◊ **shadow** to follow someone closely but without being seen; ***the drugs dealer was shadowed by two undercover policemen***

◊ **tail** to follow closely behind someone; ***the police tailed the lorry from the harbour to the warehouse***

◊ **trail** to follow the tracks left by an animal or person; ***the police trailed the group across Europe***

food

noun things which you eat; ***this hotel is famous for its food***; ⇨**nourishment**

◊ **diet** the kind of food you eat; ***during the war people were healthier than now because their diet was much simpler***

◊ **nutrition** the study of food; ***we are studying nutrition as part of the food science course***

◊ **provisions** food and drink for a journey or a long stay; ***people going on long expeditions need to plan very carefully what provisions they will take***

◊ **refreshments** food and drink, often as part of a social, leisure or business occasion; ***light refreshments will be served after the meeting***

◊ **supplies** stock of food, etc., which is needed; ***after two months at sea their supplies were running out***

fool

noun stupid person; ***I was a fool to lend him money***; ⇨**idiot**

◊ **buffoon** person who acts in a funny or stupid way; ***did you see how he behaved at the party? - he's a real buffoon***

◊ **bungler** person who continually makes a mess of any job they try to do; ***she's a bungler, but people keep on asking her to do things for them because she is such a nice person***

◊ **crackpot** person with silly or mad ideas; ***he is very clever but his ideas are so strange everyone takes him for a crackpot***

◊ **halfwit** stupid fool; ***you halfwit - that was my best coat you've just thrown away***

◊ **laughing stock** person who is laughed at by everyone; ***if my friends knew what really happened I would be the laughing stock of the school***

foreign

adjective not from your own country; ***there are lots of foreign medical students at our college***; ⇨**alien**

◊ **exotic** unusual, referring to a strange, foreign often tropical place, person or thing; ***spices can be used to make meat dishes more exotic***

◊ **imported** brought in from another country; ***she prefers imported beer to the local variety***

forget

verb not to remember; ***I have forgotten how you play chess***

◊ **neglect (i)** to fail to look after someone or something properly; ***she neglected her three children*** **(ii)** not to do something which you ought to have done; ***he neglected to collect the papers because he was in a hurry***

◊ **omit** to leave something out; ***she omitted the date when typing the contract***; ***he omitted to tell the police that he had lost the documents***

◊ **overlook** not to notice, to pretend not to notice; ***in this instance the bank will overlook the delay***

formal

adjective done officially or according to certain rules; ***the formal opening of the building was made by the mayor***

◊ **ceremonial** with an important official style; ***the guard of honour all wore ceremonial swords***

◊ **official** approved by an authority; ***we had an official order from the local authority***

◊ **proper** right and correct; ***it is always necessary to wear the proper dress for an official function***

free

adjective

(a) not in use, unoccupied; ***the room is free, you can move in straight away***; ⇨**empty**; ⇨**unoccupied**; ⇨**vacant**

(b) able to do what you want, not forced to do anything; ***he's free to do what he wants***

◊ **emancipated** having been made free, having been made equal; ***emancipated women expect to participate fully in all levels of society***

◊ **exempt** free from rules or laws which apply to others; ***children's clothes are exempt from VAT***

◊ **independent** free, not owned or run by anyone else; ***Slovenia has been independent since 1991***

◊ **unbridled** *or* **unchecked** *or* **unrestrained** without any restraint; ***the unbridled use of power always leads to tyranny***

(c) not costing any money; ***adults pay the entrance fee but children are admitted free***; ⇨**gratis**

◊ **complimentary** given free to a friend or business associate for goodwill; ***we got two complimentary tickets for the show from the firm***

◊ **tax-free** with no tax payable; ***he has been offered a tax-free job in the European Union***

friend

noun person whom you know well and like; ***we're going on holiday with some friends from work***; ⇨**mate** *(informal)*

◊ **acquaintance** person you know; ***she has many acquaintances in the publishing industry***

◊ **ally** person or country which is on the same side; ***she's a close ally of the leader of the opposition***; ***when one of our allies is attacked we have to come to their defence***

◊ **colleague** person who works in the same office, company, school, etc., as you; ***his colleagues gave him a present when he got married***

◊ **companion** person or animal who keeps someone company; ***his constant companion was his old white sheepdog***

◊ **comrade** friend or companion, especially of soldiers; ***we remember old comrades buried in foreign cemeteries***

◊ **neighbour** person who lives near you, who is sitting next to you, etc.; ***he skidded and broke down his neighbour's fence***; ***help yourself and then pass the plate on to your neighbour***

◊ **patron** person who protects or supports someone or something; ***she's a great patron of young artists***

friendly

adjective like a friend; ***don't be frightened of the dog - he's very friendly***; ⇨**cordial**

◊ **amicable** done in a friendly way; ***following an amicable discussion he accepted the cancellation of the agreement***

◊ **benevolent** good and kind, giving freely to others; ***how benevolent to give all that money to charity!***; ***a benevolent uncle gave her quite a lot of money***; ***he's in a particularly benevolent mood this morning***

◊ **benign** kind and pleasant; ***the police officer looked at the little boy with a benign smile and took him to find his mother***

◊ **devoted** loyal and faithful; ***she was devoted to her family***

◊ **faithful** trusting and loyal; ***his faithful old dog was his constant companion***

◊ **sympathetic** showing that you understand someone's problems; ***her sympathetic manner meant that many people came and told her their problems***

friendship

noun knowing and liking someone who knows and likes you; ***she formed several lasting friendships at school***

◊ **affection** liking or love; ***she felt great affection for her youngest grandson***

◊ **devotion** deep love; ***his devotion to his father***

◊ **fondness** liking for; ***his fondness for beer is not good for his waistline***

◊ **liking** pleasant feeling towards someone or something; ***she has a liking for chocolate***

◊ **love** great liking for someone or something; ***her great love is opera***

frighten

verb to make someone afraid; ***the cat has frightened all the birds away***; ⇨**scare**

◊ **bully** to be unkind or pick on someone who is weaker; ***he was bullied by the other children at school***

◊ **intimidate** frightening someone by threatening them or appearing to threaten them; ***the professor didn't realize that he intimidated his students***

◊ **startle** to make someone suddenly surprised; ***I'm sorry, I didn't mean to startle you***

◊ **terrify** to make someone very frightened; ***the sound of thunder terrifies me***

◊ **terrorize** to frighten someone very much by threatening to use violence; ***a gang of youths had been terrorizing the neighbourhood***

◊ **threaten** to warn that you are going to do something unpleasant, especially if someone doesn't do what you want; ***the teacher threatened the noisy class with punishment***

◊ **torment** to make someone suffer; ***he was constantly tormented by doubt***

full

adjective

(a) with as much inside as possible; ***the first bus was full so we had to wait for another one***

(b) complete, with nothing missing; ***you must give the police full details of the accident***; ⇨**complete;** ⇨**total**

◊ **entire** *or* **whole** all of something; ***we spent the entire day gardening***

◊ **universal** without exception, which is understood or experienced by everybody; ***there is a universal desire for peace in the region***

funny

adjective

(a) which makes you laugh; ***she made funny faces and all the children laughed***; ⇨**comical;** ⇨**humorous** *(formal)*

◊ **absurd** *or* **ridiculous** *or* **farcical** *or* **ludicrous** silly, which everyone should laugh at; ***it's absurd to want everyone to wear suits in the office when it's so hot***

◊ **amusing** which makes you laugh; ***it was amusing to hear about your journey***; ***the story in the paper was amusing but it wasn't really true***

◊ **facetious** silly or badly timed attempts at being funny; ***his facetious remarks were quite out of place at the meeting***

◊ **hilarious** very funny; ***the laughter from the audience showed that they found the play hilarious***

◊ **preposterous** silly and quite unbelievable; ***it's preposterous that he should claim to be an expert after only six weeks' training***

◊ **witty** clever and funny; ***his witty column in the daily paper was enjoyed by all the readers***

(b) strange or odd; ***she's been behaving in a funny way since the accident***; ⇨**odd;** ⇨**strange;** ⇨**peculiar**

◊ **bizarre** very strange; ***I find it bizarre that no one told her that the house had been sold***

Gg

game

noun match or pastime between individuals or teams which is played according to rules; ***football is probably the most widely played game in the world***

◊ **competition** sport or game where several teams or people enter and each tries to win; ***he won first prize in the piano competition***

◊ **event** single sporting competition; ***the last event was the 100m hurdles***

◊ **match** game between two teams, etc.; ***she won the last two table tennis matches she played***

◊ **rally** competition where cars have to go through difficult country in a certain time or as a race; ***only strong high performance cars stand any chance of winning the rally***

◊ **pastime** something you do to pass the time or enjoy yourself; ***one of our favourite pastimes as a family is playing cards***

◊ **sport** all games taken together; ***do you like watching sport on TV?***

◊ **tournament** sporting competition with many games where competitors who lose drop out until only one is left; ***the Wimbledon Tennis Tournament***

garden

noun piece of ground near a house used for growing vegetables, flowers, etc.; ***we grow all the vegetables we need in the back garden***

◊ **allotment** plot of land which belongs to a local council and which can be rented for growing plants; ***he grows vegetables on his allotment***

◊ **herb garden** part of a garden set aside for growing herbs; ***it makes such a difference to the cooking when you can get fresh herbs straight out of your own herb garden***

◊ **kitchen garden** part of a garden where fruit and vegetables are grown; ***you need to have a lot of land to have a kitchen garden as well as lawns and a flower garden***

◊ **market garden** small farm which grows vegetables or fruit often sold in a local town; ***he specialized in vegetables and fruit in his market garden***

◊ **ornamental garden** pretty rather than useful garden; ***the ornamental garden was a blaze of colour during the summer***

◊ **plot** small area of land for growing vegetables, etc.; ***he was lucky to have a small plot of land in such a built up area***

get

verb to receive or obtain; ***we got a letter from the bank***; ***go and get your coat***; ⇨**acquire** *(formal)*; ⇨**gain**; ⇨**obtain**; ⇨**procure** *(formal)*; ⇨**receive**

◊ **earn** to get by working or by doing something; ***he earns £150 a week***; ***she earned praise because she had made a great effort***; ***he earned a reprimand from the teacher for his silly behaviour***

◊ **win** to get (a prize, etc.); ***she won first prize in the art competition***

gift

noun present, something given to someone; ***the wedding gifts were displayed on a table***

◊ **bonus** extra money or advantage; ***salesmen can earn big bonuses if they sell more than their quota***

◊ **donation** gift, especially of money to a good cause; ***I can't afford to make a big donation to charity this Christmas***

◊ **grant** sum of money given to help someone; ***the student was able to get a grant to help him carry on his studies at university***

◊ **gratuity** sum of money given to someone who leaves a job; ***she received a tax free gratuity of £10,000 when she retired***

◊ **present** thing which you give to someone as a gift; ***the office gave her a present when she got married***

◊ **reward** money given to someone as a prize for finding something, or for information about something; ***when he took the purse he had found to the police station the owner gave him a £25 reward***

◊ **tip** extra money given to someone who has provided a service; ***we left a tip for the waiter because the service had been really good***

give

verb to send or pass something to someone; ***we gave her flowers for her birthday***; ⇨**bestow** *(formal)*

◊ **award** to give a prize, compensation, etc., to someone; ***he was awarded damages by the court after winning his case against the hospital***

◊ **bequeath** to give to someone by means of making a will; ***he bequeathed his shares to his son***

◊ **confer** to give power or responsibility to someone, to give an honour to someone at a ceremony; ***when he went into hospital the chairman conferred his executive powers to his deputy***

◊ **donate** to give a gift, usually of money, to a cause or charity; ***she donated a substantial amount to support the campaign***

◊ **grant** *(formal)* to agree to give something; ***the government has granted them a loan***

◊ **present** to give formally, a prize, certificate, etc.; ***when he retired after thirty years the firm presented him with a clock***

◊ **provide** to supply; ***our hosts provided us with a car and driver***

◊ **reward** to give someone money as a prize for finding something or for doing something; ***all her efforts were rewarded when she won first prize***

◊ **subsidize** to help by giving money; ***the government has agreed to subsidize developments in energy conservation***

go

verb to leave, to move from one place to another; ***when the play was over it was time to go home***; ***he has gone to work in Washington***; ⇨**move**

◊ **depart** to go away, to leave; ***the coach departs from Victoria Coach Station at 0900***

◊ **escape** to get away from prison or an unpleasant situation; ***he escaped from the dull party by claiming he had a headache***

◊ **flee** to run away, to escape from some danger or disaster; ***as the fighting spread the village people fled into the jungle***

◊ **leave** to go away from somewhere; ***Eurostar leaves Waterloo for Brussels every day at 8.25***

◊ **travel** to move from one place to another; ***he travels from town to town as part of his work***

god

noun the most important supernatural being, the being to whom people pray; ***most religions are based on the idea of a god***; ⇨**deity;** ⇨**divinity;** ⇨**supreme being**

good

adjective

(a) being of a satisfactory or high standard of quality; ***these are good shoes, they're very well made***

◊ **excellent** *or* **first-rate** *or* **first class** *or* **super** very good indeed, of the highest quality, the best available; ***his meals are really wonderful, he's an excellent chef***

◊ **flawless** without any trace of error, mistake or poor quality; ***he gave a flawless performance and everyone clapped enthusiastically***

◊ **impeccable** perfectly correct; ***we had everything - sun, sea and a lovely hotel, it was an impeccable holiday***

◊ **great** of such outstanding quality that it is rare or unusual; ***this is one of the great wines, there weren't many years as good as this***

◊ **reliable** which can be relied on, can be trusted; ***it's a very reliable car, it has never let me down***

◊ **suitable** which fits or is convenient for the purposes intended; ***I can write here, this table is quite suitable***

◊ **wholesome** healthy, good for your health; ***on a wholesome diet you will soon recover your strength***

◊ **workable** which can work or be carried out as planned; ***I don't think her idea is really workable***

(b) well-behaved; ***she's never naughty, always very good***

◊ **dutiful** who does what should be done; ***he is a very dutiful son, he always checks to see if his mother needs anything***

◊ **dependable** that can be relied upon; ***people living in villages need a dependable bus service***

◊ **obliging** willing to help; ***it was very obliging of you to wait for me***

◊ **sensible** making good sense, showing good judgement; ***staying indoors during the storm was the sensible thing to do***; ***I have a sensible pair of shoes for long walks***

◊ **trustworthy** who can be depended upon; ***you are lucky to have such trustworthy staff***

◊ **well-behaved** with good manners, behaving properly; ***the football fans were very well-behaved***

(c) living by values that are respected or admired; ***she was a good woman who had spent her life in the service of others***; ⇨**righteous;** ⇨**upright;** ⇨**virtuous**

◊ **blameless** who cannot be blamed; ***she lived a blameless life and was loved by everyone***

◊ **benevolent** good and kind, giving freely to others; ***how benevolent to give all that money to charity!***; ***a benevolent uncle gave her quite a lot of money***; ***he's in a particularly benevolent mood this morning***

◊ **commendable** which should be praised; ***his honesty is very commendable***

◊ **honourable** who or which can be respected; ***he did the honourable thing and resigned***

◊ **ethical** with good moral standards; ***it wasn't ethical to borrow money without telling anyone***

◊ **kind** *or* **considerate** giving thought to the needs of others; ***it was very kind of you to remember my birthday***

◊ **reputable** known to be reliable; ***it's a very reputable firm, you can trust them***

◊ **tolerant** allowing others to have different views or ideas; ***he accepts that not everyone will agree with him, he's quite tolerant***

(d) who performs well, has a high level of ability; ***the figures show he's a good salesman***; ⇨**able;** ⇨**effective;** ⇨**skilful**

◊ **beneficial** advantageous, which improves chances of success, or gives an advantage; ***it was advantageous to have that information before we made the deal***

◊ **capable** *or* **competent** able to do the job well; ***it was a competent repair job and it kept the machine working***

◊ **efficient** able to work well and do what is necessary without wasting time, money or effort; ***how can we make our working methods more efficient?***

◊ **favourable** will lead to a satisfactory outcome; ***it was a favourable moment to buy those shares***

◊ **fortunate** *or* **propitious** favourable, lucky; ***this is a fortunate time to be able to buy shares in the stock market***

◊ **profitable** will make a profit or produce a good result; ***that was a profitable tip, it made us a lot of money***

(e) superior or in some way special; ***that's a very good diamond***

◊ **delicious** very good to eat, of excellent taste; ***this is a good restaurant, the food's delicious***

◊ **exclusive** *or* **select** available only to a few people, not available to the wider public; ***it's an exclusive club, the members are all well-known writers and artists***

◊ **expensive** costing a lot of money; ***it was an expensive holiday but it was so good it was worth it***

◊ **dear** costing a lot of money; ***these cakes are very dear***

◊ **exquisite** very exceptional quality; ***it's an exquisite piece of carving, so delicate, so beautiful***

◊ **fabulous** almost unbelievably good; ***no one knows how rich she is, her wealth is fabulous***

◊ **luxurious** very expensive, providing richness and comfort; ***it's a top hotel, the rooms are really luxurious***

◊ **timeless** always good whatever the fashion; ***that style of dress always looks good, its beauty is timeless***

govern

verb to rule a country; ***the country is governed by an elected government***; ⇨**rule**

◊ **administer** to manage or organize (a country, an office, a company); ***the province is administered by a local governor***

◊ **be in power** to hold the office of government; ***the army will remain in power until elections are held***

◊ **hold office** to have a position of importance or authority; ***she held office in the last government***

◊ **reign** to rule a country as a king, queen or emperor; ***Queen Victoria reigned for sixty years***

government

noun group of people who rule a country; ***the president asked the leader of the largest party to form a new government***; ⇨**administration**

◊ **communism** social system in which all property is owned and shared by the society as a whole and not by individual people; ***it is hard to***

imagine people who have property or wealth choosing to live under communism

◊ **democracy** system of government by freely elected representatives of the people; ***democracy is the system of government which many countries choose so that the people can be involved***

◊ **dictatorship** rule of a country by one person; ***the leader of the army led the dictatorship after the overthrow of the elected government***

◊ **federation** grouping of provinces or states with a central government; ***federation is becoming more attractive as a form of government***

◊ **monarchy** system of government which involves a hereditary ruler such as a king or queen; ***Britain is a monarchy but the king or queen has little say in government***

◊ **reign** period when a king, queen or emperor rules; ***during the reign of Elizabeth I***

◊ **republic** system of government which has an elected or nominated head of state; ***France is a republic with a president as head of state***

greed

noun too much love of food, money, etc.; ***his greed for popularity makes him do all sorts of silly things***

◊ **avarice** *(formal)* desire to have and keep a lot of money; ***her avarice meant that although she was rich she spent hardly anything***

◊ **gluttony** *(formal)* eating and drinking too much; ***gluttony almost always leads to health problems***

◊ **selfishness** doing things only for yourself and not for other people; ***his selfishness left him without any friends at all***

greedy

adjective wanting food or other things too much; ***don't be greedy, you've already had two pieces of cake***

◊ **avaricious** *(formal)* wanting to have and to keep a lot of money; ***she was so avaricious that she spent hardly anything even though she was rich***

◊ **covetous** *(formal)* wanting something which belongs to someone else; ***he cast covetous glances at his neighbour's new car***

◊ **envious** feeling or showing that you would like to have something that someone else has; ***she was envious of her sister's good luck***

◊ **miserly** mean, not wanting to spend any money; ***he's a very miserly man***

◊ **selfish** doing things only for yourself and not for other people; ***don't be so selfish - pass the chocolates round***

group

noun number of people or things taken together; ***a small group of houses in the valley***

◊ **cluster** small group; ***there was a cluster of people round the noticeboard***

◊ **crowd** mass of people; ***after the election there were crowds of people dancing in the streets***

◊ **flock** group of similar animals together, such as sheep, goats or birds; ***a flock of sparrows***

◊ **gang** band of criminals, youths, etc.; ***gangs of football supporters wandered around the streets after the match***

◊ **herd** group of animals especially cows; ***herds of cattle were grazing on the hillside***

◊ **pack** group of wild animals together, group of dogs; ***a pack of wild dogs***

◊ **team** group of people who play a game together, group of people who work together; ***in this job you need to be able to work as a member of a team***; ***there are eleven players in a football team***

grow

verb

(a) to make plants grow, to cultivate; ***he grows vegetables in his garden***

◊ **cultivate** to dig and water the land to grow plants; ***fields are cultivated in early spring ready to grow corn***

◊ **farm** to grow crops, raise animals, etc., on a farm; ***he farms 250 acres in Devon***

◊ **raise** to grow crops or breed animals; ***he raises horses on his farm as a hobby***

(b) to become taller or bigger or more mature; ***she's grown a lot since I last saw her***

◊ **develop** to grow and change; ***eventually, a caterpillar will develop into a butterfly***

◊ **grow up** to become an adult; ***what does your son want to do when he grows up?***

◊ **mature** to become older, more fully developed; ***whiskey is matured for years before it is ready***

◊ **ripen** to become ready to be eaten or harvested; ***those apples will ripen in October***

guard

noun person who protects, often a soldier; ***security guards patrol the factory at night***

◊ **bodyguard** person who guards someone; ***the attacker was overpowered by the president's bodyguards***

◊ **escort** person or group of people accompanying someone; ***the president had a police escort to the airport***

◊ **guardian** person who protects, especially someone who has been legally appointed to look after a child; ***when his parents died his uncle became his guardian***

◊ **lifeguard** person who is on duty on a beach or at a swimming pool, and who rescues people who get into difficulty in the water; ***lifeguards have raised red flags to show that the sea is dangerous***

◊ **patron** person who protects or supports someone or something; ***she's a great patron of young artists***

◊ **police** organization which controls traffic, tries to stop crime and tries to catch criminals; ***the police are looking for the driver of the car***

◊ **sentry** soldier on duty at a gate, etc.; ***sentries were posted at each gate***

◊ **warden** person who looks after or guards something; ***the warden of the safari park tried to catch the poachers***

◊ **watchdog** **(i)** person or committee that examines public spending, public morals, etc.; ***the report of the watchdog committee on water pricing*** **(ii)** dog used to guard a house or other buildings; ***Alsatians are often used as watchdogs***

guard

verb to watch over, to protect with soldiers, fences, etc.; ***the prison is guarded at all times***

◊ **escort** to accompany someone; ***the police escorted the group into the hotel***

◊ **patrol** to keep guard by walking or driving up and down; ***armed security guards are patrolling the warehouse***

◊ **police** to make sure that rules or laws are obeyed; ***we need more constables to police the area***

◊ **protect** *or* **safeguard** to keep someone or something safe; ***the cover protects the machine against dust***

guess

noun trying to give the right answer; ***he made a guess at the answer but he was wrong***

◊ **assumption** supposing something is true; ***we must go on the assumption that we will have enough money to get home***

◊ **conjecture** guesswork; ***I had no real idea, it was all conjecture on my part***

◊ **instinct** feeling rather than a reason for deciding or doing something; ***his instinct told him that the building was dangerous so he left***

◊ **intuition** thinking of or knowing something naturally, without it being explained; ***she had an intuition the interview would go badly before she opened the door of the room***

◊ **opinion** what someone thinks about something; ***ask the lawyer for his opinion about the letter***

◊ **supposition** something which is assumed but cannot be proved; ***we can only make a supposition regarding the fate of the ship and her crew***

◊ **suspicion** general feeling that something is going to happen; ***I have a suspicion that he is coming to see me because he wants to borrow some money***

◊ **theory** explanation of something which has not been proved but which you believe is true; ***I have a theory which explains why the police never found the murder weapon***

guess

verb to try to give the right answer; ***I would guess it's about six o'clock***; ⇨**conjecture**

◊ **assume** to suppose something is true; ***we must assume that we will have enough money to get home***

◊ **imagine** to picture something in your mind; ***imagine yourself sitting on a beach in the hot sun***

◊ **speculate** to make guesses about; ***we are all speculating about what's going to happen***

◊ **suppose** to think something is probable; ***I suppose she will be late as usual***

◊ **suspect** to guess, to think something is likely; ***I suspect it's going to be more difficult than we thought at first***

guest

noun person paying a visit to a home, hotel or function; ***the guests gathered in the dining room for the meal***

◊ **lodger** person who rents a room in a house; ***she has taken in three lodgers for the summer***

◊ **occupant** person or company occupying a property; ***the occupant of the flat downstairs is very noisy***

◊ **visitor** person who comes to make a short stay; ***how many visitors come to this museum each year?***

guide

noun person who shows the way; ***they used local farmers as guides through the forest***

◊ **adviser** *or* **counsellor** person who says what should be done; ***he is consulting his financial adviser***

◊ **consultant** specialist who gives advice; ***her tax consultant advised her to sell her shares***

◊ **expert** person who knows a great deal about a subject or is very good at doing something; ***a TV gardening expert***

◊ **mentor** person who teaches, or helps younger people starting their careers; ***he was my mentor when I started out in show business***

◊ **teacher** person who shows someone how to do something, especially in a school; ***Mr Jones is our maths teacher***

guide

verb to show the way; ***she guided us round the castle***

◊ **advise** *or* **counsel** to suggest what should be done; ***he advised her to put her money into a deposit account***

◊ **lead** to go in front to show the way; ***she led us to the secret room***

◊ **recommend** to suggest that someone should do something; ***I would recommend you to talk to the bank manager***

◊ **urge** to advise someone strongly to do something; ***he urged her to do what her father said***

◊ **warn** to inform someone in advance of danger or difficulty; ***the weather forecast warned of storms***

gun

noun weapon which shoots bullets or shells; ***he kept a gun in the house but it didn't make him feel any safer***

◊ **airgun** gun which uses compressed air; ***the boy took his airgun out to the field to shoot at birds***

◊ **anti-aircraft gun** gun to fire at attacking aircraft; ***the ship was equipped with three anti aircraft guns***

◊ **anti-tank gun** gun used to fire at tanks; ***the anti tank gun required three soldiers to fire it***

◊ **artillery** *(plural)* military guns that fire shells; ***the army was short of artillery and had to rely on light weapons***

◊ **automatic** handgun which goes on firing as long as the trigger is being pressed; ***we heard automatic fire in the distance***

◊ **cannon** large gun (usually old-fashioned muzzle-loading); ***the children had their photo taken next to the cannon on the old castle walls***

◊ **field gun** light gun which can be moved around where a battle is taking place; ***they brought up more field guns to the top of the hill***

◊ **handgun** *or* **pistol** small gun which is carried in the hand; ***she kept a handgun in her bag***

◊ **revolver** small handgun where the bullets are kept in a revolving chamber; ***some people use revolvers, others prefer automatics***

◊ **rifle** gun with a long, grooved, barrel; ***hunting with a rifle is a popular sport in some countries***

◊ **shotgun** gun with one or two long smooth barrels which fires pellets from a cartridge; ***shotguns are popular hunting weapons***

◊ **side arm** handgun kept in a holster by military personnel; ***side arms, other than swords, are not normally worn on ceremonial occasions***

Hh

happiness

noun feeling of being very pleased; ***a feeling of happiness came over her at the ceremony***

◊ **bliss** *or* **ecstasy** very great happiness; ***it was sheer bliss to be walking in the countryside away from the office***

◊ **delight** *or* **enjoyment** pleasure; ***the news was greeted with delight by the waiting crowds***

◊ **euphoria** burst of extreme happiness; ***euphoria swept through the crowd when their team scored a goal in the last seconds of the game***

◊ **joy** great happiness; ***we all wished them great joy on their wedding day***

◊ **pleasure** pleasant feeling; ***his greatest pleasure is sitting by the river***

◊ **satisfaction** good feeling, sense of comfort or happiness; ***she felt a great sense of satisfaction when she finished writing the book***

◊ **thrill** feeling of great excitement; ***it gave me a thrill seeing you all again after so many years***

happy

adjective very pleased, pleasant; ***I'm so happy to hear that you are feeling better***; ⇨**cheerful;** ⇨**contented;** ⇨**glad;** ⇨**pleased**

◊ **blissful** very pleasant or happy; ***it's blissful sitting on the beach when everyone else is working in the office***

◊ **delighted** very pleased; ***he's delighted with his present***

◊ **elated** very excited and pleased; ***she was elated by her exam results***

◊ **joyful** very happy; ***I could tell by his joyful look that the interview had gone well***

◊ **merry** happy and cheerful; ***it was a merry time when all the family celebrated his 90th birthday***

◊ **optimistic** feeling that everything will work out for the best; ***we were optimistic about the plan***

◊ **satisfied** feeling full of comfort and happiness; ***he gave a satisfied smile and put down his pen when he had finished writing***

hard

adjective not soft; ***the hard chair was very uncomfortable to sit on for very long***

◊ **firm** solid or fixed; ***you must put the ladder on firm ground***

◊ **frozen** made solid by freezing; ***it was impossible to dig in the frozen ground***

◊ **rigid** stiff, inflexible, which doesn't bend; ***the scaffolding had to be rigid or it would collapse when any weight was placed on it***

have

verb to own or possess; ***she has a lot of money***; ⇨ **own;** ⇨**possess**

◊ **keep** *or* **retain** to remain in possession of something; ***can I keep the newspaper that I borrowed from you?***

◊ **occupy** to own or live in; ***they occupy the flat on the first floor***

healthy

adjective not ill, which creates a good physical or mental state; ***he is keeping to a healthy diet***; ⇨**fit;** ⇨**well**

◊ **hygienic** which is clean and free of germs; ***we decided not to eat at the restaurant as the kitchen didn't look at all hygienic***

◊ **robust** strong and vigorous; ***this young tree is robust and should survive the winter***

◊ **sound** in good condition, not rotten; ***the walls of the old house were still sound***

◊ **strong** *(of a person)* with a lot of strength; ***I'm quite strong enough to carry that box***

◊ **vigorous** very energetic, very strong; ***she went for a vigorous run round the park before breakfast***

heavy

adjective which weighs a lot; ***this suitcase is so heavy I can hardly lift it***; ***the heavy responsibilities of his office sometimes caused him great worry***; ⇨**weighty**

◊ **crushing** which takes away all hope; ***they suffered a crushing defeat at the last election***

◊ **cumbersome** large and heavy, difficult to handle; ***this big bag is very cumbersome, you should get something smaller***

◊ **massive** very large, huge; ***the company went bankrupt because of massive losses***

◊ **onerous** *(formal)* being a burden, of heavy importance; ***the duties of the post were very onerous***

◊ **overloaded** loaded in too heavy a way; ***she was overloaded with work at the office and had to work at weekends***

◊ **ponderous** heavy and slow-moving; ***he disliked the ponderous way the orchestra played the music***

◊ **unbearable** which cannot be borne; ***the pressure of work became unbearable and he became ill***

help

noun thing which makes it easier to do something; ***she finds the word processor a great help in writing her books***; ⇨**aid**; ⇨**assistance**

◊ **comfort** thing which helps to make you feel happier; ***it was a comfort to know the children were safe***

◊ **protection** shelter, being protected; ***the trees offered some protection from the rain***

◊ **reinforcement** act of making stronger or more solid; ***one of the walls of the old house needed reinforcement***

◊ **relief** reducing pain or stress, assisting after a disaster; ***an aspirin should bring relief***; ***relief was brought in to the earthquake area***

◊ **rescue** action which saves somebody or something; ***no one could swim well enough to go to her rescue***

◊ **service** favour, something done for someone; ***you would do me a great service by carrying my suitcases for me***

◊ **support** help and encouragement; ***I gave him my support in his bid to get the chairmanship***

help

verb to make it easier for someone to do something, to give aid or assistance; ***he helped the old lady up the steps***; ⇨**aid**; ⇨**assist**

◊ **advise** *or* **counsel** to suggest what should be done; ***she advised him to put all his money in a deposit account***

◊ **comfort** to make someone feel happier; ***he was comforted when we told him the children were safe***

◊ **oblige** to do something useful or helpful as a favour; ***she obliged her elderly neighbour by agreeing to weed the garden***

◊ **reinforce** to make stronger or more solid; ***we reinforced one of the walls of the old house***

◊ **support** to give help and encouragement; ***I supported him in his bid to get the chairmanship***

hide

verb to put something where no one can find or see it; ***she hid the children's presents in the kitchen***; ⇨**conceal;** ⇨**secrete**

◊ **camouflage** to hide the shape of something by using colours and patterns; ***the soldiers camouflaged the gun position with branches of trees***

◊ **disguise** to change the appearance of someone or something so as to hide the real identity; ***he came into the country disguised as a woman***

◊ **mask** to cover up or to hide; ***she masked her face with her scarf***

◊ **suppress** to stop something being made public; ***all opposition newspapers have been suppressed***

high

adjective reaching above others; ***high mountains usually are snow-capped all year***; ***he has a very high position in the government***; ⇨**elevated** *(formal)*

◊ **eminent** very highly respected because of position or work; ***an eminent judge***

◊ **exalted** in a high position in authority; ***in his exalted position he should be able to afford a larger car***

◊ **soaring** rising rapidly; ***the soaring cost of living***

◊ **steep** which rises or falls sharply; ***the car climbed the steep hill with some difficulty***

◊ **sublime** of so high a quality as to cause wonder and awe; ***the sublime sight of the snow-capped mountains towering over the lake***

◊ **tall** high, usually higher than normal; ***the bank building is the tallest building in London***

◊ **towering** very tall; ***towering cliffs***

hire

verb

(a) to pay money to use a car, boat, piece of equipment or other item for a time; ***he hired a car to get away for the weekend***

◊ **borrow** to take something for a short time, usually with permission; ***can I borrow your car to go to the shops?***

◊ **charter** to hire a plane, bus, boat, etc.; ***a fleet of chartered coaches took the group to the beach***

◊ **lease** to be used under the terms of a contract; ***he leased the shop to an Australian company***

◊ **lend** *or* **loan** to let someone use something for a certain period of time; ***she asked me to lend her £5 until Monday***

◊ **let** to allow someone to borrow a house or office for a while and pay for it; ***we're letting our cottage to some friends for the month of August***

◊ **sublet** to let a property you are renting to another tenant; ***we have sublet part of our office to a financial consultant***

(b) to engage someone to work for you; ***we've hired three more sales assistants***

◊ **conscript** to order someone to join the armed services; ***all men under 35 were conscripted into the armed forces***

◊ **employ** to give someone regular paid work; ***she is employed in the textile industry***

◊ **engage** to employ a worker; ***we have engaged a lawyer to represent us***

◊ **enlist** to get someone to help; ***we enlisted our neighbours' help to cut down the tree***

◊ **recruit** to encourage someone to join (often the armed services) or take a job; ***we are recruiting staff for our new store***

hit

verb to knock into; ***the car hit the tree***; ⇨**strike**

◊ **batter** to hit often and violently; ***he was accused of battering the baby to death***

◊ **beat** to hit hard; ***she hung the carpet on the line and beat it with a stick to remove the dust***

◊ **flog** to beat hard, usually with a whip; ***he could not get the donkey to go any further no matter how much he flogged it***

◊ **hammer** to hit hard, as with a hammer; ***she hammered on the table with her fist***

◊ **punch** to hit someone with your fist; ***he punched me on the nose***

◊ **slap** *or* **smack** to hit with your hand flat; ***she slapped his face***

◊ **tap** to hit gently; ***he tapped him on the knee with his finger***

◊ **thrash** to beat with a stick; ***she could not get the donkey to go any further no matter how she thrashed it***

◊ **whip** to hit someone or an animal with a whip; ***he whipped the horse to make it go faster***

hole

noun opening, space in something; ***you've got a hole in your shoe***; ⇨**cavity**

◊ **burrow** rabbit hole; ***the rabbits all popped down their burrow when we came near***

◊ **cave** large underground hole in rock or earth; ***when the tide went out we could explore the cave***

◊ **cavern** very large cave, formed by water which has dissolved limestone or other rock; ***the police discovered a cavern which had been used to hide weapons***

◊ **crater (i)** hole made by a bomb; ***over the winter the bomb craters filled up with rainwater*** **(ii)** round hollow at the top of a volcano; ***a group of scientists flew over the crater to monitor the activity of the volcano***

◊ **ditch** long trench for taking away water; ***the car swerved and went into the ditch***

◊ **excavation** hole or investigation made by archaeologists; ***we went to see the excavations on the site of the old town hall***

◊ **grave** hole in the ground where a dead person is buried; ***at the funeral the whole family stood by the grave***

◊ **hollow** sunken part of a flat surface; ***they made a hollow in the ground for a camp fire***

◊ **mine** deep hole in the ground from which coal, etc., is taken out; ***the coal mine has stopped working after fifty years***

◊ **niche** rounded hollow place in a wall; ***there are statues in niches all round the garden***

◊ **pit** deep hole in the ground; ***they dug a pit to bury the rubbish***

◊ **pothole** hole in a road surface; ***the council still hasn't filled in the potholes in our street***

◊ **quarry** place where stone, etc., is dug out of the ground; ***if you hear an explosion it is because they are blasting in the quarry***

◊ **shaft** deep hole; ***the mine ventilation shaft had become blocked***

◊ **trench** long narrow ditch; ***they dug trenches for drainage round the camp***

◊ **tunnel** long passage under the ground; ***the Channel Tunnel links Britain to France***

holiday

noun day or period when you don't work but rest or go away and enjoy yourself; ***we always spend our holidays in the mountains***; ⇨**vacation**

◊ **feast** special religious day or celebration; ***the Patron Saint of Ireland is St Patrick and his feast is kept as a holiday***

◊ **festival (i)** religious celebration which comes at the same time each year; ***the tour will visit Hong Kong for the Lantern Festival*** **(ii)** celebration or entertainment which is put on annually, on special occasions or at regular intervals; ***the church looked marvellous with all the displays during the annual flower festival***

◊ **leave** permission to be away from work; ***he has six weeks annual leave***

◊ **leisure time** free time when you can do what you want; ***she plays a lot of tennis in her leisure time***

◊ **sabbatical** break from work for rest and study; ***he decided to take a sabbatical at Berkeley University in California***

holy

adjective sacred, associated with religion; ***they went to ask a holy man for his advice***; ⇨**sacred**

◊ **divine** referring to God; ***she prayed for divine help***

◊ **mystical** in contact with God by some process which cannot be understood; ***he wrote about his mystical vision of the universe***

◊ **providential** seeming to come from God; ***it was providential that we came home and found the gas leak before there was a disaster***

◊ **religious** referring to belief in gods or in one God; ***she's very religious, she goes to church every day***

◊ **spiritual** referring to the spirit or the soul; ***the church's main task is to give spiritual advice and comfort to its members***

◊ **transcendental** concerned with what is beyond experience; ***he said that in a transcendental state he seemed out of time and space***

honest

adjective truthful and trustworthy; ***I wouldn't buy a car from that garage - I'm not sure they're completely honest***; ⇨**truthful;** ⇨**trustworthy**

◊ **scrupulous** very careful, very honest; ***he was very scrupulous in all his dealings with the bank***

◊ **sincere** very honest and genuine; ***we send you our sincere wishes for a speedy recovery***

◊ **wholehearted** complete and total; ***I found it difficult to give her my wholehearted attention***

honour

noun acting according to what you think is right; ***he's a man of honour***

◊ **decency** *or* **integrity** doing what is right, good morals; ***she had the decency to apologize for her mistake***

◊ **goodness** being good; ***he did it out of pure goodness of heart***

◊ **reliability** ability to be trusted to give support or do the right thing; ***her reliability makes her a very valuable employee***

◊ **sincerity** being honest and genuine; ***his sincerity makes up for his lack of ability***

◊ **veracity** truthfulness; ***the veracity of the report cannot be doubted***

hope

noun wanting and expecting something to happen; ***they have given up hope of rescuing any more earthquake victims***

◊ **ambition** *or* **aspiration** desire to do something, to become great, rich or famous; ***his great ambition is to ride on an elephant***

◊ **anticipation** excitement, because you think something will happen; ***he was full of anticipation at the thought of seeing her again***

◊ **belief** feeling sure that something is true; ***his firm belief in the power of the law***

◊ **conviction** being certain that something is true; ***it was a common conviction, in the Middle Ages, that the earth was flat***

◊ **dreams** things that you hope and imagine will happen in the future; ***the results surpassed our wildest dreams***

◊ **expectation** feeling that something will happen; ***she lived up to our expectations***

◊ **intention** aim or plan to do something; ***I can assure you that I have no intention of going to the party***

◊ **vision** ability to look and plan ahead; ***his vision of a free and prosperous society***

hope

verb to want and expect something to happen; ***they hoped they might rescue more earthquake victims***

◊ **anticipate** to expect something will happen; ***we are anticipating bad weather***

◊ **aspire** to have an ambition to get something; ***she aspires to great success as an actress***

◊ **await** to wait for; ***we are awaiting the decision of the court***

◊ **believe** to be sure that something is true although you can't prove it; ***people used to believe that the earth was flat***

◊ **dream** to imagine that something will happen in the future; ***she dreamt of buying a farm and raising goats***

◊ **expect** to think, to hope, to assume that something is going to happen; ***I expect that you are tired after your long train journey***

◊ **intend** to plan to do something; ***we intended to get up early but we all overslept***

◊ **wish** to want something to happen; ***she sometimes wished she could live in the country***

hotel

noun building where travellers can rent a room for the night, eat in a restaurant, drink in a bar, etc.; ***they are staying at a hotel while they are visiting the Lake District***

◊ **B & B** bed and breakfast accommodation; ***we want to find a B & B away from the main road***

◊ **hostel** cheap place where people can live; ***the students looked for a hostel near the railway station***

◊ **inn** small hotel; ***we stayed at an inn when we visited the mountains***

◊ **motel** hotel for car drivers where there is a parking space for every room; ***they checked into the motel last Saturday***

◊ **pub** *(informal)* place where you can buy beer and other alcoholic drinks, as well as snacks, meals, etc.; ***we had a sandwich and some beer in the pub***

house

noun building in which someone lives; ***he has bought a house in London***

◊ **apartment** separate set of rooms for living in; ***she has an apartment in downtown New York***

◊ **bungalow** house with only a ground floor; ***my grandparents bought a bungalow by the sea***

◊ **castle** large building with strong defensive walls; ***the soldiers felt safe from their enemies as soon as they were in the castle***

◊ **chalet** small (holiday) house, usually made of wood; ***a mountain landscape dotted with chalets***

◊ **cottage** little house in the country; ***we have a weekend cottage in the mountains***

◊ **detached house** house which stands alone, not attached to another; ***they lived in a pleasant detached house with a big garden***

◊ **dwelling** place to live; ***they have permission to build a dwelling on this site***

◊ **flat** separate set of rooms for living in; ***she has bought a flat in the West End of London***

◊ **lodge** small house at the gates of a large building; ***if the lodge is as big as that, just imagine the size of the main house!***

◊ **maisonette** flat on two floors in a larger building; ***they've bought a maisonette near the High Street***

◊ **manor** country house and the land surrounding it; ***the lord of the manor owns most of the land round the village***

◊ **mansion** very large private house; ***he's bought a mansion overlooking the golf course***

◊ **palace** large building where a king, queen, president, etc., lives; ***the presidential palace is in the centre of the city***

◊ **semi-detached house** house which is joined to another similar house on one side, but is not joined to a house on the other; ***a street of 1930s semi-detached houses***

◊ **shack** rough wooden hut; ***she lived for years in a little shack in the woods***

◊ **terraced house** one of a series of houses built all in a similar style and joined in a row; ***the street was lined with attractive terraced houses***

◊ **vicarage** house of the priest in charge of a parish; ***the village fete was held in the vicarage gardens***

humour

noun seeing what is funny; ***he has a good sense of humour***

◊ **farce** absurd situation; ***the meeting rapidly became a farce***

◊ **joke** thing said or done to make people laugh; ***they all laughed at her jokes***

◊ **sarcasm** sharp unpleasant remarks which mean the opposite of what they say; ***he was hurt by the sarcasm in her review of his book***

◊ **satire** way of attacking people in speaking or writing by making them seem ridiculous; ***Gulliver's Travels is a satire on 18th century England***

◊ **whimsy** odd or fanciful ideas; ***the whole silly story was just a piece of whimsy***

hungry

adjective wanting to eat; ***you must be hungry after that game of football***

◊ **famished** *(informal) or* **ravenous** very hungry; ***I'm famished - is there anything in the fridge?***

◊ **peckish** slightly hungry; ***hurry up with the sandwiches - I'm feeling peckish after my long walk***

◊ **starving (i)** without enough to eat; ***relief workers tried to bring food to the starving people*** **(ii)** *(informal)* very hungry; ***isn't dinner ready yet? I'm starving***

hurry

verb to go, do or make something fast, to make someone go faster; ***she hurried across the room***; ***don't hurry me, I like to take my time***; ⇨**rush**

◊ **accelerate** *or* **quicken** to go faster, to make something go faster; ***he pressed down the pedal and the car accelerated***

◊ **expedite** *(formal)* to make something happen faster; ***we hope you will be able to expedite delivery of this order***

◊ **gallop** to go fast; ***the riders galloped through the woods***; ***he galloped through his lecture***

◊ **speed** to move quickly; ***the ball sped across the ice***

hurt

verb to have pain, to give pain; ***my tooth hurts***; ⇨**injure**

◊ **afflict** to make someone very sad or suffer; ***the country was afflicted by civil wars***

◊ **annoy** to trouble or disturb someone or something; ***the constant noise of the traffic annoyed the man sitting in the park***

◊ **bully** to be unkind or pick on someone who is weaker; ***he was bullied by the other children at school***

◊ **distress** to make someone very sad and worried; ***the news of her grandmother's death distressed her very much***

◊ **harm** to damage; ***the bad publicity has harmed our reputation***

◊ **torment** to make someone suffer; ***he was constantly tormented by doubt***

Ii

idea

noun something which you think of, a plan which you make in your mind; ***I had an idea about where we might go on holiday***; ⇨**notion**

◊ **brainwave** sudden brilliant idea; ***I don't know how the problem can be solved, if any of you has a brainwave let me know***

◊ **concept** philosophical idea; ***it is difficult for some countries to grasp the concept of democratic government***

◊ **impression** to have a feeling that; ***I got the impression that she wanted to leave us***

◊ **thought** idea which you have when thinking; ***he had an awful thought - suppose they'd left the bathroom taps running***

ill

adjective sick, not well; ***if you're feeling ill you ought to see a doctor***; ⇨**ailing;** ⇨**sick**

◊ **bedridden** unable to leave your bed because of illness or infirmity; ***she was bedridden for two years after her stroke***

◊ **feverish** suffering from a high temperature; ***he felt feverish and took an aspirin***

◊ **indisposed** *(formal)* slightly ill; ***my father is indisposed and cannot see any visitors***

◊ **terminal** in the last period of a fatal illness; ***she has terminal cancer***

illness

noun not being well; ***she developed a serious illness***; ⇨**ailment;** ⇨**complaint;** ⇨**disorder;** ⇨**sickness**

◊ **disease** serious illness; ***it is a disease which can be treated with antibiotics***

◊ **infirmity** being old and weak; ***infirmity is often the result of old age***

important

adjective which matters a great deal, (person) who holds a high position; ***it is important to be in time for the meeting***; ***he has an important government job***

◊ **crucial** *or* **vital** extremely important; ***it is crucial that the story be kept out of the papers***

◊ **decisive** which brings about a result; ***her action was decisive in obtaining the release of the hostages***

◊ **fundamental** *or* **primary** basic, essential; ***good air quality is fundamental for children's health***

◊ **grave** important, worrying; ***he is in court facing grave charges***

◊ **key** most important; ***the key person in the company is the sales manager***

◊ **serious** important and possibly dangerous; ***the storm caused serious damage***

improve

verb to make something better; ***we are trying to improve our image with a series of TV commercials***; ⇨**refine**

◊ **cure** to make a patient or disease better; ***that is very good medicine, it cured my cough very quickly***

◊ **develop** to plan and produce or build; ***they a planning to develop the site as an industrial estate***

◊ **enhance** to increase the beauty, value or power of something; ***the facade of the building was considerably enhanced by re-painting***

◊ **modernize** to make something up to date; ***if we want to modernize the factory, we'll have to throw out all the old equipment***

◊ **reform** to change to make better; ***they want to reform the educational system***

income

noun money which you receive, especially as pay for your work, or as interest on savings; ***their weekly income is not really enough to live on***; **⇨earnings; ⇨pay; ⇨salary; ⇨wages**

◊ **commission** percentage of sales value given to a salesman; ***she gets 15% commission on everything she sells***

◊ **compensation** payment for damage or loss; ***the airline refused to pay any compensation for his lost luggage***

◊ **gratuity** sum of money given to someone who leaves a job; ***she received a tax-free gratuity of £10,000 when she retired***

◊ **pension** money paid regularly to someone who has retired from work, to a widow, etc.; ***he has a good pension from his firm***

◊ **reward** money given to someone as a prize for finding something, or for information about something; ***when she took the purse she had found to the police station she got a £25 reward***

increase

verb to make something become bigger; ***the boss increased his salary***; ⇨**expand**; ⇨**swell**

◊ **gain** to increase in value; ***the pound gained six cents on the exchange markets***

◊ **grow** to become taller or bigger; ***he's grown a lot taller since I last saw him***

◊ **multiply** to increase in numbers; ***the insects multiplied as the weather became warmer***

◊ **spread** to move over a wide area; ***the cholera epidemic has spread to the towns***

informal

adjective not done according to certain rules; ***the guide gave us an informal talk on the history of the castle***; ⇨**casual**

◊ **relaxed** calm, not upset; ***he failed his test, but seems very relaxed about it***

◊ **unconventional** not usual; ***the treatment may be unconventional but it seems to work***

information

noun facts about something; ***can you send me information about holidays in Greece?***

◊ **advice** saying what should be done; ***she went to the bank manager for advice on how to pay her debts***

◊ **common knowledge** something everyone knows; ***it is common knowledge that he is having an affair with his secretary***

◊ **data** statistical information; ***the data is stored in our main computer***

◊ **facts** things that are true; ***did you check all the facts before you wrote the article?***

◊ **gossip** *or* **hearsay** stories or news about someone which may or may not be true; ***have you heard the latest gossip about Sue?***

◊ **hint** piece of advice, hidden suggestion or clue; ***she gave some useful hints about painting furniture***

◊ **instructions** indication of how something is to be done or used; ***he gave us detailed instructions on how to get to the church***

◊ **intelligence** information provided by the secret services; ***intelligence gathered by our network of agents is very useful to us in planning future strategy***

◊ **news** spoken or written information about what has happened; ***what's the news of your sister?***

◊ **report** description of what has happened or what will happen; ***we read the report of the accident in the newspaper***

◊ **statistics** facts in the form of figures; ***these statistics on their own do not prove your case***

◊ **warning** information about a possible danger; ***he shouted a warning to the children***

insurance

noun agreement with a company by which you are paid compensation for loss or damage in return for a payment or regular payments of money; ***do you have insurance for your travel?***

◊ **bail** money paid to a court as a condition for the release of someone waiting to be tried; ***she was released on bail of £5,000***

◊ **deposit** money given in advance so that the thing you want to buy will not be sold to someone else; ***he had to pay a deposit on the watch***

◊ **guarantee** firm promise that something will happen; ***I will give a guarantee that the car will give you no trouble***

◊ **protection** being kept safe from something; ***the injection should give some protection against measles***

◊ **warranty** written guarantee that goods purchased will work properly or that an item is of good quality; ***the warranty covers spare parts but not labour costs***

interesting

adjective which attracts your attention; ***there's an interesting article in the paper on European football***

◊ **dramatic** with great force and interest; ***the dramatic effects of the storm were shown on TV***

◊ **fascinating** *or* **gripping** very interesting indeed; ***the book gives a fascinating description of London in the 1930s***

◊ **sensational** which causing great excitement; ***his sensational discovery shocked the world of archaeology***

◊ **thrilling** which makes you very excited; ***it was thrilling to land in New York for the first time***

island

noun piece of land with water all round it; ***they live on a little island in the middle of the river***; ⇨**isle**

◊ **atoll** coral island shaped like a ring; ***the atolls of the pacific Ocean***

◊ **reef** long ridge of rocks or coral just above or beneath the surface of the sea; ***the Great Barrier Reef is a coral reef off the north-east coast of Australia***

Jj

job

noun regular work which you get paid for; ***she's got a job in a supermarket***; **⇨appointment; ⇨employment; ⇨position; ⇨post**

◊ **assignment** job of work; ***he was given the assignment of reporting on the war***

◊ **calling** *or* **vocation** work you feel you have been called to do or for which you have a special talent; ***for her, nursing is a calling***

◊ **chore** piece of routine work, especially housework; ***it's a real chore, having to save our computer files every day***

◊ **errand** being sent out to buy something; ***he sent the girl out on an errand***

◊ **profession** work which needs special training, skill or knowledge; ***members of the legal profession protested against the new regulations***; ***they are negotiating a new pay structure for the teaching profession***

◊ **task** job of work which has to be done; ***there are many tasks which need to be done in the garden***

join

verb to put things together, to come together; ***you have to join the two pieces of wood together***; ***the two rivers join about four kilometres beyond the town***; **⇨assemble; ⇨connect; ⇨link**

◊ **attach** to fasten something to something else; ***the gate is attached to the post***

◊ **blend** to mix; ***blend the eggs, milk and flour together***

◊ **combine** to join together with; ***the cold weather combined with the high winds have made it a dreadful harvest***

◊ **couple** to join two things together; ***high tides coupled with strong winds caused flooding along the coast***

◊ **fuse** to join things together to form a single thing; ***the heat had fused the metal seats together***

◊ **merge** to join together with something; ***the two motorways merge here***

◊ **unite** to join together into a single body; ***the office staff united in asking for better working conditions***

◊ **weld** to join two pieces of metal together by heating them; ***the chassis can be repaired by welding the two pieces together***

joke

noun thing said or done to make people laugh; ***they all laughed at his jokes***; ⇨**gag**

◊ **practical joke** trick played on someone to make other people laugh; ***his practical joke made them laugh but unfortunately someone got hurt***

◊ **pun** play with words which have several different meanings; ***he made an awful pun about 'ploughing on' with his book on agriculture***

judge

noun

(a) person appointed to make legal decisions in a court of law; ***he was convicted for stealing but the judge let him off with a fine***

◊ **coroner** public official, either a doctor or a lawyer, who investigates sudden or violent deaths; ***deaths of prisoners are investigated by a coroner***

◊ **Justice of the Peace (JP)** local magistrate (unpaid); ***she has been appointed a JP***

◊ **magistrate** judge who tries cases in a minor court; ***she appeared before the magistrates***; ***he was fined £500 by the magistrates***

(b) person who decides which is the best entry in a competition; ***the three judges of the beauty contest couldn't agree***

◊ **censor** person who reads documents or looks at films to see if they are fit to be published or shown; ***the censor has refused permission for the film to be shown***

◊ **referee** *or* **umpire** person who supervises a game, making sure that it is played according to the rules; ***the referee sent several players off***

judge

verb to make decisions in a court of law or competition, etc.; ***her painting was judged the best and she won first prize***

◊ **arbitrate** to act as an official judge in a dispute; ***he has been asked to arbitrate in the dispute between the company and the union***

◊ **censor** to read documents or look at films to see if they are fit to be published or shown; ***parts of the film have been censored and are not to be shown***

◊ **condemn (i)** to declare a building to be unfit to use; ***the whole block of flats has been condemned and will be pulled down*** **(ii)** to sentence a criminal; ***she was condemned to life imprisonment***

◊ **referee** *or* **umpire** to supervise a game, making sure it is played according to the rules; ***there is no one to referee the match this afternoon***

◊ **try** to hear a civil or criminal case in court; ***the case will be tried by a judge and jury***

jump

verb to move upwards suddenly; ***the horses jumped over the fence***; ⇨**leap**

◊ **hop** to jump on one leg; ***he hurt his toe and had to hop around on one foot***

◊ **vault** to jump over something by putting one hand on it to steady yourself; ***she vaulted over the fence***

Kk

keep

verb to have for a long time or for ever; ***can I keep the newspaper I borrowed from you?***; ⇨**retain** *(formal)*

◊ **detain** to stop someone from leaving; ***I'm sorry I'm late - I was detained by a phone call***

◊ **hold** to keep tight, especially in your hand; ***she was holding the baby in her arms***

◊ **preserve** to look after and keep in the same state; ***our committee aims to preserve the wildlife in our area***

◊ **secure** to make safe, to attach firmly; ***secure all the doors and windows before the storm comes***

◊ **store** to keep something for use later; ***we store all our personnel records on computer***

◊ **withhold** to refuse to let someone have something; ***they suspect him of withholding important information from the police***

kill

verb to make someone or something die; ***the lack of rain has killed all the crops***; ⇨**slay**

◊ **assassinate** to kill a famous person for political reasons; ***do you remember the day the President was assassinated?***

◊ **butcher** to kill brutally; ***the soldiers set fire to the village and butchered the inhabitants***

◊ **decimate** to kill in large numbers; ***the German forests have been decimated by acid rain***

◊ **execute** to kill someone who has been condemned to death; ***murderers are no longer executed in this country***

◊ **massacre** to kill many people or animals; ***the soldiers massacred hundreds of innocent civilians***

◊ **murder** to kill someone illegally and deliberately; ***he was accused of murdering a policeman***

◊ **slaughter (i)** to kill animals for meat; ***here's the shed where the animals are slaughtered*** **(ii)** to kill many people at the same time; ***many civilians were slaughtered by the advancing army***

kind

noun sort or type; ***an ant is a kind of insect***

◊ **category** classification of things or people; ***if there is no room in the hotel shown in the brochure, we will put you into a similar category of hotel***

◊ **variety** different type of plant or animal of the same species; ***you have this new variety of rose?***

kind

adjective wanting to help, thinking about other people; ***it's very kind of you to offer your help***; ⇨ **friendly;** ⇨**helpful**

◊ **benevolent** good and kind; ***a benevolent uncle gave her quite a lot of money***; ***he's in a particularly benevolent mood this morning***

◊ **generous** very willing to give your money, time, etc.; ***it was a generous birthday present***

◊ **good** living by values that are respected or admired; ***she was a good woman who had spent her life in the service of others***

◊ **hospitable** welcoming and friendly to guests; ***the people in the village were very hospitable***

◊ **humane** kind to people or animals; ***they were praised for their humane treatment of the captured soldiers***

◊ **merciful** kind and forgiving; ***they confessed their crimes and hoped the king would be merciful***

◊ **sympathetic** showing that you understand someone's problems; ***her sympathetic manner meant that many people came and told her their problems***

◊ **tolerant** allowing others to have different views or ideas; ***he accepts that not everyone will agree with him, he's quite tolerant***

kindness

noun being kind; ***she was touched by his kindness***

◊ **benevolence** being good and kind; ***his benevolence is most noticeable this morning***

◊ **charity** help, usually money, given to the poor; ***he lost his job and his family have to rely on the charity of their neighbours***

◊ **generosity** being glad to give your money, time, etc.; ***she showed great generosity to her grandchildren***

◊ **goodwill** kind feeling; ***the charity relies on the goodwill of people who give money regularly***

◊ **help** thing which makes it easier to do something; ***she finds the word processor a great help in writing her books***

◊ **mercy** being kind and forgiving; ***they decided to confess their crime and hope for mercy from the king***

◊ **sympathy** showing that you understand someone's problems; ***he showed no sympathy for her when she said she felt ill***; ***her sympathy meant a lot to the people who came to her with their problems***

know

verb to have learned something, to have information about something; ***do you know how to start the computer programme?***

◊ **comprehend** *(formal) or* **grasp** *or* **understand** to know what something means; ***it is difficult to comprehend how he could have done such a stupid thing***

◊ **realize** to get to a point where you understand clearly; ***we soon realized we were on the wrong road***

◊ **recognize** to know someone or something because you have seen him or it before; ***do you recognize the handwriting on the letter?***

knowledge

noun general facts or information that people know

◊ **information** facts about something; ***can you send me information about holidays in Greece?***

◊ **learning** *or* **scholarship** deep study; ***the article shows sound learning about the subject***

◊ **wisdom** being able to make good use of knowledge, having sound good sense; ***he had the wisdom not to be taken in by all the publicity***

laugh
noun sound you make when you think something is funny; ***she's got a lovely deep laugh***

◊ **chuckle** quiet laugh; ***we all had a good chuckle over our chairman's speech***

◊ **smile** showing that you are pleased by turning your mouth up at the corners; ***he had a big smile as he gave her the news***

laugh
verb to make a sound to show that you think something is funny; ***we all laughed at his jokes***

◊ **giggle** to make a little laugh; ***when she saw her mother's hat she started giggling***

◊ **grin** to smile broadly; ***she grinned when we asked her if she liked the job***

◊ **smile** to show that you are pleased by turning your mouth up at the corners; ***he smiled as he gave her the news***

◊ **snicker** *or* **snigger** to laugh quietly in an unpleasant way; ***they sniggered as the teacher came into the room***

law
noun the set of rules by which a country is governed; ***everybody is supposed to obey the law***

◊ **by-law** rule or law made by a local authority or public body but not by central government; ***a local by-law says that this path is a public right of way***

◊ **canon law** religious rules or instructions; ***is there anything in canon law about the burial of non-practising Catholics?***

◊ **charter** legal document giving rights or privileges to a town or university; ***the university received its charter in 1846***

◊ **code** set of laws, rules of behaviour; ***the hotel has a strict dress code, and people wearing jeans are not allowed in***

◊ **command** *or* **order** instruction to someone to do something; ***the general gave the command to attack***

◊ **commandment** *or* **regulation** *or* **rule** strict order of the way to behave; ***the Ten Commandments*** = the ten rules given by God to Moses

◊ **common law** law as laid down in decisions of courts, rather than by statute

◊ **constitution** laws and principles under which a country is ruled, which give the people rights and duties, and which give the government powers and duties; ***unlike most countries, Britain does not have a written constitution***

◊ **decree** legal order which has not been voted by Parliament; ***the President has issued a decree banning short dresses***

◊ **directive** official instruction; ***the ministry has issued a new directive on animal feeds***

◊ **statute** written law, established in an Act of Parliament; ***unlicensed trading is prohibited by a statute of 1979***

lazy

adjective not wanting to do any work; ***she's just lazy - that's why the work never gets done on time***; ⇨**idle;** ⇨**indolent;** ⇨**slothful;** ⇨**work-shy**

leader

noun person who shows the way, who has the most important place; ***he is the leader of the Labour Party***

◊ **boss** person in charge, owner (of a business); ***if you want a day off ask the boss***

◊ **chief (i)** person in charge in a group of people or a business; ***she's been made the new chief buyer*** **(ii)** leader of a tribe; ***all the chiefs came together at a meeting***

◊ **commander** officer in charge of an army corps or ship; ***the commander must make sure that all his soldiers know what to do***

◊ **commander-in-chief** person who is in charge of all the armed services of a country; ***the President is also the Commander-in-Chief***

◊ **director** person who is in charge of an organization, project, official institute, etc.; ***he's just started his job as the director of an international charity***

◊ **head** most important person; ***she's head of the sales department***

◊ **manager** person in charge of a department, shop or business; ***the bank manager wants to talk to you about your account***

◊ **official** person holding a recognized position; ***they were met by an official from the embassy***

◊ **superior** person in a higher rank; ***each manager is responsible to his superior***

◊ **supremo** *(informal)* person in charge of a very large organization; ***he has been named World Fair supremo***

learn

verb to find out about something, or how to do something; ***he's learning to ride a bicycle***

◊ **ascertain** *(formal)* to check facts to see if they are true; ***when will you be able to ascertain if the figures are correct?***

◊ **assimilate** to learn and understand; ***she quickly assimilated the instructions she had been given***

◊ **know** to have learned something, to have information about something; ***do you know how to start the computer programme?***

◊ **research** to study, to try to find out facts; ***research your subject thoroughly before you start writing the article***

◊ **revise** to study a lesson again; ***I'm revising for my history test***

◊ **study** to examine something carefully to learn more about it; ***we are studying the possibility of setting up an office in New York***; ***he is studying medicine because he wants to be a doctor***

◊ **understand** to know what something means; ***it is difficult to understand how he could have done such a stupid thing***

leave

verb to go away from somewhere; ***Eurostar leaves Waterloo for Brussels every day at 8.25***; ⇨**go away**

◊ **abandon** to leave and give up; ***the crew abandoned the sinking fishing boat***

◊ **abscond** to run away; ***two of the prisoners have absconded***

◊ **emigrate** to leave your country to live in another; ***my daughter and her family have emigrated to Australia***

◊ **escape** to get away from prison or an unpleasant situation; ***he escaped from the dull party by claiming he had a headache***

◊ **evacuate** to make people, troops, etc., leave a dangerous place; ***the office staff were evacuated by the fire service***

◊ **go** to move from one place to another; ***when the play was over it was time to go home; he has gone to work in Washington***

◊ **quit** *(informal)* to leave a job, a house, etc.; ***when the boss criticized her, she quit***

◊ **retire** to stop work and take a pension; ***he will retire from his job as manager next April***

level

adjective flat, even; ***are these shelves level or do they slope to the left?***

◊ **flat** level, not sloping or curved; ***you can have a flat roof on a building but the water will not run off so quickly as on a sloping roof***

◊ **horizontal** flat, level with the ground; ***he drew a horizontal line under the text***

◊ **true** accurately adjusted so that it is perfectly flat; ***you have to get the floor true so that the machine will work properly***

liar

noun person who says something knowing it to be untrue; ***don't trust him - he's a liar***

◊ **cheat** person who breaks the rules or acts dishonestly in order get what they want or to gain an advantage; ***the cheat took notes with him into the exam***

◊ **conman** *or* **confidence trickster** person who tricks people to get money by making them believe something; ***the conman got her to sign the papers***

◊ **hypocrite** person who pretends to be what they are not; ***you hypocrite, you say that I'm lazy but do no work yourself***

◊ **impostor** person who pretends to be someone else; ***the priest who married them turned out to have been an impostor, so they had to get married again***

◊ **swindler** person who makes illegal deals in which someone is cheated out of money; ***the swindler managed to get £50,000 from the company before he was caught***

licence

noun document which gives official permission to possess something or to do something; ***she has applied for an export licence for these paintings***

◊ **authorization** official permission; ***do you have authorization for this expenditure?***

◊ **permission** freedom which you are given to do something; ***he asked the manager for permission to take a day off***

◊ **permit** paper which allows you to do something; ***you have to have a permit to sell ice cream from a van***

◊ **warrant** official document from a court permitting to do something; ***the magistrate issued a warrant for her arrest***

lie

noun something which is not true; ***someone has been telling lies about him***; ⇨**falsehood** *(formal)*

◊ **perjury** crime of telling lies when you have sworn an oath to tell the truth in court; ***she appeared in court on a charge of perjury***

◊ **pretence** making believe something which is untrue, the action of pretending; ***they made a pretence of being interested***

◊ **understatement** statement which does not tell the facts forcefully enough; ***saying that the government has had a few difficulties is the understatement of the year***

◊ **white lie** lie not meant to do any harm; ***I told him his painting was wonderful - it was only a white lie***

life

noun time when you are alive; ***she spent her whole life working on the farm***; ⇨**existence**

◊ **reality** what is real and not imaginary; ***the grim realities of living in an industrial town***

light

adjective

(a) having a lot of light so that you can see well; ***the big windows make the kitchen very light***

◊ **bright** *or* **radiant** shining strongly, clear and sunny; ***there will be bright sunshine during the afternoon***

◊ **brilliant** shining very strongly; ***she stepped out into the brilliant sunshine***

◊ **dazzling** very bright (light); ***he covered his eyes against the dazzling floodlights***

◊ **glittering** which sparkles brightly; ***a glittering diamond crown***

◊ **luminous** which gives out light in the dark; ***the luminous hands of her bedside clock glowed faintly in the dark***

◊ **sparkling** shining with little lights; ***a necklace of sparkling diamonds***

(b) not heavy; ***I can lift this box easily - it's quite light***

◊ **buoyant** which can float easily; ***the raft became waterlogged and was no longer buoyant***

◊ **lightweight** made of light material; ***at last we have some hot weather and a chance to wear some lightweight clothes***

◊ **portable** which can be carried; ***he carried a small portable radio to listen to the cricket match***

◊ **weightless** having no weight; ***the weightless astronauts floated in space***

light

noun brightness, the opposite of darkness; ***I can't read the map by the light of the moon***; ⇨**brightness**

◊ **daylight** light during the daytime; ***three men robbed the bank in broad daylight***

◊ **flash** short sudden burst of light; ***flashes of lightning lit up the sky***

◊ **glare** very bright light; ***the glare of the sun on the wet road blinded me***

◊ **glimmer** little light; ***there was a glimmer of light in one of the upstairs windows***

◊ **glitter** bright sparkle of light; ***the glitter of the sun on the sea***

◊ **moonlight** light from the moon; ***we could see the path clearly in the moonlight***

◊ **sunlight** *or* **sunshine** light which comes from the sun; ***sunlight was pouring into the room***

◊ **twilight** time when the light is weak, between sunset and night; ***the twilight hours are dangerous for drivers***

like

verb to have pleasant feelings about something or someone; ***do you like the new manager?***; ***would you like to go to the cinema?***

◊ **admire** to look at someone or something with respect; ***he was admired for his skill as a violinist***

◊ **adore** to like very much; ***he adored his father***

◊ **appreciate** to recognize the value of; ***shoppers always appreciate good value***

◊ **befriend** *(formal)* to become friendly with someone and help them; ***he befriended a lonely student whom he met at Waterloo Station***

◊ **idolize** to admire someone very much; ***she idolized her art teacher***

◊ **love** to have strong feelings for someone or something; ***she loves little children***

◊ **respect** to admire or to honour someone; ***everyone respected her decision to emigrate***

◊ **sympathize** to show that you understand someone's problems; ***I sympathize with you, my husband snores too***

◊ **value** to consider something as being valuable; ***she values her friendship with him***

◊ **worship** to praise and love someone; ***he absolutely worships his girlfriend***

list

noun number of items, names, addresses, etc., written or said one after another; ***we've drawn up a list of people to invite to the party***

◊ **checklist** list of things which have to be done or dealt with before something can be done; ***I must go through my checklist to see if we have covered all the points I wanted to discuss***

◊ **index** list, usually in alphabetical order, showing the references in a book; ***look up the references to London in the index***

◊ **inventory** list of contents (of a house, etc.); ***the landlord checked the inventory when the tenants left***

◊ **register** written list of names; ***I can't find your name in the register***

◊ **table** list of figures, facts, information set out in columns; ***the times of tides are given in a table in the newspaper***

◊ **timetable** printed list which shows the times of classes in school, of trains leaving, etc.; ***we have two English lessons on the timetable today***; ***he asked for a current timetable of trains to London***

listen

verb to pay attention to someone who is talking or to something which you can hear; ***don't make a noise - I'm trying to listen to a music programme***

◊ **bug** *(informal)* to plant a hidden microphone; ***they met in Hyde park because he was afraid his flat had been bugged***

◊ **concentrate** to be very attentive; ***the exam candidates were all concentrating very hard***

◊ **eavesdrop** to listen to a conversation which you are not supposed to hear; ***she stood outside the door to eavesdrop on the interview her son had with the manager***

◊ **hear** to catch sounds with your ears; ***you could hear the sound of bells in the distance***

◊ **overhear** to hear accidentally something which you are not meant to hear; ***I couldn't help overhearing what you said***

◊ **pay attention** to note and think about something carefully; ***pay attention to the following instructions***

◊ **tap** to attach a secret listening device to a telephone line; ***the police tapped her phone***

little

adjective not big, not much; ***we drink very little milk***; ⇨ **small**

◊ **compact** small; close together; ***the computer system is very compact***

◊ **dainty** small and delicate; ***the baby has dainty little fingers***

◊ **infinitesimal** tiny, very small indeed; ***they found an infinitesimal amount of bacteria in the drinking water***

◊ **microscopic** so small as to be visible only through a microscope; ***microscopic forms of life are visible in very old rocks***

◊ **miniature** *or* **minute** very small; ***he has a miniature camera***

◊ **petite** *(of a woman)* small and dainty; ***she was petite and took a very small size in clothes***

◊ **tiny** very small; ***can I have just a tiny bit more pudding?***

loan

noun something lent, especially a sum of money; ***he bought the house with a loan from the bank***

◊ **advance** money paid as a loan or as a part of a payment to be made later; ***can I have an advance of £50 against next month's salary?***

◊ **credit** time given to pay; ***we give buyers six month's interest-free credit***

◊ **debt** money owed to someone; ***her debts are mounting up***

◊ **hire purchase** system of buying something by paying a sum regularly each month; ***we're planning to buy our new refrigerator on hire purchase***

◊ **IOU** paper promising that you will pay back money which you have borrowed; ***she gave him an IOU for £100***

◊ **mortgage** the money lent on the security of a property; ***he got a mortgage from the bank to buy his house***; ***he is behind with his mortgage repayments***

◊ **overdraft** the amount of money which you can withdraw from your bank account with the bank's permission, which is more than there is in the account, i.e. you are borrowing money from the bank; ***he has an overdraft of £500***

lonely

adjective

(a) feeling sad because of being alone; ***it's odd how lonely you can be in a big city***

◊ **alone** with no one else; ***she was all alone in the shop***

◊ **friendless** without friends; ***he found himself friendless in a foreign country***

◊ **solitary** lonely, living alone; ***my sister lives a solitary life in the country***

◊ **unpopular** not liked by other people; ***the new manager was very unpopular with the staff***

(b) *(place)* with few or no people; ***the cliff top is a lonely place at night***

◊ **desolate** bleak and deserted; ***it was a desolate place, far from civilization***

◊ **god-forsaken** *(formal)* desolate, lost; ***how do they ever manage to live in this god-forsaken place?***

◊ **isolated** separated from others; ***they live in an isolated cottage in the hills***

◊ **secluded** *(place)* which is quiet, away from the crowds; ***they tried to find a secluded beach***

long

adjective not short in length, not short in time; ***what a long programme - it lasted almost three hours!***

◊ **epic** long and difficult; ***his epic struggle against the local planning authority***

◊ **eternal** everlasting; ***her eternal complaints really annoy me***

◊ **lengthy** (very) long; ***he wrote a lengthy note, detailing all the problems involved***

◊ **long drawn-out** taking a very long time; ***there was a long drawn-out argument about who would pay the bill***

◊ **longstanding** which has been in existence for a long time; ***we have a longstanding arrangement to go for a picnic on her birthday***; ***she is a longstanding customer of ours***

◊ **long-term** planned to last for a long time; ***she asked the bank for a long-term loan***

◊ **never-ending** which seems as if it will never stop; ***the compilation of a thesaurus is a never-ending task***

◊ **perpetual** continuous, without any end; ***I'm fed up with these perpetual arguments***

look

verb to turn your eyes towards something; ***if you look out of the office window you can see our house***

◊ **discern** *(formal)* to see, to make out something with difficulty; ***in the fog, we could barely discern the oncoming traffic***

◊ **distinguish** to see clearly; to make out details; ***with the binoculars we could easily distinguish the houses on the other side of the lake***

◊ **gaze** to look steadily; ***he stood on the cliff gazing out to sea***

◊ **glare** to look angrily; ***she glared at me and went on reading her book***

◊ **glimpse** to catch sight of; ***we only glimpsed her as she was leaving***

◊ **inspect** to look at something closely; ***the kitchens are regularly inspected***

◊ **notice** to see; to take note of; ***I didn't notice you had come in***

◊ **observe** to watch or to look at; ***we observed the eclipse from the top of the mountain***

◊ **pry** to look inquisitively into something; ***he accused the press of prying into his private life***

◊ **scan** to look very carefully at something all over; ***we scanned the horizon but no ships were to be seen***

◊ **spy** to watch someone in secret, to find out what they are planning to do; ***we discovered that our neighbours had been spying on us***

◊ **stare** to look at someone or something for a long time; ***she stared unhappily out of the window***

◊ **watch** to look at and notice something; ***did you watch the TV news last night?***

loud

adjective which is very easily heard; ***turn down the radio - it's too loud***

◊ **deafening** so loud as to make you deaf; ***there was a deafening crack of thunder***

◊ **noisy** which makes a lot of noise; ***a crowd of noisy little girls***

◊ **piercing** very loud, shrill; ***they suddenly heard a piercing cry***

◊ **strident** unpleasantly loud and harsh; ***the strident horns of the fire engines***

◊ **thunderous** very loud, often referring to applause; ***the actors came back on stage to thunderous applause***

love

noun great liking for someone or something; ***her great love is opera***; ⇨**affection**; ⇨**devotion**

◊ **fondness** liking for; ***his fondness for beer is not good for his waistline***

◊ **friendship** state of being friends, knowing and liking someone who knows and likes you; ***she formed several lasting friendships at school***

◊ **liking** pleasant feeling towards someone or something; ***she has a liking for chocolate***

◊ **passion** very strong emotion or enthusiasm; ***she has a passion for motor racing***

love

verb to have strong feelings for someone or something; ***she loves little children***

◊ **adore** to like very much; ***he adored his father***

◊ **appreciate** to recognize the value of; ***shoppers always appreciate good value***

◊ **cherish** to love; to treat kindly; ***she cherished the ring given to her by her grandmother***

◊ **idolize** to admire someone very much; ***she idolized her art teacher***

◊ **like** to have pleasant feelings about something or someone; ***do you like the new manager?***; ***would you like to go to the cinema?***

◊ **treasure** to value something; ***I treasure the calm life of the fishing village where I live***

◊ **value** to consider something as being valuable; ***she values her friendship with him***

◊ **worship** to praise and love someone; ***he absolutely worships his girlfriend***

Mm

machine

noun thing which works with a motor; ***we have bought a machine for putting leaflets in envelopes***

◊ **appliance** electrical machine which is used in the home, such as a washing machine; ***household appliances should be properly earthed***

◊ **engine** machine which powers or drives something; ***the lift engine has broken down again - we will have to use the stairs***

◊ **gadget** useful tool; ***a useful gadget for taking the tops off bottles***

◊ **machinery** many machines, taken as a group; ***the factory has got rid of a lot of old machinery***

◊ **mechanism** working parts of a machine; ***if you take the back off the watch you can see the delicate mechanism***

mad

adjective having a serious mental disorder; ***she became mad and had to be put in a special hospital***; ⇨**demented;** ⇨**deranged;** ⇨**insane;** ⇨**lunatic**

◊ **crazy** acting wildly; ***it was a crazy idea to go mountain climbing in sandals***

◊ **delirious** suffering from a confused mental state where the person sees imaginary scenes or hears imaginary sounds; ***she collapsed and became delirious***

◊ **frenzied** wild and uncontrollable; ***the group launched a frenzied attack on the driver of the bus***

◊ **hysterical** in a fit of panic or excitement; ***he was hysterical and I had to slap his face to stop him screaming***

◊ **manic** excited and violent; ***because of her manic behaviour she had to be restrained***

◊ **neurotic** worried and obsessed with something; ***he has a neurotic dislike of cats***

◊ **paranoid** suffering from a fixed illusion of being persecuted; ***her paranoid behaviour about the neighbours became impossible to ignore***

◊ **schizophrenic** suffering from delusions and loss of contact with the real world; ***their schizophrenic son had to stay in hospital but visited them occasionally***

magazine

noun illustrated paper which comes out regularly; ***the gardening magazine comes out on Fridays***

◊ **booklet** *or* **pamphlet** small book with not many pages usually giving information; ***you will find booklets about the town at the Tourist Information Office***

◊ **brochure** pamphlet which provides information about goods, holidays, etc.; ***we got a holiday brochure in January to choose our summer holiday***

◊ **comic** children's paper with cartoon stories; ***he spends his pocket money on comics and sweets***

◊ **daily** newspaper published every weekday; ***the story was on the front page of most of the dailies***

◊ **journal** periodical magazine, especially one on a learned subject; ***she edits the journal of the Historical Society***

◊ **monthly** magazine which is published each month; ***I buy all the computer monthlies***

◊ **newspaper** publication consisting of loose folded sheets of paper, which usually comes out each day, with news of what has happened; ***we saw your picture in the local newspaper***

◊ **periodical** magazine which appears regularly; ***she writes for several London periodicals***

◊ **publication** book, newspaper or magazine which has been published; ***he asked the library for a list of gardening publications***

◊ **review** monthly or weekly magazine which contains articles of general interest; ***his first short story appeared in a Scottish literary review***

◊ **weekly** magazine published once a week; ***she gets a gardening weekly every Friday***

magic

noun spells, conjuring tricks, etc., which do not appear to follow normal scientific rules; ***the conjurer made a rabbit come out of his hat, and the children thought it was magic***

◊ **conjuring** doing tricks in which things appear and disappear; ***conjuring can use cards, small animals or even glasses of water***

◊ **illusion** trick in which something impossible appears to take place; ***the audience gasped in amazement at the illusion***

◊ **sorcery** *(in fairy tales)* witchcraft, wicked magic; ***it wasn't done honestly, it was done by sorcery***

◊ **superstition** belief in magic and that some thing are lucky and others unlucky; ***he always refuses to walk under ladders out of superstition***

◊ **witchcraft** art of magic (not for entertainment); ***she was accused by her neighbours of using witchcraft***

mail

noun letters, service provided by the post office; ***the mail hasn't come yet***; ***the cheque was lost in the mail***

◊ **airmail** mail sent by air; ***we sent her birthday present by airmail***

◊ **correspondence** letters; ***she has kept up her correspondence with her old teacher***

◊ **GPO** General Post Office

◊ **letter** piece of writing sent by one person or organization to another to pass on information; ***don't forget to write a letter to your mother to tell her how we all are***

◊ **post** letters, etc., sent; ***the morning post comes around nine o'clock***

◊ **surface mail** mail sent by ship, van or train but not by air; ***the letter wasn't urgent, so we sent it by surface mail***

mail

verb to send something by the postal services; ***we mailed the catalogue to addresses all over Europe***

◊ **redirect** to send a letter you have received on to another address; ***letters are redirected automatically to our new address***

make

verb

(a) to put together, to build; ***he made a boat out of old pieces of wood***; ⇨**produce**

◊ **build** *or* **construct** to assemble and fit pieces together materials to make something; ***he built a perfect model of the plane from the kit he bought in the model shop***

◊ **compose** to write something using your intelligence; ***it took Mozart only three days to compose his fifth piano concerto***

◊ **create** to build or make something which has not been made before; ***the scientists finally created a rocket capable of reaching the moon***

◊ **erect** to put up something upright such as a mast or tall building; ***they are planning to erect a monument to the dead president***

◊ **generate** to produce power, etc.; ***we use wind to generate electricity***

◊ **invent** to create a new process or machine; ***she invented a new type of computer terminal***

◊ **manufacture** to make products commercially; ***we no longer manufacture tractors here***

(b) to force someone to do something; ***his mother made him clean his room***; ⇨**coerce**; ⇨**compel**; ⇨**force**; ⇨**oblige**

◊ **dictate** to tell someone what to do; ***the army commander dictated the terms of the surrender***

◊ **insist** to state firmly that something must be done or given; ***I insist on an immediate explanation***

◊ **necessitate** to make necessary; ***the new model will necessitate a complete change of machinery***

man

noun adult male human being; ***that tall man is my brother***; ***two men came to the door***; ⇨**bloke** *(informal)*; ⇨**chap** *(informal)*; ⇨**guy** *(informal)*

◊ **bachelor** man who is not married; ***she's going out with a bachelor she met at a party***

◊ **brother** boy or man who has the same mother and father as someone else; ***my brother John is three years older than me***

◊ **father** man who has a son or daughter; ***her father is a well-known artist***

◊ **gentleman** man, especially a well behaved or upper class man; ***he's such a gentleman, he always opens the door for me***

◊ **godfather** man who sponsors a child at baptism; ***he was godfather to four children***

◊ **grandfather** father of your mother or father; ***my grandfather always gives me money for my birthday***

◊ **husband** man to whom a woman is married; ***her husband is a schoolteacher***

◊ **uncle** brother of your father or mother, husband of your father's or mother's sister; ***Uncle George is coming to see us***

manage

verb to be in charge of something; ***she manages all our offices in Europe***; ⇨**administer**

◊ **arrange** *or* **direct** *or* **organize** to put into good order; ***we have put him in charge of organizing the city archives***

◊ **command** *(usually military)* to be in charge of something; ***he commands a minesweeper***

◊ **influence** to make someone or something change; ***the price of oil has influenced the price of industrial goods***

◊ **orchestrate** to organize a demonstration, etc.; ***they orchestrated the protest marches in such a way as to get them on the TV news***

◊ **preside** to be in control of; ***she presided over one of the world's richest corporations***

◊ **regulate** to maintain something by law; ***speed on the motorway is strictly regulated***

◊ **supervise** to watch carefully, to see that work is well done; ***he supervises six trainee receptionists***

manager

noun person in charge of a department, shop or business; ***the bank manager wants to talk to you about your account***

◊ **administrator** person who runs an organization; ***we are advertising for a new chief administrator for the society***

◊ **controller** person who directs how things are done; ***the strike by air traffic controllers caused widespread disruption***

◊ **director** person who is in charge of an organization, project, official institute, etc.; ***he's just started his job as the director of an international charity***

◊ **executive** businessman or businesswoman who makes decisions; ***top executives make the hard decisions and get the top salaries***

◊ **leader** person who shows the way, who has the most important place; ***he is the leader of the Labour Party***

◊ **official** person holding a recognized position; ***they were met by an official from the embassy***

◊ **principal** head (of a school, a college); ***the principal wants to see you in her office***

◊ **supervisor** person who watches carefully to see that work is well done; ***if you have any questions, ask your supervisor***

many

adjective large number of things or people; ***many old people live on the south coast***

◊ **abundant** in large quantities; ***the cottage has abundant stocks of wood for the stove***

◊ **ample** sufficient; ***four hours should be ample time to get to Glasgow***

◊ **considerable** quite large; ***he lost a considerable amount of money betting on horse races***

◊ **innumerable** very many, which cannot be counted; ***we have had innumerable complaints about this product***

◊ **numerous** very many; ***he has been fined for speeding on numerous occasions***

◊ **prolific** producing a lot of something; ***she is a prolific writer of travel guides***

◊ **several** more than a few but not a lot; ***we've met several times***

map

noun drawing which shows a place, such as a town, a country or the world as if it is seen from the air; ***here's a map of Europe***

◊ **atlas** book of maps; ***can you find Montserrat in the atlas?***

◊ **chart** map of the sea, a river or a lake; ***you will need an accurate chart of the entrance of the river***

◊ **road map** map showing all the roads of a place or country; ***we'll need a good road map to find the cottage***

◊ **street plan** map showing the streets in a town, with their names; ***I was trying to find Cambridge Road on my street plan***

meal

noun occasion when people eat food at a special time; ***most people have three meals a day***

◊ **banquet** formal dinner for important guests; ***the president gave a banquet for the visiting Prime Minister***

◊ **barbecue** meal where food is cooked on a metal grill out of doors; ***we had a barbecue for twenty guests***

◊ **breakfast** first meal of the day; ***I had a boiled egg for breakfast***

◊ **dinner** main meal of the day (usually eaten in the evening); ***we were having dinner when the telephone rang***

◊ **feast** very large meal; ***that wasn't an ordinary meal - it was a feast!***

◊ **lunch** meal eaten in the middle of the day; ***we always have lunch at twelve thirty***

◊ **picnic** open air meal where the food is usually cold and people sit on the ground; ***if it's fine, let's go for a picnic***

◊ **refreshments** food and drink (usually at a function, meeting, etc.); ***light refreshments will be served after the meeting***

◊ **snack** light meal, a small amount of food; ***we just had a snack during the journey***

◊ **spread** *(informal)* attractive mass of food; ***you should have seen the spread at the wedding reception***

◊ **supper** meal which is eaten late or before going to bed; ***don't eat a big supper, it will stop you sleeping well***

◊ **tea** afternoon meal at which you drink tea and eat bread, cake, etc.; ***why don't you come for tea tomorrow?***

measure

verb to find out the length or quantity of something; ***he measured the size of the garden***

◊ **calculate** to find the answer to a problem using numbers; ***the bank clerk calculated the rate of exchange for the dollar***

◊ **count** to find out a total; ***he counted up the sales for the last twelve months***

◊ **gauge** to measure or to calculate; ***this is an instrument which gauges the speed of the wind***

◊ **survey** to measure land in order to produce a plan or map; ***they are surveying the area where the new runway will be built***

medicine

noun drug taken to treat a disease; ***the chemist told me to take the medicine four times a day***; ⇨**drug**

◊ **antidote** substance which counteracts the effects of a poison; ***there is no satisfactory antidote to cyanide***

◊ **medication** drug taken by a patient; ***are you taking any medication?***

◊ **painkiller** drug which stops someone feeling pain; ***I'll get you a painkiller for your migraine***

◊ **remedy** thing which may cure; ***it's an old remedy for hayfever***

◊ **stimulant** substance which makes the body function faster; ***caffeine is a stimulant***

◊ **tonic** something which makes you stronger; ***he's taking a course of iron tonic tablets***

meet

verb to come together; ***she met him at the railway station***; ⇨**encounter**

◊ **assemble** *or* **collect** *or* **congregate** to come together as a group; ***the fans assembled at the football ground***

◊ **convene** to call a meeting; ***he convened a meeting of local shopkeepers***

◊ **converge** to come together at a certain place or point; ***crowds of protesters converged on the main square***

◊ **muster** *or* **rally** to gather together; ***she tried to muster her supporters before the vote***

meeting

noun the coming together of people in a group; ***the club will hold its next meeting on Thursday***; ⇨**assembly;** ⇨**encounter**

◊ **conclave** assembly of people held in private to make a decision; ***a conclave of senior politicians met to decide on a new leader***

◊ **conference** meeting of a group or society; ***the annual conference of the Electrician's Union***

◊ **convention** general meeting of an association or political party; ***they are holding their annual convention in Chicago***

◊ **council** official group or elected committee; ***the town council privatized the refuse service***

◊ **gathering** group of people who have come together; ***a speaker addressed the gathering***

◊ **party** special occasion when several people meet, usually in someone's house; ***we're having a party on New Year's Eve***

◊ **rally** large meeting of members of an association or political party; ***they held a rally to protest against the job cuts***

◊ **reunion** meeting of people who have not met for a long time; ***we are holding a reunion of past students next year***

member

noun person who belongs to a group; ***three members of staff are away sick***

◊ **associate** person who works in the same business as someone; ***she is a business associate of mine***

◊ **fellow** member of a college (at Oxford and Cambridge Universities) or of a research institute or academic society; ***he is a fellow of Pembroke College Oxford***

◊ **partner** person who works in a business and has a share in it with others; ***she became a partner in a firm of solicitors***

◊ **sympathizer** person who agrees in general with the policies of a group, without being a member of it; ***the government is made up of communists and communist sympathizers***

message

noun information which is sent or left; ***I will leave a message with his secretary***

◊ **communication** official message; ***we have had a communication from the local tax inspector***

◊ **e-mail** message sent from one computer to another, using telephone lines; ***I found two e-mails on my computer when I went into work this morning***

◊ **letter** piece of writing sent from one person or organization to another to pass on information; ***there were two letters for you in the post***

◊ **note** short written message; ***he wrote me a note to say he could not come***

◊ **postcard** piece of card (often with a picture on one side) which you send to someone with a short message on it; ***send us a postcard when you arrive in China***

◊ **reminder** message to remind someone to do something; ***we had a reminder from the gas company that we hadn't paid our bill***

◊ **voice mail** messages left on a telephone answering machine; ***I always check my voice mail first when I come into the office***

middle

adjective in the centre; half way between two ends; ***they live in the middle house of a row of five***; ⇨**central;** ⇨**median**

◊ **average** *or* **mean** calculated by dividing the total by the number of quantities; ***his average speed was 30mph***

◊ **intermediate** half way between two points; ***we are at an intermediate stage in our research work***

◊ **mid-** *(prefix)* the middle part; ***mid-life***; ***the mid-1980s***; ***the factory is closed until mid-July***

mind

noun part of the body which controls memory, reasoning; ***her mind always seems to be on other things***

◊ **brain** nerve centre in the head, which controls all the body; ***the brain is the most important part of the body***

◊ **consciousness** being aware of things happening around you; ***he never regained consciousness after the accident***

◊ **intellect** power of the brain, ability to think or reason; ***you could see at once she was a person of superior intellect***

◊ **mentality** way of thinking which is typical of someone or a group; ***I don't understand the mentality of people who are cruel to animals***

◊ **reason** the power of thought; ***he used his reason to solve the problem***

◊ **subconscious** part of your mind which has ideas or feelings of which you are not aware; ***somewhere, deep in her subconscious, was a feeling of hatred for his family***

mistake

noun act or thought which is wrong; ***he made a mistake in typing the address***; ⇨**blunder;** ⇨**error;** ⇨**miscalculation;** ⇨**slip**

◊ **fallacy** false argument; ***it's a common fallacy that American companies are more efficient than British ones***

◊ **lie** something which is not true; ***someone has been telling lies about him***

◊ **misjudgement** wrong opinion formed about something or someone; ***selling the house was a serious misjudgement***

◊ **misunderstanding** not understanding something correctly; ***there was a misunderstanding over my tickets***

◊ **oversight** mistake made by not doing something because you forgot it or did not notice it; ***through an oversight, the minutes of the meeting were not sent out***

mix

verb to blend or to mingle things together; ***she made the cake by mixing eggs and flour***; ⇨**blend**; ⇨**mingle**

◊ **amalgamate** to combine together; ***the two paragraphs are so short that they can be amalgamated into one***

◊ **intersperse** to scatter among or alternate with; ***the play consisted of short conversations interspersed with long periods of silence***

◊ **jumble** to mix in a confused way; ***his thoughts were all jumbled up in his head***

◊ **merge** to join together with something; ***the two motorways merge here***

◊ **shuffle** to mix playing cards; ***shuffle the cards then we can begin the game***

modern

adjective referring to the present time; ***it is a fairly modern invention - it was patented only thirty years ago***

◊ **avant-garde** new, experimental and not traditional music, painting, etc.; ***during his lifetime he was regarded as an avant-garde author***

◊ **brand-new** completely new; ***these shoes are brand-new for the wedding***

◊ **contemporary** modern, present-day; ***contemporary art has made a decisive break with the past***

◊ **new** made quite recently, never used before; ***this is the new model, it's just come out***

◊ **newfangled** modern and complicated; ***I don't like these newfangled ideas of his***

◊ **recent** which took place not very long ago; ***we will mail you our most recent catalogue***

◊ **revolutionary** very new; ***a revolutionary treatment for cancer is being tested***

◊ **up-to-date** with very recent information; ***I don't have an up-to-date timetable***

money

noun coins or notes which are used for buying things; ***how much money have you got in your wallet?***

◊ **capital** money which is invested; ***a company with £100,000 capital***

◊ **cash** money in coins and notes, not in cheques or any other form; ***I prefer to use cash rather than my credit card***

◊ **cash flow** rate at which money comes into and is paid out from a business; ***the company had a very healthy cash flow and was able to invest***

◊ **currency** the money which a country uses; ***we changed our money into the local currency***

◊ **finance** money used to promote projects, businesses, etc.; ***how will you raise the finance for the expansion?***

◊ **funds** money which is available for spending; ***he started a course at college and then ran out of funds***

◊ **pocket money** money which parents give to their children each week; ***she spends her pocket money on comics and sweets***

◊ **wealth** large amount of money; ***his wealth was inherited from his grandfather***

mountain

noun piece of very high land; ***Everest is the highest mountain in the world***

◊ **highlands** mountain region; ***they live in the Highlands of Scotland***

◊ **hill** piece of high land, but lower than a mountain; ***the hills are covered with spring flowers***

◊ **peak** *or* **summit** top of a mountain; ***can you see that snow-covered peak in the distance?***

◊ **plateau** area of high, flat land; ***the high plateau region of southern Argentina***

◊ **range** series of mountains in line; ***they looked out at the vast mountain range***

◊ **upland** mountainous area of a country; ***heather is common in upland areas***

move

verb to change the place of something, to change your position; ***move the chairs to the side of the room***; ***some animal was moving about outside the tent***

◊ **carry** to take something and move it to another place; ***they had to carry the chest of drawers up the stairs***

◊ **deport** *or* **expel** to throw someone out from a country; ***he was deported when his visa expired***

◊ **displace** to move something from its usual place; ***someone has displaced the ornaments on the mantelpiece***

◊ **eject** to throw out; ***they ejected the troublemakers from the meeting***

◊ **evict** to force someone, especially a tenant, to leave a property; ***she was evicted from her house***

◊ **go** to leave, to move from one place to another; ***when the play was over it was time to go home***; ***he has gone to work in Washington***

◊ **leave** to go away from somewhere; ***Eurostar leaves Waterloo for Brussels every day at 8.25***

◊ **pull** to move something towards you or after you; ***the truck was pulling a trailer***; ***he pulled a gun out of his pocket***

◊ **push** to make something move away from you or in front of you; ***we'll have to push the car to get it to start***

◊ **send** to make someone or something go from one place to another; ***my mother sent me to the baker's to buy some bread***

◊ **shift** to move, to change the position of something; ***we've shifted the TV from the kitchen to the dining room***

◊ **transfer** to move something or someone to another place; ***the money will be transferred directly to your bank account***

◊ **transport** to move goods or people from one place to another in a vehicle; ***the visitors will be transported to the factory by helicopter***

murder

noun illegal act of deliberately killing someone; ***the murder was committed during night***; ⇨**homicide;** ⇨**killing**

◊ **assassination** political killing; ***an assassination attempt against the president***

◊ **euthanasia** mercy killing, the killing of a sick person to put an end to his or her suffering (legal in some countries); ***euthanasia can be a difficult dilemma for doctors and relatives***

◊ **execution** legal killing of a person sentenced to death; ***in the 19th century there were still public executions***

◊ **manslaughter** the offence of killing someone without having intended to do so or killing someone intentionally but with circumstances which reduce the seriousness of the crime; ***he was acquitted of murder but found guilty of manslaughter***

◊ **massacre** *or* **slaughter** killing of a large number of people or animals; ***in the massacre, soldiers killed hundreds of innocent civilians***

◊ **suicide** act of killing yourself; ***he killed his two children then committed suicide***

museum

noun building you can visit to see a collection of valuable or rare objects; ***the museum has a rich collection of Italian paintings***

◊ **archives** collection of documents; ***the town's archives go back to its foundation in 1140***

◊ **art gallery** place where pictures and sculpture is shown to the public; ***the art gallery had very few really modern paintings***

◊ **exhibition** display (of works of art, flowers, etc.); ***the exhibition is open from 10am to 5pm***

◊ **gallery** shop selling pictures, antiques; ***she runs an art gallery selling pictures by local artists***

◊ **library** place where books are kept which can be borrowed; ***he forgot to take his books back to the library***

music

noun sound made when you sing or play an instrument; ***do you like Russian music?***

◊ **arrangement** music arranged for a particular instrument or to be played in a certain way; ***the band played a special arrangement of the song***

◊ **blues** sad songs from the southern USA; ***Bessie Smith, the great blues singer***

◊ **chamber music** classical music for a small group or orchestra suitable for a room rather than a large hall; ***we went to a recital of chamber music***

◊ **choral music** music sung by a choir; ***the Welsh are famous for their choral music***

◊ **classical music** traditional, serious music; ***modern classical music draws on a tradition of over four hundred years***

◊ **composition** piece of music; ***his composition was performed by a local orchestra***

◊ **concert** programme of music played in public; ***the concert included work by Mozart and Delius***

◊ **harmony** agreeable musical sounds; ***the group sang in harmony***

◊ **hymn** song sung during a Christian religious service; ***the congregation stood for the first hymn***

◊ **jazz** type of music with a strong rhythm, and solo improvizations, first played in the southern USA; ***Louis Armstrong was one of the kings of jazz***

◊ **melody** *or* **tune** series of musical notes which have a recognisable pattern; ***the song has a catchy melody***

◊ **pop music** *(informal)* modern popular music; ***do you prefer jazz to pop music?***

◊ **recital** concert given by a small group of musicians; ***we went to a Mozart recital***

◊ **rhythm and blues** mixture of pop music and blues music; ***rhythm and blues became very popular after the 1960s***

◊ **rock music** loud popular music with a strong rhythm; ***she likes to listen to rock music on his radio***

◊ **song** words which are sung; ***he was singing a song in the bath***

◊ **swing** dance music with a strong rhythm played by bands and popular in the 1940s and 1950s; ***Benny Goodman's band was one of the great swing bands***

Nn

name

noun special way of calling someone or something; ***Hello! My name's Bill***

◊ **designation** name, title or description given to someone or something; ***she has the official designation of chief medical officer***

◊ **first name** *or* **Christian name** a person's first name; ***write your surname in capitals, followed by your first names***

◊ **nickname** short or informal name given to someone; ***his real name is John but everyone calls him by his nickname - Jack***

◊ **surname** family name, shared by all people in the family; ***Smith is the commonest surname in the London telephone directory***

◊ **title (i)** word (such as Dr, Mr, Professor, Lord, Sir, Lady, etc.) put in front of a name to show an honour or a qualification; ***do not forget to put the title Doctor in front of his name*** **(ii)** name or description given to someone or something; ***she has the official title of Chief Medical Officer***

near

adjective close to, not far away from; ***he is a near neighbour of ours, he lives in the next street***

◊ **adjacent** very close to, almost touching; ***we went to the museum and parked in the adjacent car park***

◊ **adjoining** next to, touching; ***the adjoining gardens were separated by a fence***

◊ **local** referring to a place or district near where you are; ***she works as a nurse in the local hospital***

◊ **neighbouring** which is close to you; ***there are no shops in our village so we have to go to the neighbouring town***

◊ **next** nearest in place; ***the ball went over the fence into the next garden***

network

noun linked system; ***a computer network***; ***a railway network***

◊ **Internet (the net)** international network linking thousands of computers; ***he used the Internet to help with his research***

◊ **system** group of things that are linked together; ***the British motorway system***

◊ **WWW (world wide web, the web)** collection of millions of individual pages of information (containing text, images and sound) within the Internet, which users can visit; ***she found a bargain holiday advertised on the web***

new

adjective made quite recently, never used before; ***this is the new model, it's just come out***

◊ **avant-garde** new, experimental and not traditional music, painting, etc.; ***during his lifetime he was regarded as an avant-garde author***

◊ **brand-new** completely new; ***he wore brand-new shoes for the wedding***

◊ **contemporary** modern, present-day; ***contemporary art has made a decisive break with the past***

◊ **fresh** made quite recently, not used; ***let's ask for a fresh pot of coffee***

◊ **modern** referring to the present time; ***it is a fairly modern invention - it was patented only thirty years ago***

◊ **newfangled** modern and complicated; ***I don't like these newfangled ideas of his***

◊ **novel** *or* **original** new, of a new kind; ***it was a novel idea which quickly caught on***

◊ **recent** which took place not very long ago; ***we will mail you our most recent catalogue***

◊ **revolutionary** very new; ***a revolutionary treatment for cancer is being tested***

◊ **unprecedented** which has never happened before, or with such force; ***there followed a period of unprecedented prosperity***

◊ **up-to-date** with very recent information; ***I don't have an up-to-date timetable***

news

noun spoken or written information about what has happened; ***what's the news of your sister?***

◊ **bulletin** information on a situation; ***the hospital issued a daily news bulletin on the condition of the accident victims***

◊ **communiqué** official announcement; ***the government communiqué announced the president's tour***

◊ **dispatch** message sent; ***the reporters send regular dispatches from the war zone***

◊ **gossip** *or* **hearsay** stories or news about someone which may or may not be true; ***have you heard the latest gossip about Sue?***

◊ **information** facts about something; ***can you send me information about holidays in Greece?***

◊ **press release** sheet giving news about something which is sent to newspapers, TV and radio stations; ***the company sent out a press release about the launch of the new car***

◊ **report** description of what has happened or what will happen; ***we read the report of the accident in the newspaper***

◊ **rumour** story spread from one person to another but which may not be true; ***there's a rumour going round that John's finally getting married***

◊ **teletext** news, weather and other information available in text through the TV; ***I checked the teletext to find out the latest headlines***

next

adjective coming afterwards in time, nearest in place; ***next week is the start of our holiday***; ***she took the next seat in the row***

◊ **consecutive** *or* **successive** one after the other; ***the bank sent him reminders for two consecutive weeks***

◊ **ensuing** *or* **following** which follows; ***the explosion and the ensuing fire***

◊ **near** close to, not far away from; ***he is a near neighbour of ours, he lives in the next street***

◊ **subsequent** *(formal)* which comes later; ***the rain storm and the subsequent flooding disrupted the cricket match***

nice

adjective good, fine; ***we had a nice time at the seaside***; ⇨**agreeable;** ⇨**pleasant**

◊ **amusing** which makes you laugh; ***it was amusing to hear about your journey***

◊ **attractive** pleasant looking; ***they found the Lake District very attractive***

◊ **charming** with an attractive manner; ***she was a charming hostess and the evening was delightful***; ***they are a charming couple***

◊ **comfortable** soft and relaxing; ***there are some comfortable chairs in the lounge***

◊ **delightful** very pleasant; ***they are a very nice family and the evening we spent with them was delightful***

◊ **enjoyable** which pleases; ***they spent an enjoyable evening playing cards***

◊ **refreshing** exciting and new; ***our new offices are a refreshing change from the old building***

◊ **restful** which makes you feel calm and relaxed; ***we were glad to get back to the restful calm of the hotel***

◊ **satisfying** which makes someone pleased with the way things have gone; ***to grow all your own fruit and vegetables is very satisfying***

normal

adjective usual, which usually happens; ***we hope to resume normal service as soon as possible***

◊ **average** ordinary, not unusual; ***it was an average working day***

◊ **common** which happens often, which you find everywhere; ***it is very common for people to get colds in winter***

◊ **everyday** very common; ***the milkman calling was an everyday event***

◊ **natural** not unusual; ***it's natural to worry about your first baby***

◊ **ordinary** not special; ***they lead a very ordinary life***

◊ **typical** having the usual qualities of a particular group or occasion; ***it was a typical school day***

nothing

noun or pronoun not anything; ***there's nothing interesting on TV***; ⇨**nil;** ⇨**zero**

◊ **nobody** no one, no person; ***there was nobody to meet us at the airport***

◊ **none** not one; ***none of my friends are married***

nurse

verb to look after people who are ill; ***when she became ill her daughter nursed her***

◊ **comfort** to make someone happier, when they are in pain or miserable, etc.; ***she tried to comfort the little girl***

◊ **cure** to make a patient or disease better; ***it's good medicine, it cured my cough very quickly***

◊ **heal** to become healthy again; ***after six weeks the wound finally healed***

◊ **tend** to look after someone or something; ***the nurses tended the wounded soldiers***

◊ **treat** to deal with injuries or illnesses in order to cure them; ***the injured people were treated in hospital after the accident***

nurse

noun (woman or man) person who looks after sick people; ***he's training at the hospital to be a nurse***

◊ **auxiliary** helper who does general work in a hospital or clinic; ***the nurse is busy at the moment so an auxiliary will take you to the right department***

◊ **first aider** person trained to give help to a person who is hurt, before a doctor or ambulance arrives; ***first aiders often help out where big crowds gather for some event***

◊ **paramedic** person who works in a medical profession linked to that of nurse or doctor, such as ambulance men, therapists, etc.; ***the paramedics did a heart massage when the patient had a cardiac arrest in the ambulance***

◊ **psychiatric nurse** nurse who works with patients who have mental illness; ***she's a psychiatric nurse who visits patients living at home***

Oo

obey

verb to do what someone tells you to do; ***soldiers always obey the orders of an officer***

◊ **comply** to keep a rule, to obey an order; ***failure to comply with the court order will lead to prosecution***

◊ **conform** to behave in the same way as other people; ***my son is a bit of a rebel - he hates having to conform***

◊ **observe** to follow or to obey (a rule, law, custom, etc.); ***his family observes all the Jewish festivals***

obtain

verb to get; ***she obtained a copy of the will***; ⇨**acquire** *(formal)*; ⇨**gain**; ⇨ **get**; ⇨**procure** *(formal)*

◊ **appropriate** to seize property; ***the authorities appropriated the land to build a new hospital***

◊ **earn** to get by working or by doing something; ***he earns £150 a week***; ***she earned praise because she had made a great effort***; ***he earned a reprimand from the teacher for his silly behaviour***

◊ **receive** to get something which has been sent; ***we received a parcel from the supplier this morning***

◊ **win** to get (a prize, etc.); ***she won first prize in the art competition***

offence

noun

(a) crime, act which is against the law; ***he was charged with committing an offence***

◊ **crime** illegal act or acts; ***the crime he was charged with was breaking and entering***

◊ **capital offence** offence for which the death penalty can be given; ***the crime of treason is still a capital offence in some countries***

◊ **felony** crime classed as serious; ***he was told that a felony would usually result in a prison sentence***

◊ **misdemeanour** crime classed as a less serious crime; ***as he was only charged with a misdemeanour his case was heard by a magistrate not by a judge and jury***

(b) action against public opinion or against someone's feelings; ***her behaviour was an offence to the whole village***

◊ **injury** hurt; ***it caused injury to his feelings***

◊ **insult** rude words said to or about a person; ***that is an insult to the government***

◊ **sin** something bad; ***it would be a sin to waste all that meat***

◊ **transgression** overstepping a limit or breaking a rule; ***any transgression of the rules will be punished very severely***

offend

verb to be or to go against public opinion or someone's feelings; ***he offended the whole village by the article he wrote in the paper***

◊ **aggravate** to make something worse; ***the situation was aggravated by her bad manners***

◊ **antagonize** to make someone very hostile; ***don't antagonize him by telling him what he ought to do***

◊ **disgust** to give someone a strong feeling of dislike or disapproval; ***the smell of boiling cabbage disgusted her***

◊ **displease** not to please; ***his reply seemed to displease her***

◊ **enrage** to make someone very angry; ***she was enraged by the attitude of the council***

◊ **insult** to say rude words to or about a person; ***he insulted the team in a newspaper article***

◊ **repel** to be so unpleasant as to drive people away; ***the smell repelled me so much that I could not finish my meal***

◊ **scandalize** to make people angry by doing something which they think is wrong; ***she scandalized her neighbours by the clothes she wore***

◊ **shock** to give someone a sudden unpleasant surprise; ***the conditions in the hospital shocked the new doctor***

◊ **sicken** to make someone disgusted; ***it sickens me to think of foxes being hunted***

◊ **upset** to make someone worried or unhappy; ***don't upset your mother by telling her you're planning to go to live in Russia***

offer

noun thing which is proposed; ***he accepted her offer of a job in Paris***

◊ **bid** offer to buy (especially at an auction); ***his bid for the painting was too low***

◊ **overture** cautious offer to begin negotiations; ***they made overtures with a view to forming an alliance***

◊ **proposal** suggestion, plan which has been suggested; ***the committee made a proposal to rebuild the club house***

◊ **tender** offer to do something at a certain price; ***the firm's tender for the work was unacceptable***

office

noun room or building where you carry on a business or where you organize something; ***I'll be working late at the office this evening***; ⇨**bureau**

◊ **premises** building which houses an office or shop; ***we must move to new premises, the business has outgrown the old building***

◊ **workplace** place where work is done; ***more work gets done if the workplace is in pleasant surroundings***

official

noun person holding a recognized position; ***they were met by an official from the embassy***

◊ **bailiff** court official whose responsibility is to see that court orders are obeyed; ***the court ordered the bailiff to seize his property because he had not paid his debts***

◊ **bureaucrat** *or* **civil servant** *or* **public servant** person who works in a government department; ***she works as a bureaucrat in Brussels***

◊ **magistrate** judge who tries cases in a minor court; ***she appeared before the magistrates***; ***he was fined £500 by the magistrates***

official

adjective done or approved by someone in authority or by the government; ***we had an official order from the local authority***

◊ **authoritative** which demands respect; ***this is an authoritative work on Shakespeare's 'Macbeth'***

◊ **correct** right, without any mistakes; ***can you tell me the correct time?***

◊ **factual** referring to facts; ***he presented a straightforward factual report***

◊ **governmental** referring to a government; ***he chairs the governmental committee on unemployment***

◊ **mandatory** which has to be done, which has to take place because of a rule or law; ***attendance at meetings is mandatory for all committee members***

often

adverb many times, frequently; ***I often have to go to town on business***; ⇨**frequently**

◊ **daily** happening every day; ***he travelled daily by train***

◊ **monthly** happening every month; ***she is paid £1000 monthly***

◊ **regularly** done in a way that is repeated at the same time; ***he is regularly the first person to arrive at the office***

◊ **repeatedly** again and again; ***she repeatedly broke the law***

◊ **weekly** happening every week; ***he visits his father weekly***

old

adjective not young, having existed for a long time; ***my uncle is an old man - he's 84***; ***this old painting is valuable, it dates from the 17th century***; ⇨**elderly**

◊ **ancient** very old; ***she's studying ancient history***

◊ **antique** old and valuable; ***an antique Chinese vase***

◊ **antiquated** very old and out-of-date; ***he still drives that antiquated old car he bought years ago***

◊ **medieval** referring to the Middle Ages; ***the ruins of a medieval castle dominate the town***

◊ **old-fashioned** not in fashion, out-of-date; ***she wore old-fashioned clothes***

◊ **prehistoric** belonging to the time before there was a written history; ***prehistoric people used flints to make knives***

◊ **senile** *(person)* whose mind is getting muddled because of age; ***his father is getting a bit senile***

◊ **traditional** according to the beliefs, customs and stories which are passed from one generation to the next; ***villagers still wear their traditional dress on Sundays***

◊ **venerable** very old and likely to be respected; ***he died at a venerable age***

open

adjective not shut; ***the safe door is open***

◊ **accessible** easily reached, easily entered into; ***the countryside is easily accessible from the town***; ***his writing is very accessible to all readers***

◊ **ajar** slightly open; ***we left the door ajar to let some air into the hot room***

◊ **gaping** *or* **yawning** wide open; ***a gaping hole appeared in the street***

◊ **unfenced** not fenced in; ***large areas of unfenced countryside are open to walkers***

open

verb to make something not shut any more; ***we opened the door and went into the house***

◊ **break open** to open something by using force; ***the police broke open the door to get into the house***

◊ **prise open** to open using something as a lever; ***he prised open the lid using a screwdriver***

◊ **uncork** to open a bottle by removing the cork; ***he uncorked the champagne at the wedding***

◊ **uncover** to take a cover off something; ***if you uncover the jam pots it will encourage wasps***

◊ **unfasten** to open by undoing a fastening; ***she unfastened her jacket and sat down***

◊ **unlock** to open something which was locked; ***I can't unlock the car door - I've got the wrong key***

opinion

noun what someone thinks about something; ***ask the lawyer his opinion about the letter***

◊ **belief** feeling sure that something is true; ***his firm belief in the power of the law***

◊ **conviction** being certain that something is true; ***her religious convictions do not allow her to eat shellfish***

◊ **estimate** calculation of the approximate worth of something; ***can you give me an estimate of how much time you spent on the job?***

◊ **feeling** something which you sense with your mind; ***I had a feeling that the strange man knew who I was***

◊ **idea** something which you think of, a plan which you make in your mind; ***I have had an idea about where we might go on holiday***

◊ **impression** sensing or getting a feeling about something; ***I got the impression that she wanted us to leave***

◊ **view** way of thinking about something; ***in his view the government ought to act now***

◊ **viewpoint** particular way of thinking about something; ***she looks at the project from the viewpoint of a mother***

opportunity

noun chance or circumstances which allow you to do something; ***did you have an opportunity to visit St. Paul's Cathedral in London?***; ⇨**chance;** ⇨**opening**

◊ **possibility** being likely to happen; ***there is no possibility of the bank lending us any more money***

orchestra

noun large group of musicians who play together; ***the school orchestra played at the prize-giving***

◊ **chamber orchestra** small orchestra which plays music which can be played in a room rather than a hall; ***he plays the violin in a chamber orchestra***

◊ **ensemble** small group of musicians or singers; ***an ensemble played music by Mozart***

◊ **quartet** four musicians playing together; ***a string quartet played music by Bach***

◊ **quintet** five musicians playing together; ***he plays the cello in a string quintet***

◊ **symphony orchestra** large orchestra which has enough musicians to be able to play large scale musical works; ***the London Symphony Orchestra***

◊ **trio** three musicians playing together; ***the concert has been postponed because one of the trio is ill***

order

verb

(a) *(usually by someone in authority)* to tell someone to do something; ***they ordered the protesters to leave the parliament building***; ***the doctor ordered him to take complete rest***; ⇨**command;** ⇨**direct**

◊ **decree** to state as a legal order; ***the president decreed that it would be a national holiday***

◊ **demand** to ask firmly for something; ***she demanded a refund***

◊ **instruct** to tell someone officially to do something; ***the fireman instructed everyone to leave the building***; ***the inspectors instructed the restaurant to replace its kitchen equipment***

◊ **tell** to give instructions; ***give a shout to tell us when to start***

(b) to arrange for something to be bought or delivered; ***we ordered our meal and had a drink while we waited***

◊ **buy** to get something by paying money; ***what did you buy your mother for her birthday?***

◊ **put a deposit on** to pay money given in advance so that the thing will not be sold to someone else; ***she had to put a deposit on the watch***

◊ **requisition** to place a written official order for the supply of something; ***the official requisitioned all the supplies that were needed***

◊ **reserve** to keep for use at a later date; ***we reserved two good seats at the theatre for her birthday next week***

order

noun instruction to someone to do something; ***he shouted orders to the workmen***; ⇨**command**

◊ **court order** direction for action issued by a court; ***the judge issued a court order to ensure the payment of the debt***

◊ **decree** legal order which has not been voted by parliament; ***the president issued a decree declaring a public holiday***

◊ **demand** firm request for something; ***we received a demand for payment***

◊ **directive** official instruction; ***the ministry has issued a new directive on animal feeds***

◊ **injunction** court order compelling someone to do something or not to do something; ***he got an injunction preventing his wife from selling the car***

◊ **law** the set of rules by which a country is governed; ***everybody is supposed to obey the law***

◊ **regulations** *or* **rules** strict order of the way to behave or do something; ***the new government regulations on housing standards***

◊ **requisition** written official order for the supply of something; ***the captain wrote out a requisition order for stores for the journey***

◊ **subpoena** court order telling someone to appear in court; ***she has been served a subpoena to appear in court next month***

◊ **summons** official command to appear in court to be tried for a criminal or civil offence; ***he answered the summons and appeared in court the following month***

◊ **ultimatum** final demand or proposal after which action will be taken if no agreement is reached; ***the union delivered an ultimatum to the management***

ordinary

adjective not special; ***they lead a very ordinary life***; ⇨**conventional**

◊ **average** normal, not unusual; ***it was an average working day***

◊ **common** *or* **commonplace** which happens often, which you find everywhere; ***it is very common for people to get colds in winter***

◊ **everyday** very common; ***the arrival of the post is an everyday event***

◊ **familiar** heard or seen often before; ***we saw several familiar faces at the party***

◊ **natural** not unusual; ***it's natural to worry about your first baby***

◊ **normal** *or* **standard** usual, what usually happens; ***we hope to resume normal service as soon as possible***

◊ **typical** having the usual qualities of a particular group or occasion; ***it was a typical school day***

organize

verb to put into good order; ***we have asked her to organize the city archives***; ⇨**arrange;** ⇨**direct**

◊ **administer** to manage, to organize (a country, an office, a company); ***the province was administered by Portugal for many years***

◊ **manage** to be in charge of something; ***she manages all our offices in Europe***

◊ **manipulate** to influence people or situations so that you get what you want; ***by manipulating the media the government made sure its message got across to the people***

◊ **orchestrate** to organize a demonstration, etc.; ***they orchestrated the protest marches in such a way as to get them on the TV news***

◊ **prearrange** to organize in advance; ***we prearranged our holiday***

◊ **prepare** to get something ready; ***he is preparing for his exam***

◊ **preside** to be in control of; ***she presided over one of the world's richest corporations***

◊ **regulate** to maintain something by law; ***speed on the motorway is strictly regulated***

◊ **supervise** to watch carefully, to see that work is well done; ***he supervises six trainee receptionists***

owe

verb to be due to pay someone some money; ***she still owes me the £10 she borrowed last month***; ⇨**be in debt;** ⇨**be in the red** *(informal)*

◊ **borrow** to take money for a time, usually paying interest; ***I borrowed money from the bank to pay for the holiday***

own

verb to have, to possess; ***he has his own business***; ⇨ **have;** ⇨**possess**

◊ **buy** to get something by paying money; ***what did you buy your mother for her birthday?***

◊ **keep** *or* **retain** *(formal)* to have for a long time or for ever; ***can I keep the newspaper I borrowed from you?***

Pp

pain

noun feeling of being hurt; ***if you have a pain in your chest, you ought to see a doctor***; ⇨**ache**

◊ **agony** *or* **torment** extreme pain; ***after the accident, she was in agony for weeks***

◊ **discomfort** lack of comfort; ***we suffered acute physical discomfort on the flight***

◊ **distress** great sorrow or pain; ***I don't want to cause the family any distress***

◊ **headache** pain in your head; ***I must lie down, I have a bad headache***

◊ **migraine** sharp severe headache (sometimes accompanied by vomiting and seeing bright lights); ***he had an attack of migraine and couldn't come to work***

◊ **spasm** sudden painful contraction of a muscle; ***she had stomach spasms and went to lie down***

◊ **suffering** feeling pain over a long period of time; ***the doctor gave him an injection to relieve his suffering***

◊ **torture** making someone suffer pain as a punishment or to make them reveal a secret; ***they accused the police of using torture to get information***

◊ **twinge** short sharp pain; ***he sometimes has a twinge in his right shoulder***

painting

noun picture done with paints; ***do you like this painting of the old church?***

◊ **abstract** painting which is not a representation of anything; ***the shapes and colours of the abstract were attractive but didn't mean anything to him***

◊ **daub** *(informal)* very bad painting; ***this daub shouldn't be in an art gallery***

◊ **diptych** two paintings done on panels hinged together

◊ **landscape** painting of a country scene; ***he collects 18th century English landscapes***

◊ **oil painting** picture painted in oil paints; ***he bought an old oil painting at a sale***

◊ **old master** painting by a very famous long dead artist; ***there are several old masters in her collection***

◊ **original** not a copy; ***this is a copy - the original is in the Prado, Madrid***

◊ **pastiche** picture deliberately painted in the style of another artist; ***he did this pastiche as a sort of joke***

◊ **portrait** painting of a person; ***she has painted a portrait of the Queen***

◊ **still life** painting of objects, such as fruit, bottles, flowers, food, etc.; ***Dutch still lifes are well-known***

◊ **triptych** set of three painted panels, hinged together

◊ **watercolour** *or US* **watercolor** picture painted using paints which are mixed with water; ***she exhibited several watercolours in the local gallery***

park

noun open space with grass and trees; ***Hyde Park and Regents Park are in the middle of London***

◊ **amusement park** open-air park with various types of entertainment, such as roundabouts, shooting galleries, etc.; ***we went to the amusement park when we went to the seaside***

◊ **car park** place where cars are left when not being used; ***there's a multi-storey car park next to our office***

◊ **nature reserve** area of land where animals and plants are protected; ***we often go to the nature reserve to do some birdwatching***

◊ **playground** place at a school or in a public area where children can play; ***children were playing in the playground***

◊ **playing field** large field where sports can be played; ***our playing field is large enough for two rugby matches to be played at the same time***

◊ **public gardens** place in a town where there are flowers and trees and grass, where people can walk around and enjoy themselves; ***the public gardens are in the centre of town near the river***

◊ **recreation ground** public area with playgrounds for children and sports fields for adults; ***the recreation ground is always full of people during summer weekends***

◊ **theme park** amusement park based on a single theme (such as a medieval castle, etc.); ***a visit to the theme park is included in the tour***

part

noun less than the whole amount of something; ***parts of the film were very good***; ⇨**piece**; ⇨**portion**

◊ **bit** *or* **fragment** small part; ***would you like a bit of cake?***

◊ **clause (i)** part of a sentence; ***the sentence had two clauses joined by the word 'and'*** **(ii)** section of a treaty or legal document; ***according to clause 6, payments will not be due until next year***

◊ **excerpt** small part (of a larger piece of music or writing); ***they played an excerpt from a Mozart symphony***

◊ **extract** thing taken from something larger; ***he will be reading extracts from his latest book***

◊ **fraction** very small amount; ***sales are up a fraction this month***

◊ **instalment** regular payment of part of a total sum owed; ***they are paying for the new kitchen by monthly instalments***

◊ **percentage** figure shown as proportion of a hundred; ***a low percentage of the population voted***

◊ **quotation** words spoken or written by someone else which are repeated; ***the article ended with a quotation from one of Churchill's speeches***

◊ **section** part of something which, when joined to other parts, goes to make up a whole; ***the brass section of the orchestra***; ***she works in the legal section of the company***

◊ **segment** part of something which seems to be formed by natural divisions; ***30- to 40-year-olds are the most affluent segment of the population***

◊ **share** part of something that is divided between two or more people; ***take your share of the cake and I will keep the rest***

partner

noun

(a) person who works in a business and has a share in it with others; ***she became a partner in the firm of solicitors***

◊ **accomplice** person who helps another person commit a crime; ***his brother acted as his accomplice***

◊ **ally** person who is on the same side; ***she's a close ally of the leader of the opposition***

◊ **associate** person who works in the same business as someone; ***he is a business associate of mine***

◊ **assistant** person who helps; ***his assistant prepares his materials next door***

◊ **co-worker** person who works alongside someone; ***I was her co-worker on that project***

◊ **backer** person who supports a project with money; ***one of the company's backers has withdrawn***

◊ **colleague** person who works in the same company, office, school, etc., as you; ***his colleagues at the office gave him a present when he got married***

◊ **comrade** friend or companion, especially a soldier; ***we remembered old comrades buried in foreign cemeteries***

◊ **confederate** person who has joined with others, usually to do a crime; ***all over Europe people are looking for her and her confederates***

◊ **helper** person who helps; ***she works two mornings a week as helper in a playgroup***

◊ **supporter** person who encourages; ***it sounds a good idea - I'm surprised it hasn't attracted more supporters***

◊ **sympathizer** person who agrees in general with the policy of a group, without being a member of it; ***the government is made up of communists and communist sympathizers***

(b) person you live with, without necessarily being married; ***we invited him and his partner for drinks***

◊ **husband** man to whom a woman is married; ***her husband is a schoolteacher***

◊ **lover** person, especially a man, who is having a sexual relationship with someone; ***she spent the weekend with her lover***

◊ **mistress** woman who is having a sexual relationship with a man; ***he spent the weekend with his mistress***

◊ **wife** woman to whom a man is married; ***his wife runs an employment agency***

past

noun time before now; ***in the past we always had an office party just before Christmas***

◊ **antiquity** ancient times; ***lost in the mists of antiquity***

◊ **bronze age** period of history when tools, etc., were made of bronze

◊ **history** study of the past, of past events; ***she teaches history at London University***

◊ **iron age** period of history when tools, etc., were made of iron

◊ **olden days** *(informal)* long ago, in historical times; ***in the olden days there were no cars or TV***

◊ **prehistory** time before written history started; ***the finds in the cave shed light on the prehistory of the region***

◊ **stone age** period of history when tools, etc., were made from stone

pay

verb to give money for something; ***I'll pay you to wash my car***

◊ **award** to give a prize, compensation, etc., to someone; ***he was awarded damages by the court after winning his case against the hospital***

◊ **compensate** to pay for damage, for a loss; ***they agreed to compensate him*** for the damage to his car

◊ **refund** to pay money back; ***they refunded 50% of the price of the holiday***

◊ **reimburse** to pay someone back for money he has spent; ***your expenses will be reimbursed***

◊ **repay** to pay back money that is owed; ***I'll repay the loan next month***

◊ **reward** to give money as a prize for finding something, or doing something; ***he was rewarded for finding the box of important papers***

◊ **tip** to give money (not payment) to someone who has provided a service; ***I tipped the waiter £10 because the service had been really good***

pay

noun money earned for doing a job; ***the workers were on strike for more pay***; ⇨**earnings;** ⇨**salary;** ⇨**wages**

◊ **commission** percentage of sales value given to a salesman; ***she gets 15% commission on everything she sells***

◊ **compensation** payment for damage or loss; ***the airline refused to pay any compensation for his lost luggage***

◊ **gratuity** sum of money given to someone who leaves a job; ***she received a tax-free gratuity of £10,000 when she retired***

◊ **income** money which you receive, especially as pay for your work, or as interest on savings; ***their weekly income is not really enough to live on***

◊ **pension** money paid regularly to someone who has retired from work, to a widow, etc.; ***he has a good pension from his firm***

◊ **reward** money given to someone as a prize for finding something, or for information about something; ***when she took the purse she had found to the police station she got a £25 reward***

◊ **tip** extra money given to someone who has provided a service; ***we left a tip for the waiter because the service had been really good***; ***the taxi driver was annoyed because I didn't give him a tip***

peace

noun

(a) state of not being at war; ***the troops are trying to keep peace in the area***

◊ **armistice** agreement to stop fighting; ***the two generals signed an armistice***

◊ **coexistence** living side by side peacefully; ***coexistence needs some effort and understanding on both sides***

◊ **neutrality** not taking sides in a war; ***Switzerland maintained its neutrality through two world wars***

◊ **pacifism** refusing to use violence in the support of any cause; ***is pacifism a choice when your country is at war?***

◊ **truce** agreement between two armies or enemies, etc., to stop fighting for a time; ***when it got dark, they decided to call a truce***

(b) quiet state; ***the peace of the village is being ruined by noisy motorcycles***; ⇨**calm;** ⇨**peacefulness**

◊ **hush** time of silence; ***a hush fell over the people in the hall as the speaker stood up***

◊ **quiet** calm and without noise; ***all I want is a bit of peace and quiet***

◊ **rest** being quiet and peaceful; ***I'm having a well-earned rest after working hard all week***

◊ **tranquillity** calm and peace; ***it is the tranquillity of the mountains that I like most***

people

noun men, women, children, taken as a group; ***there were twenty people waiting to see the doctor***; ⇨**folk**

◊ **clan** family tribe, especially in Scotland; ***the clan name was Campbell***

◊ **community** group of people living in one area; ***the local community is worried about the level of violence in their streets***

◊ **ethnic group** people sharing the same race; ***the ethnic group forms a minority of the total population***

◊ **humanity** *or* **mankind** all people; ***a crime against humanity***

◊ **nation** people living in a country; ***the Prime Minister spoke to the nation about the declaration of war***

◊ **population** number of people who live in a place; ***Paris has a population of over three million***

◊ **public** people in general; ***the public have the right to know what is going on***

◊ **race** large group of people with similar skin colour, hair, etc.; ***the government is trying to stamp out discrimination on grounds of race***

◊ **society** large group of people, usually all the people living in a country, considered as an organized community; ***society needs to be protected against criminals***; ***we live in a free society***

◊ **tribe** group of people with the same race, language and customs; ***she went into the jungle to study the jungle tribes***

perform

verb

(a) to act or entertain in public; ***the group will perform at the arena next week***

◊ **act** to take part in a film, play, etc.; ***he acted the part of Hamlet in the film***

◊ **busk** to perform (usually music) in the street, asking for money; ***the music student went busking in the high street to help pay his fees at college***

◊ **dance** to move in time to music; ***she dances in the Royal Ballet***

◊ **entertain** to amuse; ***we hired a clown to entertain the children***

◊ **mime** to tell a story or convey emotions through gestures without words; ***the clowns mimed the scene and the audience loved it***

◊ **sing** to make music with your voice; ***she sang a funny song about elephants***

◊ **star** to appear as a main character in a film or play; ***he starred in the new production of Guys and Dolls***

(b) to carry out an action; ***she performed a perfect dive***

◊ **do** *(something)* to perform some action; ***I'll do the cleaning***

◊ **operate** to make something work; ***he knows how to operate the machine***

◊ **work** to use your strength or brain to do something; ***he's working well at school***

performance

noun public show; ***the next performance will start at 8 o'clock***

◊ **ballet** public entertainment where dancers perform a story to music; ***Tchaikovsky's ballet Swan Lake***

◊ **cabaret** entertainment given in a restaurant or club; ***there's a cabaret at the club tonight***

◊ **concert** programme of music played in public; ***I'm sorry, the concert's sold out***

◊ **opera** performance on the stage with music, in which the words are sung not spoken; ***'The Marriage of Figaro' is one of Mozart's best-known operas***

◊ **operetta** opera with an amusing plot in which some words are spoken; ***'The Merry Widow' is Lehar's most famous operetta***

◊ **pantomime** funny Christmas play for children, with songs and dances on a traditional fairy-tale subject; ***we took the children to pantomime as a Christmas treat***

◊ **play** written text which is acted in a theatre or on TV; ***did you see the play on TV last night?***

◊ **show** something which is on at a theatre; ***the show starts at 7.30 so let's have dinner early***

performer

noun person who gives a public show; ***in Covent garden street performers entertain the tourists***

◊ **accompanist** person who plays an instrument to accompany a soloist; ***she always used the same accompanist on her tours***

◊ **acrobat** person who performs spectacular physical movements for the public; ***the circus acrobats were amazing***

◊ **actor** *or* **actress** person who acts in the theatre, in films, on television; ***a famous TV actor***

◊ **busker** person who performs (usually music) in the street, asking for money; ***they are trying to ban buskers from playing in Underground stations***

◊ **clown** man who makes people laugh in a circus; ***the clown had a big red nose and baggy trousers***

◊ **comedian** person who tells jokes to make people laugh; ***a well-known TV comedian***

◊ **conductor** person who directs an orchestra; ***the conductor asked the horns to play more softly***

◊ **dancer** person who moves in time to music; ***there were twenty dancers in the chorus of the show***

◊ **entertainer** person who amuses at a public performance, on TV, etc.; ***my brother hired an entertainer for his daughter's birthday party***

◊ **film star** *or* **movie star** well-known film actor or actress; ***there are pictures of film stars in the cinema entrance***

◊ **illusionist** person who performs tricks in which something impossible appears to take place; ***the illusionist made his wife disappear and then reappear***

◊ **juggler** person who throws and catches several things, such as balls, so that most of them are in the air at the same time; ***the jugglers in Covent Garden market attract a good audience***

◊ **magician** person who performs tricks with cards, rabbits, etc.; ***they hired a magician to entertain the children***

◊ **musician** person who plays music professionally; ***a group of young musicians played at the concert***

◊ **pop star** well-known performer of modern popular music; ***the pop star was famous for about a year and then was never heard of again***

◊ **singer** person who makes music with his or her voice; ***she is training to be a professional singer***

◊ **soloist** musician who plays or sings alone; ***she was the soloist in Elgar's Cello Concerto***

◊ **star** famous performer who is very well-known to the public; ***the star of the show was ill and it was difficult to find a suitable replacement***

permanent

adjective lasting for ever; supposed to last for ever; ***he has found a permanent job***

◊ **durable** which lasts, which does not wear away; ***you need a really durable floor covering in a kitchen***

◊ **enduring** which continues for a long time; ***our enduring impression of the holiday was of long white beaches and tall palm trees***

◊ **immemorial** ancient beyond the reach of memory; ***the immemorial oak trees stood in the park***

◊ **lasting** which lasts for a long time; ***his visit to China made a lasting impression on him***

◊ **longstanding** which has been in existence for a long time; ***we have a longstanding arrangement to go for a picnic on her birthday***; ***she is a longstanding customer of ours***

◊ **perpetual** continuous, without any end; ***I don't drive in London because of the perpetual traffic jams***

person

noun single human being; ***his father is a very interesting person***; ⇨**individual**

◊ **child** young boy or girl; ***as a child he was brought up in China***

◊ **man** male human being; ***two men came to the door***; ***that tall man is my brother***

◊ **somebody** *or* **someone** *(pronoun)* certain person; ***somebody was sitting by the window***

◊ **woman** female human being; ***that tall woman is my sister***; ***a woman stopped us and asked to see our tickets***

picture

noun drawing, painting, photo, etc.; ***she drew a picture of the house***

◊ **caricature** funny drawing which exaggerates a person's appearance; ***he drew a caricature of the Prime Minister***

◊ **cartoon** funny, often political, drawing in a newspaper; ***he draws cartoons for the Evening Standard***

◊ **drawing** picture done with a pen or pencil; ***I've bought an old drawing of the church***

◊ **engraving** picture made by printing from a metal plate which has a picture cut on it; ***he has a collection of engravings of 18th century London***

◊ **fresco** painting done on wet plaster on a ceiling or inside wall; ***some 13th century frescos were damaged in the earthquake***

◊ **icon** picture of Christ or a saint in an Eastern Christian church; ***there is a exhibition of Russian icons in the British Museum***

◊ **illustration** picture in a book; ***the book has twenty-five colour illustrations***

◊ **mosaic** picture made of tiny pieces of coloured stone stuck to a wall or floor; ***the floor mosaic showed scenes from Greek mythology***

◊ **mural** painting on a wall; ***the murals were painted by Giotto in the 14th century***

◊ **painting** picture done with paints; ***do you like this painting of the old church?***

◊ **photocopy** copy made on a machine which scans the original; ***he took six photocopies of the page***

◊ **photograph** picture taken with a camera; ***I've found an old black and white photograph of a steam train***

◊ **print** picture or photograph which has been printed; ***I'm going to have some more prints made of this photo***

◊ **reproduction** copy of a painting, etc.; ***this painting is not a real Picasso, it's only a reproduction***

◊ **sketch** rough quick drawing; ***he made a sketch of the church***

◊ **tapestry** thick woven cloth with a picture, usually hung on walls; ***from the clothes of the people shown in the tapestry we were able to work out its age***

◊ **woodcut** print made from an engraving cut on wood; ***the poetry book was illustrated with simple woodcuts***

pity

noun feeling of sympathy for someone unfortunate; ***have you no pity for the homeless?***; ⇨**compassion**

◊ **charity** help, usually money, given to the poor; ***he has lost his job, and his family have to rely on the charity of their neighbours***

◊ **clemency** mercy shown to someone who has done something wrong; ***she appealed for clemency for her son***

◊ **condolences** expressions of regret, especially at the death of someone; ***we expressed our condolences to him on the death of his father***

◊ **mercy** kindness towards unfortunate people; ***the parents of the little boy pleaded with the kidnappers for mercy***

◊ **sympathy** feeling of understanding of someone's problems, or after someone's death; ***he showed no sympathy for her when she said she felt ill***; ***her sympathy meant a lot to the people who came to her with their problems***; ***we received many messages of sympathy when my wife died***

place

noun where something is, or where something happens; ***here's the place where we saw the cows***

◊ **birthplace** place where someone was born, place where something was invented; ***they visited Shakespeare's birthplace in Stratford***; ***Ironbridge is regarded as the birthplace of the industrial revolution***

◊ **district** *or* **locality** part of a town, a small rural area; ***a district well-known for its Italian restaurants***

◊ **location** position in an area; ***the hotel is in a very central location***

◊ **region** area of a country; ***the south west region is famous for apple growing***

◊ **site** place where something is or will be, place where something happened or once existed; ***here is the site for the new factory***; ***this was the site of the battle of Hastings in 1066***

◊ **territory** large stretch of land, land which belongs to a country; ***they occupied all the territory on the east bank of the river***

◊ **zone** area or part which is different from others or which has something special; ***police cars are patrolling the inner city zones***

plan

verb to arrange how you will do something; ***she is busy planning her holiday in Greece***

◊ **anticipate** to expect something to happen; ***I anticipate a delay if the bad weather continues***

◊ **organize** to arrange; ***she is responsible for organizing the meeting***

◊ **outline** to make a broad description of a plan; ***he outlined the plan to the bank manager***

◊ **prearrange** to organize in advance; ***we prearranged our holiday***

◊ **prepare** to get something ready; ***he is preparing for his exam***

◊ **propose** to say that you intend to do something; ***they propose to pay the loan back at £20 per month***

play

noun written text which is acted in a theatre or on TV; ***did you see the play on TV last night?***

◊ **comedy** play which makes you laugh; ***'A Midsummer Night's Dream' is one of Shakespeare's comedies***

◊ **drama** serious performance in a theatre; ***the 'Globe' theatre has put on an unknown Elizabethan drama***

◊ **farce** comic play based on ridiculous situations; ***we went to see a 19th century French farce***

◊ **musical** play with songs and popular music; ***musicals such as 'Cats' and 'Evita' can play for years***

◊ **pantomime** funny Christmas play for children, with songs and dances on a traditional fairy-tale subject; ***we took the children to pantomime as a Christmas treat***

◊ **revue** stage show with satirical sketches, songs, etc.; ***they put on a revue when they were still at university***

◊ **show** something which is on at a theatre; ***the show starts at 7.30 so let's have dinner early***

◊ **tragedy** serious play which ends sadly; ***Shakespeare's tragedy 'King Lear' is playing at the National Theatre***

play

verb

(a) to take part in a game; ***the whole side played well and they won the game easily***

(b) to make music on an instrument; ***she plays the violin in a string quartet***

please

verb to make someone happy or satisfied; ***she's not difficult to please***; ⇨**gratify**

◊ **amuse** to make someone laugh or make the time pass pleasantly; ***the story about the Prime Minister's cat will amuse you***

◊ **cheer up** *or* **comfort** to make someone happier when they are unhappy; ***he made her a good meal to try to cheer her up***

◊ **satisfy** to make someone pleased with what he has bought or with the service he has received; ***our aim is to satisfy our customers***

plenty

noun large quantity; ***you have plenty of time to catch the train***; ⇨**abundance**

◊ **profusion** very large quantity; ***in May, there's a profusion of flowers in the fields***

◊ **wealth** large quantity (usually of money); ***there's a wealth of talent just waiting to be discovered***; ***he inherited his wealth from his grandfather***

police

noun organization which controls traffic, tries to stop crime and tries to catch criminals; ***the police are looking for the driver of the car***

◊ **bobby***(informal)* *or* **copper** *(informal)* policeman; ***watch out, there's a copper coming!***

◊ **C.I.D (Criminal Investigation Department)** department of the police force which uses non-uniformed officers for criminal investigations

◊ **military police** police force which is part of the army; ***the military police were patrolling the harbour***

◊ **special** part-time volunteer uniformed policeman; ***the regular police were accompanied by a group of specials***

◊ **Special Branch** section of the British police dealing with terrorism, spies, crimes against the government

◊ **traffic police** police who deal with traffic and patrol roads; ***the traffic police regularly drive along motorways***

◊ **uniformed officer** police officer who wears a uniform; ***three uniformed officers stood outside the club***

politics

noun ideas and methods used in governing a country; ***he studied politics and economics at university***

◊ **democracy** system of government by freely elected representatives of the people; ***democracy is the system of government in many countries***

◊ **government** group of people who rule a country; ***the president asked the leader of the largest party to form a new government***

◊ **House of Commons** *(also the Commons)* lower house of the British Parliament; ***the Bill will come before the House of Commons***

◊ **House of Lords** *(also the Lords)* upper house of the British Parliament; ***the House of Lords made several amendments to the Bill***

◊ **law** the set of rules by which a country is governed; ***everybody is supposed to obey the law***

◊ **MP (Member of Parliament)** elected member of the House of Commons; ***our MP spoke in Parliament yesterday***

◊ **parliament** group of elected representatives who vote the laws of a country; ***Parliament has passed a law forbidding the sale of dangerous drugs***

◊ **party politics** working to promote the interests of a political party, by taking power in a local or national government; ***the head of state should be above party politics***

◊ **political party** organization of people with similar political opinions and aims; ***which political party does he belong to?***

poor

adjective with little or no money; ***the family is very poor now that neither of the parents has any work***

◊ **bankrupt** *or* **insolvent** not able to pay your debts; ***he has been declared bankrupt***

◊ **broke** *(informal)* *or* **penniless** with no money; ***it's the end of the month and, as usual, I'm broke***

◊ **destitute** with no money or belongings; ***when her husband died he left her destitute***

◊ **hard up** with very little money; ***I can't lend you anything because I'm rather hard up at the moment***

◊ **impoverished** made poor; ***after years of famine and war the impoverished population were starving***

◊ **needy** very poor; ***an organization dedicated to helping needy people in Africa***

popular

adjective liked by a lot of people; ***the department store is popular with young mothers***

◊ **celebrated** very famous; ***the city of Bath gets its name from its celebrated Roman Baths***

◊ **famous** well-known; ***he's a famous footballer***

◊ **fashionable** being of the most admired style at a particular moment; ***she lives in the fashionable West End of London***

port

noun harbour, or town which has a harbour; ***the port of Liverpool is busier now than it has been for some years***

◊ **anchorage** stretch of water where ships can anchor safely; ***the harbour provided a safe anchorage***

◊ **dock** *or* **quay** place where ships load or unload; ***we used to go down to the docks to watch the ships come in***

◊ **ferry terminal** place where ferries begin and end their journeys; ***Dover is a busy ferry terminal***

◊ **harbour** place where boat can come and tie up; ***the yacht moved away from the harbour***

◊ **marina** special harbour with floating platforms where a large number of pleasure boats, such as yachts, can tie up; ***his yacht was moored in the marina***

power

noun the ability to control people or happenings; ***it is in not my power to ban the demonstration***

◊ **ability** having the force to do something; ***he has many abilities but singing isn't one of them***

◊ **authority** power to do something; ***she has the authority to act on our behalf***

◊ **force** *or* **might** strength or power; ***the police had to use force to push back the demonstrators***

◊ **government** group of people who rule a country; ***the president asked the leader of the largest party to form a new government***

◊ **influence** being able to change someone or something; ***he has had a good influence on the other staff***

◊ **politics** ideas and methods used in governing a country; ***he studied politics and economics at university***

◊ **strength** power of action or resistance; ***the strength of the pound increases the possibility of higher inflation***

prayer

noun speaking to God; ***she says her prayers every night before going to bed***

◊ **contemplation** deep thought; ***he was deep in contemplation and did not notice that I had come in***

◊ **devotions** *(formal)* prayers; ***she is at her devotions***

◊ **intercession** pleading (to God or someone in authority) for another person or persons; ***he made many intercessions on behalf of his brother***

◊ **litany** series of prayers with repeated responses, used in church; ***the priest and congregation recited the litany***

◊ **meditation** silent, calm state, as part of religious practice; ***she's deep in meditation***

◊ **petition** prayer asking God for something; ***she offered many petitions in church***

◊ **worship** praise and respect to God; ***prayer is the most important part of worship***

prepare

verb to get something ready; ***he is preparing for his exam***

◊ **anticipate** to expect something to happen; ***I anticipate a delay if the bad weather continues***

◊ **organize** to arrange; ***she is responsible for organizing the meeting***

◊ **outline** to make a broad description of a plan; ***he outlined the plan to the bank manager***

◊ **plan** to arrange how you will do something; ***she is busy planning her holiday in Greece***

◊ **practise** to do repeated exercises in order to improve; ***he's practising catching and throwing***

◊ **prearrange** to organize in advance; ***we prearranged our holiday***

◊ **prime** to get something prepared; ***the bomb had been primed and would have exploded in ten minutes***

◊ **train** to become fit by practising for a sport; ***he's training for the 100m***

◊ **warm up** to practise just before an event; ***the orchestra is warming up before the concert***

press

noun newspapers taken as a group; ***the election wasn't reported in the British press***

◊ **journalism** profession of writing for newspapers or periodicals; ***she took a journalism course to help her get a job on a newspaper***

◊ **media** means of passing information to a large number of people, such as newspapers, TV, radio; ***the book attracted a lot of interest in the media***

◊ **news** spoken or written information about what has happened; ***what's the news of your sister?***

◊ **newspaper** publication consisting of loose folded sheets of paper, which usually comes out each day, with news of what has happened; ***we saw your picture in the local newspaper***

◊ **press agent** person employed to promote someone or something in the press; ***once she became a star she got a press agent***

◊ **stop press** the very latest news printed in brief in a newspaper; ***the accident appeared in the stop press at the bottom of the page***

pretend

verb to make someone believe you are something, so as to deceive them; ***he got into the house by pretending to be a telephone engineer***

◊ **deceive** to trick someone, to make someone believe something which is not true; ***he deceived everyone into thinking that he was a policeman***

◊ **fantasize** to imagine doing or having something which is impossible; ***he often fantasizes about living on a tropical island***

◊ **imagine** to picture something in your mind; ***imagine sitting on a beach in the hot sun***

◊ **imitate** to copy something or someone; ***he made us all laugh by imitating the head teacher***

◊ **lie** to tell someone something which is not true; ***someone has been lying about him to the manager***

◊ **make believe** *(often with children)* to agree to pretend; ***let's make believe that this is a jungle and we are explorers***

prevent

verb to stop something happening, to stop someone doing something; ***the police prevented anyone from leaving the building***

◊ **cancel** to stop something that has been planned; ***the trip was cancelled because the weather was too bad***

◊ **control** to keep in order, to direct or restrict; ***the police were out in force to control the crowds***

◊ **counteract** to act against the actions or effects of something; ***the lotion should counteract the irritant effect of the spray***

◊ **hinder** to make it difficult for something to be done or happen; ***the economic situation is hindering any increase in living standards***

◊ **inhibit** *or* **limit** *or* **restrict** not to allow something to go beyond a certain point; ***the government has limited the number of new motorways that can be built***

◊ **neutralize** to cancel the effect of something; ***we acted immediately to neutralize the threat from their navy***

◊ **oppose** to try and prevent something from happening; ***several groups oppose the new law***

◊ **prohibit** to say that something must not be done; ***the rules prohibit singing in the dining room***

◊ **regulate** to control by using rules or laws; ***speeds are strictly regulated on all classes of roads***

◊ **restrain** to try and stop someone doing something; ***it took six policemen to restrain the man who became violent***

◊ **stop** to make someone or something not do something any more, to prevent someone or something being done; ***the rain stopped the picnic***; ***we stopped the children from buying unwrapped sweets***

◊ **suppress** to not allow to continue; ***all opposition newspapers have been suppressed***

price

noun money which you have to pay to buy something; ***the price of petrol is going up***; ⇨**charge (for)**; ⇨**cost (of)**

◊ **estimate** *or* **quotation** calculation of the price before supplying an item or doing a job; ***the estimate for the job was high and we couldn't afford it***

◊ **expense** the amount of money involved in buying something; ***I can't afford the expense of a holiday just now***

◊ **fare** price you have to pay for a journey; ***rail fares have increased by 10%***

◊ **fee** money paid to doctors, schools and lawyers, etc., for work done; ***private school fees are very high***

◊ **rate** level of payment; ***he accepted the rate he was offered***

◊ **rent** money paid to live in a house, flat, to use an office, etc.; ***rents are high in the centre of town***

◊ **rental** money paid to hire a room, car, etc.; ***the telephone rental has gone up this year***

◊ **retail price** price charged to the general public; ***the retail price is double the wholesale price***

◊ **supplement** *or* **surcharge** additional payment added to the price; ***the hotel charged a supplement for single occupancy of a room***

◊ **tariff** list of prices for gas, water, electricity, etc.; ***the new winter tariff will be imposed next week***

◊ **wholesale price** price charged to a distributor of goods; ***the wholesale price is half the retail price***

pride

noun very high opinion of yourself; ***his pride would not let him admit he had made a mistake***

◊ **arrogance** feeling that you are much better than others; ***his arrogance makes him disliked***

◊ **conceit** high opinion of yourself; ***his conceit in saying he is the only person who can help us is astonishing***

◊ **contempt** feeling of not respecting someone; ***you have shown contempt for the feelings of our family***

◊ **ostentation** being showy and expensive so as to impress; ***the press criticized the ostentation of the new government offices***

◊ **pomposity** using dignified language to make yourself sound more important; ***I can't stand his arrogance and pomposity***

◊ **snobbery** only liking people who are of a higher social class; ***I can't stand the snobbery of the old universities***

◊ **vanity** being excessively proud of your appearance, feeling that you are very good-looking; ***his vanity made him dye his hair and wear some very odd clothes***

principal

noun head, senior administrator (of a school, a college); ***the principal wants to see you in her office***

◊ **chancellor** head of a university; ***he became chancellor of the university four years ago***

◊ **head teacher** teacher who is in charge of a school; ***the head teacher plans to retire next year***

◊ **leader** person who shows the way, who has the most important place; ***he is the leader of the Labour Party***

◊ **rector** head of certain Oxford colleges, head teacher of certain colleges in Scotland, head of a training college for Catholic priests; ***he was elected rector of St Andrews University***

◊ **superior** person in a higher rank; ***each manager is responsible to his superior***

prison

noun building where people are kept when they are being punished for a crime; ***the judge sent him to prison for five years***; ⇨**jail** *(also spelled gaol)* ⇨**penitentiary** *(US)*

◊ **cell** room in a prison; ***there were two prisoners to each cell***

◊ **detention centre** centre where young criminals are kept; ***she gives English lessons in the detention centre***

◊ **open prison** prison which does not have a high level of security for offenders who are not dangerous nor likely to escape; ***as his sentence was for repeated speeding offences he spent three months in an open prison***

◊ **remand centre** prison where people are held while awaiting trial; ***as he was refused bail he had to wait in a remand centre until his trial***

◊ **secure institution** mental hospital in which dangerous prisoners are kept; ***as a murderer who had been found not responsible for his actions he was committed to a secure institution by the court***

prisoner

noun person kept in a secure building or prison as a punishment for a crime, someone held against their will; ***there were two prisoners to each cell in the prison***; ⇨**captive**

◊ **convict** criminal who has been sent to prison; ***the police are searching for two escaped convicts***

◊ **detainee** person held by the authorities; ***the government has promised to release all political detainees***

◊ **hostage** person who is captured and held by someone or an organization, which threatens to kill him unless certain demands are met; ***three of the hostages will be freed tomorrow***

◊ **political prisoner** person kept in prisoner because he or she is an opponent of the government; ***she was held as a political prisoner for fourteen years***

prize

noun something given to a winner; ***she won first prize in the music competition***

◊ **citation** words used in giving someone an award or honour explaining why the award is being made; ***he received a citation for bravery***

◊ **consolation prize** prize for making an effort but not winning; ***she got a goldfish as a consolation prize***

◊ **cup** tall silver bowl given as a prize; ***he has won three silver cups for golf***

◊ **decoration** medal; ***she went to Buckingham palace to receive her decoration***

◊ **medal** metal disc, usually attached to a ribbon, made to commemorate an important occasion or battle, and given to people who have performed well; ***the old soldiers put on all their medals for the parade***

◊ **prize money** money given to the person who wins a competition; ***there is £10,000 in prize money at stake***

problem

noun something which is a difficult question; ***the police are trying to solve the problem of how the thieves got into the house***; ⇨**difficulty**

◊ **aggravation** when something is made worse; ***the treatment was an aggravation to the illness not a cure***

◊ **crisis** serious situation where decisions have to be taken rapidly; ***an international crisis has developed in the area***

◊ **hindrance** something which makes it difficult for something else to happen; ***having six children is something of a hindrance when arranging holidays***

◊ **impasse** when two sides cannot come to an agreement; ***negotiations have reached an impasse***

◊ **impossibility** something which cannot be done; ***getting him to change his mind is an impossibility***

◊ **inconvenience** when difficulties are caused; ***losing my car keys was a real inconvenience***

◊ **predicament** trouble or difficult situation; ***she's got herself into an awful predicament***

◊ **trouble** something that makes you worry, something that causes upset; ***the trouble with old cars is that they don't always start***

product

noun thing which is manufactured; ***Germany is helping her industry to sell more products abroad***

◊ **creation** thing which has been made; ***for desert they served some sort of chocolate and cream creation***

◊ **end product** manufactured product, result of a production process; ***the end product did not reach an acceptable standard***

◊ **handiwork** work done or made by yourself; ***I was just admiring your handiwork***

◊ **harvest** ripe crops which have been gathered; ***a bumper harvest of wheat***

◊ **output** amount which a firm, machine or person produces; ***the factory has doubled its output in the last three months***

◊ **produce** crops grown on the land; ***vegetables and other garden produce are sold in the market***

◊ **result** something which happens because of something else; ***what was the result of the police investigation***

◊ **yield** quantity of a crop or produce produced from a plant or area of land; ***what is the normal yield per hectare?***

profession

work which needs special training, skill or knowledge; ***members of the legal profession protested against the new regulations***; ***they are negotiating a new pay structure for the teaching profession***; ⇨**employment**

◊ **assignment** job of work; ***he was given the assignment of reporting on the war***

◊ **calling** *or* **vocation** work you feel you have been called to do or for which you have a special talent; ***for her, nursing is a calling***

◊ **job** regular work which you get paid for; ***she's got a job in a supermarket***

professional

adjective good, skilled or trained at doing something; ***they did a very professional job in designing the new office***; ⇨**expert**

◊ **proficient** skilful, able to do something well; ***by the summer I had become proficient in speaking German***

◊ **qualified** with the right qualifications; ***she's a qualified doctor***

◊ **specialist** *or* **specialized** which deals with or knows about one thing in particular; ***he has a specialized knowledge of international currency***

profit

noun money you gain which is more than the money you paid for it; ***the sale produced a good profit***

◊ **commission** percentage of sales value given to a salesman; ***she gets 15% commission on everything she sells***

◊ **dividend** part of a company's profits shared out among shareholders; ***the company made a loss and there will be no dividend this year***

◊ **income** *or* **earnings** money which you receive, especially as pay for your work, or as interest on savings; ***their weekly income is not really enough to live on***

◊ **proceeds** money which you receive when you sell something; ***she sold her house and invested the proceeds in a little shop***

◊ **profit margin** percentage of money gained against money paid out; ***we have to work on a very small profit margin so we need a lot of sales***

◊ **return** income from money invested; ***this account should bring in a good return on your investment***

◊ **takings** cash received in a shop or business; ***this week's takings were less than last week's***

◊ **turnover** amount of sales of goods or services by a business; ***our turnover is rising each year***

◊ **winnings** money which has been won at betting; ***he collected all his winnings and went to book a holiday in Spain***

promise

verb to give your word that you will definitely do something; ***they promised to be back for supper***

◊ **contract** to agree to do some work under a legally binding agreement; ***they contracted to supply spare parts for the vehicles for two years***

◊ **swear** to make a solemn public promise; ***the witnesses swore to tell the truth***

◊ **underwrite** to accept responsibility for something; ***the share issue was underwritten by one of the merchant banks***

◊ **vouch for** to guarantee that something is true, that someone will behave well; ***we can't vouch for the statement put out by the publicity department***

◊ **vow** *(formal)* to make a solemn promise to do something; ***he vowed to pay the money back***

promise

noun act of saying that you will definitely do something; ***I'll pay you back on Friday - that's a promise***; ⇨**assurance;** ⇨**guarantee;** ⇨**pledge;** ⇨**undertaking**

◊ **bond** contract; ***his word is his bond***

◊ **commitment** agreement to do something; ***she made a firm commitment to be more punctual in future***

◊ **compact** *(formal)* agreement; ***the two companies signed a compact to share their research findings***

◊ **contract** legal agreement; ***I don't agree with some of the conditions of the contract***

◊ **oath** solemn legal promise that someone will say or write only what is true; ***the lords swore an oath of allegiance to the king***

◊ **vow** solemn promise to do something; ***he made a vow to go on pilgrimage to Jerusalem***

◊ **word** promise which you have made verbally; ***she kept her word and paid the money back***; ***he gave his word that the matter would remain confidential***

proof

noun thing which shows that something is true; ***the police have proof that she committed the murder***

◊ **clarification** making clear; ***we have asked for clarification of the demand for payment***

◊ **conclusive proof** something which definitely shows that something is true; ***the photograph was conclusive proof that he was there***

◊ **evidence** fact which indicates that something really exists or has happened; ***the blood stains on his coat were evidence of the crime***

◊ **verification** check which shows that documents or statements are correct; ***we had to wait for verification of the documents before we could collect the papers***

property

something which belongs to someone; ***the management is not responsible for personal property left in the restaurant***

◊ **inheritance** property which is received from a dead person; ***my grandparent's old home is part of my inheritance***

protect

verb to keep someone or something safe; ***the cover protects the machine against dust***; ⇨**safeguard**

◊ **escort** to accompany someone; ***the police escorted the group into the hotel***

◊ **guard** to protect with soldiers, fences, etc.; ***the prison is guarded at all times***

◊ **immunize** to protect someone against a disease by an injection or treatment; ***I was immunized against tetanus three years ago***

◊ **patrol** to keep guard by walking or driving up and down; ***armed security guards are patrolling the warehouse***

◊ **police** to make sure that rules or laws are obeyed; ***we need more constables to police the area***

◊ **shelter** to give someone protection; ***the school sheltered several refugee families***

◊ **shield** to protect from danger, to protect someone who has done wrong; ***he tried to shield her from the wind***; ***she's just shielding her father from the consequences of his actions***

protection

noun shelter, being kept safe from something; ***the trees give some protection from the rain***; ⇨**defence**

◊ **immunity (i)** ability to resist attacks from a disease; ***the injection will give immunity to malaria*** **(ii)** protection against being arrested; ***she was granted immunity from prosecution***

◊ **insurance** agreement with a company by which you are paid compensation for loss or damage in return for regular payments of money; ***do you have insurance for your travel?***

◊ **preservation** action of protecting; ***the trust is mainly concerned with the preservation of historic buildings***

◊ **safety** not being in danger, not likely to be hurt; ***the police tried to ensure the safety of the public***

◊ **security** protection against criminals; ***the security of the building is maintained by guard dogs***

proud

adjective with a very high opinion of yourself; ***he's too proud to admit he's made a mistake***

◊ **arrogant** very proud in an unpleasant way; ***I've never known such an arrogant young woman***

◊ **boastful** saying how good, etc., you are; ***he annoyed everyone with his boastful talk of his salary and new car***

◊ **cocky** *(informal)* unpleasantly confident; ***she's such a cocky little girl!***

◊ **conceited** thinking too much of yourself; ***how can he be so conceited as to think he's the only person who can run the shop?***

◊ **contemptuous** showing that you do not believe someone is important; ***he shouldn't treat patients in such a contemptuous way***

◊ **ostentatious** looking showy and expensive, so as to impress; ***she rejected the first design as too ostentatious***

◊ **pompous** using very dignified language to make yourself sound more important; ***when he talks to us about morality he always ends up sounding pompous***

◊ **pretentious** claiming to be more important than you are; ***it sounds pretentious to claim that you changed history***

◊ **selfish** doing things only for yourself and not for other people; ***don't be so selfish - pass the chocolates round***

◊ **snobbish** liking people of a higher social class; ***we don't associate with them because they are so snobbish***

◊ **vain** very proud of you appearance, clothes, achievements, etc.; ***he's very vain, and is always combing his hair***

prove

verb to show that something is true; ***I'm determined to prove that he is wrong***

◊ **clarify** to make clear; ***we will have to clarify the situation before making any more decisions***

◊ **corroborate** to show that a statement is true, especially in court; ***the witness corroborated the alibi of the accused***

◊ **establish** to show something to be true; ***we have established her reasons for resigning***

◊ **justify** to show that something is fair, to prove that something is right; ***how can you justify your behaviour?***

◊ **substantiate** to prove that something stated is true; ***she made a claim which was later substantiated***

◊ **verify** to check to see if documents or statements are true; ***is it possible to verify his statement?***

◊ **vindicate** to show that what someone thought was wrong was actually right; ***the report completely vindicated the action taken by the driver***

publish

verb to make publicly known, to bring out a newspaper, book, for sale; ***the company publishes six magazines***

◊ **broadcast** to send out on radio or TV; ***the programme will be broadcast on Monday at 8pm***

◊ **circulate** to send round to various people; ***they circulated their new list of prices to their customers***

◊ **print** to put letters or pictures on a page by machine and produce books, leaflets, newspapers, etc.; ***we printed 5,000 copies of the leaflet***

◊ **serialize** to make a book, story, etc., into a set of instalments; ***the book has been serialized on TV***

◊ **televise** to broadcast something by television; ***the football match will be televised live***

punish

verb to make someone suffer because of something he has done; ***the children must be punished for stealing apples***; ⇨**chastise** *(formal)*; ⇨**discipline**

◊ **condemn** to sentence a criminal; ***she was condemned to death***

◊ **execute** to kill someone who has been condemned to death; ***murderers are no longer executed in this country***

◊ **kill** to make someone or something die; ***the lack of rain has killed all the crops***

◊ **persecute** to treat someone badly on political or religious or racial grounds; ***early Christians were persecuted by the Romans***

◊ **reprimand** to criticize someone severely for doing something wrong; ***the report reprimanded the directors for their negligence***

◊ **sentence** to give someone an official, legal punishment; ***he was sentenced to three weeks in prison***

◊ **take revenge on** to punish someone in return for something he has done to you; ***she planned to take revenge on the boss for having insulted her in public***

◊ **torture** to inflict mental or physical pain on someone; ***the soldiers tortured their prisoners***

◊ **victimize** to treat someone more unfairly than others; ***the prison governor was accused of victimizing young prisoners***

punishment

noun treatment given to someone to make them suffer because of something they have done; ***as a punishment you'll wash the kitchen floor***; ⇨**chastisement** *(formal)*

◊ **capital punishment** killing someone as a punishment for a crime; ***capital punishment is not used in this country***

◊ **corporal punishment** punishment by beating; ***corporal punishment is illegal in state schools***

◊ **execution** legal killing of a person sentenced to death; ***in the 19th century there were still public executions***

◊ **persecution** bad treatment for political, religious or racial reasons; ***the persecution of the early Christians by the Romans***

◊ **reprimand** sharp criticism for doing something; ***she received a reprimand and lost two weeks pay***

◊ **retribution** well-deserved punishment; ***the informer suffered swift retribution from the other members of the gang***

◊ **revenge** punishing someone in return for harm he has caused you; ***they broke the windows of the judge's house in revenge for the fines he had imposed***

◊ **sentence** the official, legal punishment of a court; ***he was given a six-month prison sentence***

◊ **torture** making someone suffer pain as a punishment or to make them reveal a secret; ***they said the police used torture to extract a confession***

◊ **victimization** action of treating someone more unfairly than others; ***the victimization of one child by the others***

purpose

noun what you are trying to do; ***the purpose of the meeting is to plan the village fair***; ⇨**aim**; ⇨**intent**; ⇨**intention**

◊ **objective** *or* **target** the thing which you are trying to do; ***our long-term objective is to make the company financially sound***

◊ **plan** organized way of doing things; ***he made a plan to get up earlier in future***

Qq

qualification

noun suitability for a job, proof of having completed a specialized course of study; ***does he have the necessary qualifications for the job?***

◊ **aptitude** natural ability, readiness to learn; ***she shows great aptitude for French***

◊ **capability** skill or ability to do something; ***I'm afraid this job is way beyond my capabilities***

◊ **degree** diploma from a university; ***she has a degree in mathematics from Oxford***

◊ **diploma** document which shows that a person has reached a certain level of skill in a subject; ***he is studying for a diploma in engineering***

◊ **experience** knowledge got by working or living in various situations; ***some experience of selling is required for this job***

◊ **suitability** the extent to which someone is fit for something; ***I still have doubts about his suitability for the job***

question

noun something which calls for an answer; ***some of the questions in the exam were too difficult***; ⇨**query**

◊ **doubt** being unsure of something; ***I have my doubts about the accuracy of the figures***

◊ **examination** test or inquiry of what you know; ***the examination was very difficult***

◊ **inquiry** *or* **enquiry** question about something; ***a government inquiry into bribery in the police force***

◊ **interrogation** harsh questioning; ***she confessed to the crime during her interrogation***

◊ **interview** meeting in which one person asks another person questions; ***he gave an interview to one of the Sunday magazines***

◊ **investigation** close examination of what you know; ***a police investigation into the causes of the crash***

◊ **questionnaire** printed list of questions given to people to answer, especially used in research; ***we sent out a questionnaire to find out what people thought about the new carpet cleaner***

◊ **riddle** puzzling question to which you want to find the answer; ***where she had got to was a real riddle***

quick

adjective fast; ***this is the quick train to London***; ⇨**fast;** ⇨**rapid;** ⇨**swift**

◊ **hasty** *or* **hurried** carelessly fast; ***it was a hasty decision which he regretted afterwards***; ***we just had time to snatch a hurried lunch before catching the train***

◊ **lively** very active; ***the boss is very lively at the age of 85***

◊ **prompt** done immediately; ***thank you for your prompt reply***

◊ **rushed** done in a rush, too quickly; ***it was a rushed decision which they regretted afterwards***

◊ **speedy** very fast; ***we all wished her a speedy recovery***

quickly

adverb without taking much time; ***the fire service came quickly when we dialled 999***; ⇨**rapidly;** ⇨**swiftly**

◊ **hastily** *or* **hurriedly** quickly and roughly; ***we hastily gathered our picnic things up when the rain came***; ***he hastily hid the letter in his pocket***

quiet

noun absence of loud noise or confusion; ***noisy motorcycles ruin the quiet of the village***; ⇨**calm;** ⇨**peacefulness**

◊ **hush** time of silence; ***a hush fell over the people in the hall as the speaker stood up***

◊ **lull** quiet period; ***there was a lull in all the fuss and noise of the office***

◊ **peace** calm, quiet state; ***the peace of the village is being ruined by noisy motorcycles***

◊ **rest** being quiet and peaceful; ***I'm having a well-earned rest after working hard all week***

◊ **silence** absence of sound; ***I love the silence of the countryside at night***

◊ **stillness** absence of sound or movement; ***the stillness of a windless autumn day is very beautiful***

◊ **tranquillity** calm and peace; ***it is the tranquillity of the mountains that I like most***

quiet

adjective without any noise or fuss; ***the brochure said the rooms were quiet***; ⇨**noiseless**

◊ **calm** *or* **peaceful** *or* **tranquil** quiet, not rough or excited; ***the calm sea was almost flat and the boat stayed still, hardly moving***

◊ **hushed** quiet, so as not to make too much noise; ***she spoke in a hushed whisper***

◊ **muted** restrained, not noisy; ***the press gave the proposal a muted welcome***

◊ **silent** without sound; ***he kept silent for the whole meeting***

◊ **still** without sound or movement; ***there was no wind, and the surface of the lake was completely still***

quietly

adverb without making any noise or fuss; ***the burglar climbed quietly up to the window***

◊ **calmly** *or* **peacefully** quietly, in an unexcited way; ***the doctor explained calmly what would happen during the operation***

◊ **faintly** as if far away; ***the sound of bells could be heard faintly across the field***

◊ **noiselessly** *or* **silently** making no noise; ***they crept noiselessly up to the house***

◊ **stealthily** without anyone knowing or seeing; ***the burglar crept forward stealthily***

Rr

race

noun contest to see which person, horse, car, etc., is the fastest; ***she was second in the 200m race***

◊ **cross-country** race across fields and along paths, not on a running track; ***the cross-country champion is a favourite to win the marathon***

◊ **marathon** long distance running race; ***a marathon is run over 26 miles***; ***he's taking part in the London Marathon***

◊ **racecourse** grass-covered track where horse races are held; ***the Grand National is run at Aintree racecourse***

◊ **race meeting** series of horse races held on several days; ***there was a race meeting at Leicester racecourse***

◊ **relay** running race by teams in which one runner passes a baton to another who then runs on; ***they won the 400m relay***

◊ **sprint** fast run over a short distance; ***the 100m sprint***

rain

noun drops of water which fall from the clouds; ***the ground is dry, we've had no rain for days***

◊ **cloudburst** sudden downpour of rain; ***we went walking in the hills and got drenched in a cloudburst***

◊ **deluge** very heavy rainfall; ***it had been dry for weeks and then we had a deluge***

◊ **downpour** heavy fall of rain; ***there was a downpour and all the spectators ran inside***

◊ **drizzle** light rain; ***a drizzle was falling so we took our umbrellas***

◊ **monsoon** season of wind and rain in tropical countries; ***at last the monsoon brought relief from the dry, hot weather***

◊ **shower** slight fall of rain or snow; ***we sheltered from the shower and walked on after it finished***

◊ **thunderstorm** storm with rain, thunder and lightning; ***there was a terrible thunderstorm last night***

rain

verb to fall as drops of water from the clouds; ***as soon as we sat down it started to rain***

◊ **drizzle** to rain lightly; ***it's drizzling outside***

◊ **pour** *or* **teem** to rain hard; ***it poured all afternoon***

read

verb to look at and understand written words; ***she was reading a book when I saw her***

◊ **browse** to look through a book, newspaper or magazine, without reading it properly; ***I browsed through several magazines at the doctor's surgery***

◊ **scan** *or* **skim** to look over words or pictures very quickly; ***he scanned the newspaper to see if the report was mentioned***

ready

adjective prepared for something; ***are all the children ready to go to school?***; ⇨**prepared**

◊ **alert** *or* **vigilant** ready and expectant; ***the guard must remain alert at all times***

◊ **mature** *or* **ripe** fully grown, ready to be used or harvested; ***a mature Cheddar cheese***

◊ **poised** ready to do something; ***the army is poised to capture the city***

real

adjective existing, not imaginary or artificial; ***is that watch real gold?***; ⇨**actual**

◊ **authentic** genuine, not a copy; ***he believed the diaries to be authentic***

◊ **factual** referring to what is true; ***he presented a factual report of events***

◊ **genuine** real, true; ***a genuine leather purse will cost a lot more than a plastic imitation***

◊ **objective** considering things from a general point of view rather than your own; ***you must be objective, not too optimistic, when planning the future of your business***

◊ **tangible** which is real or can be touched; ***there is no tangible evidence that he was responsible***

reason

noun

(a) the power of thought; ***he used his reason to solve the problem***

◊ **consciousness** being aware of things happening around you; ***he never regained consciousness after the accident***

◊ **intellect** power of the brain, ability to think or reason; ***you could see at once she was a person of superior intellect***

◊ **intelligence** ability to think and understand; ***his intelligence is well above average***

◊ **intuition** thinking of something, or knowing something naturally, without it being explained; ***he had an intuition something was wrong before he opened the door***

◊ **mind** part of the body which controls memory, reasoning; ***her mind always seems to be on other things***

◊ **perception** ability to notice or realize; ***he doesn't have a very clear perception of what he is supposed to do***

◊ **understanding** ability to know what something means or why something happens; ***my understanding of how the Internet works is very limited***

(b) why something happens; ***what is the reason for the plane's late arrival?***; ⇨**cause**

◊ **incentive** thing which encourages; ***a bonus is an incentive to the sales force***

◊ **motive** reason for doing something; ***the police are trying to find a motive for the murder***

◊ **stimulus** thing which encourages someone or something to greater activity; ***what sort of stimulus is needed to revive the tourist trade?***

receive

verb to get something which has been sent; ***we received a parcel from the supplier this morning***

◊ **acquire** *(formal)* to get something by effort or over a period of time; ***she has acquired a large collection of shoes***

◊ **collect** to gather together into a group; ***he collects old golf clubs, but never uses any of them when he is playing golf himself***

◊ **get** to receive or obtain; ***we got a letter from the bank***; ***go and get your coat***

◊ **inherit** to receive money, etc., from a person who has died; ***she inherited a small fortune from her father***

◊ **take** to accept; ***if they offer you the job, take it***

record

noun written evidence of something; ***we have no record of the sale***

◊ **account** detailed records of financial affairs; ***he kept careful a account of the amount he spent each week***

◊ **archives** collection of old documents; ***the town's archives go back to its foundation in 1140***

◊ **case study** the study of a certain group, institution or person over a long period of time; ***the case study reveals that housing estates in large cities produce more cases of juvenile crime***

◊ **documentation** all papers referring to something; ***please send me all the documentation concerning the sale***

◊ **dossier** file of documents; ***she's asked to see the dossier of complaints about service***

◊ **file** holder for papers and documents; ***when you have finished with the papers put them back in the file***

◊ **minutes** notes taken of what has been said at a meeting; ***the secretary will take minutes of the meeting***

refuse

verb to say that you will not do something; ***his father refused to lend him any more money***

◊ **decline** to refuse or to turn down (an invitation); ***she declined to come to lunch***

◊ **rebuff** to refuse sharply; ***they rebuffed all offers of help***

◊ **reject** to refuse to accept something; ***they rejected the offer for the house because it was too low***

region

noun area of a country; ***the south-west region is famous for apple growing***; ⇨**belt**; ⇨**country**

◊ **district** *or* **locality** part of a town or a small rural area; ***it's a district well-known for its Italian restaurants***

◊ **place** where something is, or where something happens; ***here's the place where we saw the cows***

◊ **territory** large stretch of land, land which belongs to a country; ***they occupied all the territory on the east bank of the river***

◊ **zone** area or part which is different from others or which has something special; ***police cars are patrolling the inner city zones***

release

verb to set free; ***six prisoners were released from prison***

◊ **absolve** to set someone free from the consequences of their actions; ***he was absolved of responsibility for the injuries caused by the accident***

◊ **acquit** to declare formally that a person is not guilty; ***she was acquitted of the crime***

◊ **emancipate** to make someone free; ***they passed a law to emancipate slaves***

◊ **liberate** to set someone or something free; ***the hostages were liberated by the security forces***

◊ **open** to make something not shut any more; ***we opened the door and went into the house***

◊ **parole** to let a prisoner out of prison on condition that he or she behaves well; ***after six months he was paroled***

reliable

adjective which can be relied on, can be trusted; ***it's a very reliable car, it has never let me down***

◊ **careful** with attention and effort so you are sure to get it right; ***we were so careful that no one heard us come in***

◊ **dependable** that can be relied upon; ***people living in villages need a dependable bus service***

◊ **fair** right, giving someone what they deserve; ***it isn't fair for her to have a bigger piece of cake than me***

◊ **honest** truthful and trustworthy; ***I wouldn't buy a car from that garage - I'm not sure they're completely honest***

◊ **obedient** doing what you're told to do; ***our old dog is very obedient, he always comes when you call him***

◊ **sensible** making good sense, showing good judgement; ***staying indoors during the storm was the sensible thing to do***; ***I have a sensible pair of shoes for long walks***; ***he made a very sensible suggestion***

◊ **trustworthy** *or* **responsible** *(person)* who can be depended upon; ***you are lucky to have such trustworthy staff***

religion

noun belief in gods, or one God; ***does their religion help them to lead a good life?***

◊ **belief** feeling sure that something is true; ***her strong belief in God***

◊ **cult** small religious group; ***he joined a cult we had never even heard of***

◊ **faith** religious belief; ***we must respect people of other faiths***

◊ **worship** praise and respect being shown to God; ***prayer is the most important part of worship***

remember

verb to bring back into your mind something which you have seen or heard before; ***do you remember when we got lost in the fog?***; ⇨**recall;** ⇨**recollect** *(formal)*

◊ **commemorate** to celebrate the memory of someone or something; ***we are gathered here today to commemorate those who died in the World Wars***

◊ **memorize** to learn and remember something; ***for homework, we all had to memorize a poem***

◊ **remind** to make someone remember something; ***she reminded him that the meeting had to finish at six-thirty***

◊ **reminisce** to talk about memories of the past; ***the two old soldiers sat reminiscing about the war***

repair

verb to make something work again; ***we need someone to come and repair the telephone***; ⇨**fix;** ⇨**mend;** ⇨**put right**

◊ **amend** to change for the better; ***the Prime Minister amended his speech after taking advice on the latest situation***

◊ **correct** to take away mistakes in something; ***you must try to correct the mistakes in your driving or you will never pass your driving test***

◊ **rectify** to correct something, to make something right; ***he has been asked to rectify the incorrect entry in the catalogue***

◊ **rehabilitate** to train someone to lead a normal life again after disablement, illness or imprisonment; ***prisoners need to be rehabilitated to make sure they do not re-offend***

◊ **rejuvenate** to give something new vigour and strength; ***he hopes to rejuvenate the club by attracting younger members***

◊ **remedy** to correct something, to make something better; ***tell me what's wrong and I'll try to remedy it straightaway***

◊ **renovate** to make a building like new again; ***we plan to renovate the offices this year***

◊ **restore** to repair, to make something like new again; ***he spent many hours restoring the old car to its original condition***

◊ **revive (i)** to bring back signs of life (to a person, animal or plant); ***the paramedics managed to revive her on the way to hospital; when she came back from holiday she needed to revive all her house plants with a good watering*** **(ii)** to make something popular again; ***they decided to revive the old musical show and put it on in a modern setting***

repeat

verb to say or do something over again; ***could you repeat what you have just said?***

◊ **copy** *or* **duplicate** *or* **reproduce** to make something which looks exactly like something else; ***to make the pullover just copy this pattern***

◊ **quote** to repeat what someone has said or written; ***he started his speech by quoting from Shakespeare's Hamlet***

◊ **recapitulate** to go over again the chief points of something; ***she recapitulated the reasons for selling the shares***

◊ **retell** to tell again; ***he retold the story***

replace

verb to put something in the place of something else; ***we are replacing all our permanent staff with freelancers***; ⇨**substitute**

◊ **exchange** to give one thing back and get another thing in its place; ***I exchanged my faulty watch for a new one***

respect

noun high opinion of someone or something; ***he showed respect for his teacher***; ⇨**admiration;** ⇨**esteem**

◊ **courtesy** respectful manner; ***children should show courtesy to their elders***

◊ **deference** respectful agreement; ***she put a shawl over her head out of deference to the rules of the monastery***

◊ **honour** sign of respect; ***it is an honour for me to be here today***

◊ **reverence** great respect; ***the priest approached the altar with great reverence***

respect

verb to have a high opinion of someone or something; ⇨**admire**

◊ **appreciate** to recognize the value of; ***shoppers always appreciate good value***

◊ **honour** to show someone a special sign of respect; ***he was honoured by his colleagues at a special dinner***

◊ **revere** *(formal)* to respect someone very highly; ***she was revered by her patients for her kindness***

◊ **value** to consider something as being valuable; ***she values her friendship with him***

◊ **venerate** to respect greatly; ***his memory is venerated throughout the area***

restaurant

noun place where you can buy and eat a meal; ***the restaurant is famous for its seafood***

◊ **bar** place in a hotel or pub where you can buy and drink alcohol; ***let's meet in the bar before dinner***

◊ **brasserie** continental-style restaurant or bar; ***brasseries are popular eating places nowadays***

◊ **café** small restaurant selling snacks or light meals; ***we had a snack in the station café***

◊ **canteen** private self-service restaurant in an office block, factory, etc.; ***the canteen was busy with workers taking their lunch***

◊ **diner** *(US)* small restaurant selling simple hot food; ***we grabbed a quick bite in the diner***

◊ **snack bar** place where light meals can be bought; ***we bought sandwiches and tea at the snack bar***

◊ **teashop** small restaurant which serves mainly tea, coffee, sandwiches, scones and cakes; ***pretty villages often have a teashop for visitors***

result

noun something which happens because of something else; ***what was the result of the police investigation?***; ⇨**consequence**

◊ **conclusion** opinion reached after careful thought; ***what conclusions can you draw from the evidence?***

◊ **effect** result or influence; ***the cuts in spending will have a serious effect on the hospital***

◊ **end product** manufactured product, result of a production process; ***the end product did not reach an acceptable standard***

◊ **product** thing which is manufactured; ***Germany is helping her industry to sell more products abroad***

◊ **upshot** the final result; ***the upshot of the discussions was that we sold the shares***

rich

adjective having a lot of money; ***if only we were rich, we could buy a bigger house***

◊ **affluent** *or* **wealthy** *(person)* very rich; ***affluent people nearly always have expensive cars***

◊ **opulent** luxurious, splendid; ***this opulent hotel was only for the very rich***

◊ **plush** *(informal)* luxurious; ***the car's got a very plush interior***

◊ **prosperous** successful and well off; ***Salisbury is a very prosperous town***

river

noun large mass of fresh water which runs across the land and goes into the sea, a lake, or another river; ***London is on the river Thames***

◊ **brook** small stream; ***they crossed the brook and walked on up the hill***

◊ **stream** little river; ***can you jump over the stream?***

◊ **tributary** stream or river which flows into a larger river; ***the Mole is a tributary of the Thames***

◊ **watercourse** channel through which water flows or has flowed; ***the watercourses are often dry in summer***

◊ **waterway** canal or deep river along which boats can easily travel; ***the Rhine is a main European waterway***

road

noun hard pathway used by vehicles to travel along; ***the road to York goes directly north from London***

◊ **by-pass** road round a town; ***take the by-pass if you want to avoid the town centre***

◊ **driveway** short private road leading to a house; ***three cars were parked in the driveway***

◊ **dual carriageway** road with two lanes in each direction, with a barrier between the pairs of lanes; ***only very important roads are dual carriageways***

◊ **footpath** path for people to walk on; ***the footpath leads through the wood***

◊ **highway** main public road; ***a footbridge was built over the highway***

◊ **main road** the largest and busiest road in a place; ***you take a turning off the main road to get to their farm***

◊ **motorway** fast road with several lanes and very few junctions on which traffic can travel at high speeds; ***we drove south along the new motorway***

◊ **path** narrow track for walking; ***there's a path across the field***

◊ **route** way to be followed to get to a destination; ***we have to decide which route we will take***

◊ **street** road in a town or village, usually with houses on each side; ***her flat is on a noisy street***

◊ **track** rough path; ***we followed a track through the forest***

◊ **way** path or road which goes somewhere; ***the way to London is through St Albans***

room

noun part of a building, divided from other parts by walls; ***we want an office with at least four rooms***

◊ **attic** room at the top of a house under the roof; ***he slowly climbed up the stairs up to the attic***

◊ **bathroom** room in a house with a bath, a washbasin and usually a lavatory; ***the house has two bathrooms***

◊ **bedroom** room where you sleep; ***the hotel has twenty-five bedrooms***

◊ **cellar** underground room or rooms beneath a house; ***stone steps lead down to the cellar***

◊ **dining room** room in a house or hotel where you usually eat; ***she was doing her homework on the dining room table***

◊ **dormitory** long room full of beds; ***the scout leader sleeps in a small room off the main dormitory***

◊ **kitchen** room where you cook food; ***he put the shopping down on the kitchen table***

◊ **living room** *or* **lounge** *or* **sitting room** comfortable room for sitting in; ***let's go and watch TV in the lounge***

◊ **study** room in which someone reads, writes, works, etc.; ***he wrote most of his books in his small study***

◊ **toilet** room where body waste can be got rid of; ***we need two toilets with five people living here***

royal

adjective referring to a king or queen; ***members of the Royal Family***; ⇨**regal**

◊ **imperial** referring to an empire or emperor; ***the imperial court***

◊ **reigning** who is on the throne; ***the reigning monarch***

◊ **titled** with a title such as Lord, Sir, etc., put in front of a name; ***a titled lady has come to live in the village***

ruler

noun person who governs; ***he's the ruler of a small African state***

◊ **dictator** person who rules a country alone; ***the rebel army finally overthrew the dictator***

◊ **emperor** *or* **empress** ruler of an empire; ***Napoleon declared himself Emperor***

◊ **head of state** king, queen or president, who is the leader of a state; ***the Queen, as head of state, opens Parliament each year***

◊ **king** *or* **queen** *or* **monarch** *or* **sovereign** man or woman who rules a country by right of birth; ***the king and queen came to visit the town***

◊ **president** head of a republic; ***during his term of office as president he doubled the size of the army***

◊ **tyrant** ruler who rules by force and fear; ***the tyrant was overthrown and a democratic republic set up***

run

verb to go quickly on foot; ***I had to run to catch the train***

◊ **charge** to attack while running; ***the police charged the rioters***

◊ **chase** to run after someone to try and catch him; ***the postman was chased by a dog***

◊ **dash** *or* **rush** to hurry, to go forward fast; ***he dashed out of the office when he remembered he had left the oven on at home***

◊ **flee** to run away from danger or disaster; ***as the fighting spread the people from the villages fled into the jungle***

◊ **jog** to run at an easy pace, especially for exercise; ***he jogged along the river bank for two miles***

◊ **scamper** *or* **scurry** to run fast with little steps; ***the rabbits were scampering across the field***

◊ **sprint** to run very fast over a short distance; ***I had to sprint to catch the bus***

Ss

sad

adjective not happy; ***he's sad because the holidays have come to an end***; **⇨dejected; ⇨miserable; ⇨unhappy**

◊ **depressed** *or* **dispirited** feeling miserable and hopeless; ***she was depressed after her exam results***

◊ **disappointed** sad because things did not turn out as expected; ***she was disappointed with her exam results***

◊ **discontented** not satisfied; ***groups of discontented dock workers marched on the offices of the port authority***

◊ **gloomy** sad in mind and outlook; ***he felt gloomy about the future because he had no job***

◊ **grief-stricken** crushed with sadness; ***she was grief-stricken over the death of her father***

sadness

noun feeling of being very unhappy; ***she felt great sadness on the death of her cat***; **⇨dejection; ⇨sorrow**

◊ **anguish** great mental suffering; ***he caused his parents great anguish***

◊ **depression** mental state where you feel miserable and hopeless; ***she suffers from fits of depression***

◊ **despair** absolute hopelessness; ***when he lost his job he was filled with despair***

◊ **gloom** sadness of mind and outlook; ***the family were full of gloom when they heard the bad news***

◊ **grief** crushing sadness; ***she couldn't hide her grief at the funeral***

◊ **misery** great unhappiness; ***there were scenes of appalling human misery in the refugee camps***

safe

adjective not in danger, not likely to be hurt; ***a building society account is a safe place for your money***

◊ **immune** *(person)* **(i)** protected against infection; ***I seem to be immune from colds*** **(ii)** protected against arrest; ***as a diplomat, she is immune against arrest***

◊ **impregnable** which cannot be captured; ***after the election his position as leader of the party was impregnable***

◊ **invulnerable** which cannot be harmed; ***the press seemed invulnerable to criticism***

◊ **protected** kept safe by someone or something; ***old people are protected against flu by injections***

◊ **secure (i)** safe against attack; ***you need to make your jewels secure against theft*** **(ii)** firmly fixed; ***make sure the ladder is secure before you climb up it***

◊ **sheltered** protected from wind, cold, danger, etc.; ***our garden is very sheltered***

◊ **unassailable** which cannot be attacked; ***after five wins the team manager's position was unassailable***

safety

noun not being in danger, not likely to be hurt; ***the police tried to ensure the safety of the public***

◊ **immunity (i)** ability to resist attacks from a disease; ***the injection will give immunity to malaria*** **(ii)** protection against being arrested; ***she was granted immunity from arrest***

◊ **protection** shelter, being kept safe from something; ***the trees give some protection from the rain***

◊ **security** protection against criminals; ***the security of the building is maintained by guard dogs***

◊ **shelter** protection against the wind, cold, danger, etc.; ***the trees give shelter from the rain***

save

verb

(a) to stop someone or something from being damaged, hurt or killed; ***we must save the rain forests from destruction***

◊ **conserve** *or* **preserve** to look after and keep in the same state; ***our committee aims to conserve the wildlife in our area***

◊ **emancipate** to make someone free; ***they passed a law to emancipate slaves***

◊ **liberate** to set someone or something free; ***the hostages were liberated by the security forces***

◊ **rescue** to save someone from a dangerous situation; ***the lifeboat rescued the crew of the sinking ship***

(b) to put things such as money to one side so that you can use them later; ***I'm saving to buy a car***

◊ **amass** to collect a lot of money, information, things; ***she amassed her fortune in the 1980s***

◊ **deposit** to put money into a bank account; ***he deposited £100 in his current account***

◊ **hoard** to buy and store supplies in case of need; ***everyone has started hoarding fuel in case supplies run out***

◊ **invest** to put money into savings, property, etc., so that it will increase in value; ***he was advised to invest in government bonds***

◊ **keep** to have for a long time or for ever; ***can I keep the newspaper I borrowed from you?***

◊ **store** to keep something for use later; ***we store all our personnel records on computer***

school

noun place where students, usually children, are taught; ***our little boy is four so he will be starting school soon***

◊ **academy** college where specialized subjects are taught; ***she wanted to be a musician so she applied for a place at a music academy***

◊ **college** teaching institution (for adolescents and adults); ***she's studying accountancy at the local college***

◊ **comprehensive** state secondary school for children of all abilities; ***there were no tests for children who went to the local comprehensive***

◊ **grammar school** secondary school where students have to pass an exam to enter; ***he passed the exam for the local grammar school***

◊ **infant school** school for children aged 4-7; ***a group of children from the infant school waited to get into the swimming pool***

◊ **junior school** school for children aged 8-11; ***it's open day at our local junior school***

◊ **nursery school** first school for very small children; ***his daughter went to nursery school until she was four***

◊ **prep school (preparatory school)** private school for children up to the age of 13; ***his parents sent him to prep school when he was 6***

◊ **public school** private fee paying school for children over 13 which is not part of the state system; ***Eton and Winchester are two famous public schools***

◊ **secondary school** school for children after the age of 11; ***she's the head teacher of our local secondary school***

◊ **sixth form college** college for students between 16-18 where 'Advanced' level subjects are taught; ***she got three good 'A' levels at the sixth form college and went to Exeter University***

search

verb to examine very carefully, to try to find; ***the police searched the house***; ***I searched the Internet for information on Ireland***; ⇨**hunt**

◊ **check** to make sure by examining; ***did you lock the door? - I'll go and check***

◊ **examine** to inspect something to see if it is healthy or in good order; ***the water samples were examined for traces of pollution***

◊ **inquire** *(also enquire)* to ask questions in order to find out about something; ***the social services are inquiring about the missing girl***

◊ **probe** to examine something deeply; ***the police probed into his financial affairs***

◊ **prospect** to search for minerals; ***the team went to the desert to prospect for oil***

◊ **pry** to look inquisitively into something; ***he accused the press of prying into his private life***

◊ **ransack** to cause a lot of damage and mess while searching a place; ***while she was out someone had ransacked her room***

◊ **reconnoitre** to make a survey of enemy land to get information; ***we sent a small party of soldiers ahead to reconnoitre the town***

◊ **rummage** to search about for something; ***he rummaged in the drawer until he found his gloves***

◊ **scan** to look very carefully at something all over; ***we scanned the horizon but no ships were to be seen***

◊ **scour** to search everywhere; ***we scoured the market for fresh aubergines***

◊ **seek** to look for; ***the police are seeking a group of ladies who were in the area when the incident took place***

◊ **spy** to watch someone in secret, to find out what they are planning to do; ***we discovered that our neighbours had been spying on us***

seat

noun something which you sit on; ***he was sitting in the driver's seat***

◊ **armchair** chair with arms; ***each room in the hotel has two armchairs***

◊ **bench** long wooden seat; ***we sat on one of the park benches***

◊ **chair** piece of furniture which you can sit on which has a back; ***he pulled his chair up to the desk***

◊ **high-chair** baby's chair at a level with a table, sometimes with a tray in front of the baby; ***most restaurants provide high-chairs***

◊ **pew** long wooden seat in a church; ***we sat on an empty pew at the back of the church***

◊ **rocking chair** chair designed to rock backwards and forwards; ***rocking chairs are marvellous for relaxing***

◊ **settee** *or* **sofa** long seat with a soft back where several people can sit; ***my three aunts were sitting on the settee holding cups of tea***

◊ **stool** small seat with no back; ***when the little girl sat on the piano stool her feet didn't reach the floor***

◊ **throne** chair on which a king or queen sits during ceremonies; ***the coronation throne was very elaborate***

secret

adjective hidden, not known by other people; ***there is a secret door into the cellar***

◊ **anonymous** without stating a name; ***the police have received several anonymous phone calls***

◊ **clandestine** secret, undercover; ***a clandestine operation to smuggle pirate CDs into the country***

◊ **concealed** *or* **hidden** placed so it cannot be seen; ***the concealed camera allowed the police to watch their movements***

◊ **secluded** *(place)* which is quiet, away from crowds; ***they tried to find a secluded beach***

◊ **top secret** absolutely secret; ***he left a file of top secret documents in the taxi***

◊ **undercover** acting in disguise; ***two undercover policemen were sent to the night club to look for drugs***

secret

noun thing which is not to be known, something kept hidden; ***if I tell you a secret, promise not to repeat it to anyone***

◊ **cipher** *or* **code** secret language for sending messages; ***they sent the message in cipher***

◊ **conspiracy** *or* **plot** secret plan against someone or something; ***there was a conspiracy to murder the leader of the Liberal Party***

◊ **enigma** mystery or puzzle; ***he's an enigma, even to his friends***

◊ **mystery** thing which cannot be explained; ***it's a mystery how the box came to be hidden under her bed***

see

verb to use your eyes to notice; ***can you see that tree in the distance?***

◊ **discern** *(formal)* to see, to make out something with difficulty; ***in the fog we could barely discern the oncoming traffic***

◊ **distinguish** to see clearly, to make out details; ***with the binoculars we could easily distinguish the houses on the other side of the lake***

◊ **glimpse** to catch sight of; ***we only glimpsed her as she was leaving***

◊ **look** to turn your eyes towards something; ***if you look out of the office window you can see our house***

◊ **notice** *or* **spot** to see, to take note of; ***I didn't notice you had come in***

◊ **observe** to watch or to look at; ***we observed the eclipse from the top of the mountain***

◊ **perceive** to notice through the senses, to become aware of something; ***the changes are so slight they are almost impossible to perceive with the naked eye***

◊ **reconnoitre** to make a survey of enemy land to get information; ***we sent a small party of soldiers ahead to reconnoitre the town***

◊ **scan** to look very carefully at something all over; ***we scanned the horizon but no ships were to be seen***

◊ **sight** to see something a long way off; ***we often sight rare birds on the lake***

◊ **spy** to watch someone in secret, to find out what they are planning to do; ***we discovered that our neighbours had been spying on us***

◊ **stare** to look at someone or something for a long time; ***she stared unhappily out of the window***

◊ **visualize** to have a picture of something in your mind; ***I can just visualize myself driving a sports car down the motorway***

◊ **watch** to look at and notice something; ***did you watch the TV news last night?***

selfish

adjective doing things only for yourself and not for other people; ***don't be so selfish - pass the chocolates round***

◊ **avaricious** *(formal)* wanting to have and to keep a lot of money; ***she was so avaricious that she spent hardly anything even though she was rich***

◊ **egotistical** thinking you are better than everyone else, thinking and talking only about yourself; ***he was so egotistical that he never noticed anyone else's problems***

◊ **greedy** wanting food or other things too much; ***don't be greedy, you've already had two pieces of cake***

◊ **proud** with a very high opinion of yourself; ***he's too proud to admit he's made a mistake***

◊ **vain** very proud of your appearance, clothes, achievements, etc.; ***he's very vain, and is always combing his hair***

sell

verb to give something to someone for money; ***he sold his house to my father***; ⇨**flog** *(informal)*

◊ **auction** to sell to the person who makes the highest bid in public; ***they decided to auction all their grandmother's possessions***

◊ **market** to sell products using marketing techniques; ***this product is being marketed in all European countries***

◊ **peddle** to sell goods from door to door or in the street; ***he makes a living peddling cleaning products door-to-door***

◊ **retail** to sell goods to the public; ***the shoes retailed at £89***

◊ **undercut** to sell more cheaply than someone else; ***our prices are the lowest and we won't allow anyone to undercut us***

send

verb to make someone or something go from one place to another; ***my mother sent me to the baker's to buy some bread***; ***he sent a message to the police***; ⇨**dispatch**

◊ **broadcast** to send out on radio or TV; ***the programme will be broadcast on Monday at 8pm***

◊ **deport** *or* **expel** to throw someone out from a country; ***he was deported when his visa expired***

◊ **eject** to throw out; ***they ejected the troublemakers from the meeting***

◊ **evict** to force someone, especially a tenant, to leave a property; ***she was evicted from her house***

◊ **mail** *or* **post** to send something by the postal services; ***we mailed the catalogue to addresses all over Europe***

◊ **export** to sell goods in other countries; ***we export a lot of books to Europe***

◊ **move** to change the place of something, to change your position; ***move the chairs to the side of the room***; ***some animal was moving about outside the tent***

◊ **post** to send someone to another place, often overseas, to work; ***he was posted to an air base in East Anglia***

◊ **redirect** to send a letter you have received on to another address or a phone call to another number; ***phone calls can be redirected to my office number***

◊ **shift** to move, to change the position of something; ***we've shifted the TV from the kitchen to the dining room***

◊ **ship** to send goods (or people) but not always on a ship; ***we ship goods all over the country***

◊ **transfer** to move something or someone to another place; ***the money will be transferred directly to your bank account***

◊ **transmit** to send out a programme or a message by radio or TV; ***the message was transmitted to the ship by radio***

◊ **transport** to move goods or people from one place to another in a vehicle; ***the visitors will be transported to the factory by helicopter***

sensible

adjective showing good judgement; ***staying indoors during the storm was the sensible thing to do***; ⇨**fair;** ⇨**level-headed**

◊ **balanced** which is not excessive; ***he kept to a balanced diet while training for the marathon***

◊ **clever** *or* **intelligent** able to learn quickly; ***she is very clever at spotting bargains and saving money***

◊ **capable** able to work well; ***she's an extremely capable secretary***

◊ **discerning** having good judgement about the value or worth of things; ***he was a discerning collector and had many fine pieces in his collection***

◊ **enlightened** holding good ideas about people; ***the council has an enlightened policy about employing as many disabled people as possible***

◊ **just** fair, showing no bias; ***the decision of the court was just***

◊ **reasonable** willing to act in a sensible and fair way; ***the manager of the shop was very reasonable when she explained she had left her credit cards at home***

◊ **shrewd** *or* **smart** clever, especially at spotting an advantage or opportunity; ***it was a shrewd move to sell those shares before they fell so badly***

◊ **tolerant** allowing something to exist which you don't agree with; ***she was tolerant of her husband's mistakes when cooking***

◊ **wise** having knowledge and good sense; ***it was a wise decision to cancel the trip when you saw the weather forecast***

separate

verb to keep apart; ***the police tried to separate the two gangs***

◊ **boycott** to refuse to deal with someone; ***we are boycotting all food imports from that country***

◊ **differentiate** *or* **discriminate** to treat two things differently; ***we do not differentiate between boys and girls in the teaching of science***

◊ **divide** to separate into parts; ***the two companies agreed to divide the market between them***

◊ **divorce (i)** to separate from your husband or wife; ***they got divorced*** **(ii)** to separate two ideas, etc.; ***it is difficult to divorce religion from politics***

◊ **liberate** to set someone or something free from something; ***the hostages were finally liberated by the security forces***

◊ **segregate** to keep in separate groups; ***to avoid trouble, we will have to segregate the fans of the rival teams***

◊ **subdivide** to separate into parts something that is already separated; ***after paying the shareholders and directors, the profits were subdivided among the workers***

separate

adjective not together, not attached; ***the dogs were kept separate from the other pets***; ⇨**distinct;** ⇨**unattached**

◊ **individual** single, for a particular person; ***we treat each individual case on its merits***

◊ **insular** thinking only of your own local interests; ***people with a nationalist view are often accused of being insular***

◊ **isolated** separated from others; ***they live in an isolated cottage in the hills***

◊ **lonely** with few or no people; ***the cliff top is a lonely place at night***

separately

adverb in a way that is individual, not attached to anything else; ***each of us will pay separately***

◊ **apart** not being together; ***they are now living apart***

◊ **piecemeal** done bit by bit; ***they had bought all sorts of paintings piecemeal***

◊ **singly** one by one; ***the police interviewed the boys singly***

serious

adjective important and possibly dangerous; ***the storm caused serious damage***

◊ **crucial** *or* **vital** extremely important; ***it is crucial that the story be kept out of the papers***

◊ **dangerous** which can cause harm, injury or damage; ***be careful - that loose carpet on the stairs is dangerous***

◊ **grave** important, worrying; ***he is in court facing grave charges***

◊ **important** which matters a great deal, who holds a high position; ***it is important to be in time for the meeting***; ***he has an important government job***

◊ **key** most important; ***the key person in the company is the sales manager***

◊ **solemn** serious and formal; ***it was the most solemn moment of the ceremony***

servant

noun person who is paid to do service, especially domestic service; ***they employ two servants in their London home***

◊ **assistant** person who helps; ***the painter's assistant prepares his materials next door***

◊ **bodyguard** person who guards someone; ***the attacker was overpowered by the president's bodyguards***

◊ **civil servant** *or* **public servant** person who works in a government department; ***she works as a civil servant in Brussels***

◊ **helper** person who helps; ***she works two mornings a week as helper in a playgroup***

◊ **housekeeper** person who looks after someone else's house; ***he employs a housekeeper, a driver and two gardeners***

◊ **nanny** girl who looks after small children in a family; ***she's training to be a nanny***

◊ **slave** person who belongs to someone and works for him; ***in the old days, slaves worked on the tobacco plantations***

share

noun part of something that is divided between two or more people; ***take your share of the cake and I will keep the rest***

◊ **bit** *or* **fragment** small part; ***would you like a bit of cake?***

◊ **excerpt** small part (of a larger piece of music or writing); ***they played an excerpt from a Mozart symphony***

◊ **fraction** very small amount; ***sales are up a fraction this month***

◊ **part** *or* **piece** *or* **portion** less than the whole amount of something; ***parts of the film were very good***

◊ **percentage** figure shown as proportion of a hundred; ***a low percentage of the population voted***

◊ **sample** small part which is used to show what the whole is like; ***try a sample of the local cheese***

◊ **section** part of something which, when joined to other parts, goes to make up a whole; ***the brass section of the orchestra***

◊ **segment** part of something which seems to be formed by natural divisions; ***30- to 40-year-olds are the most affluent segment of the population***

shelter

noun place where you are kept safe from something; ***we stood in the shelter of a tree waiting for the rain to stop***

◊ **asylum** safe refuge from enemies; ***people seeking asylum in Britain***

◊ **haven** safe or peaceful place; ***the square is a haven from the noisy market***

◊ **refuge** place to be safe from danger or trouble; ***during the fighting, they were given refuge in the British Embassy***

◊ **sanctuary** place of safety; ***no hunters were allowed in the bird sanctuary***

◊ **stronghold** fortress, place which is difficult to capture; ***they attacked the enemy stronghold***

ship

noun large boat for carrying passengers or cargo on the sea; ***the first time we went to the USA we went by ship***

(a) *(commercial)*

◊ **boat** small ship; ***they sailed their boat around the lake for the weekend***

◊ **coaster** ship which sails from port to port along the coast; ***coasters carry local cargo along the coast because the area is too mountainous for good roads***

◊ **container ship** ocean-going ship designed to carry cargo already stored in commercial containers; ***the container lorries waited at the port to deliver their loads onto the container ship***

◊ **cruise liner** *or* **cruise ship** large passenger ship providing holidays at sea whilst visiting places of interest on the journey; ***the cruise liner went round the Caribbean***

◊ **factory ship** ship which can process fish caught by trawlers while still at sea; ***the factory ship sailed alongside the trawlers until they were ready to bring in their catches***

◊ **ferry** ship which carries people and vehicles to and fro across a stretch of water; ***the cars and trucks drove on to the ferry as it got ready to cross the channel***

◊ **liner** large passenger ship; ***they travelled across the Atlantic by liner because they were not in a hurry and wanted to enjoy the journey***

◊ **tanker** ship for carrying liquids, especially oil; ***only the biggest ports can take the huge oil tankers***

◊ **trawler** fishing boat which uses nets; ***the trawlers all came into the harbour to unload their catches***

◊ **tug** powerful boat which pulls other, bigger boats; ***two tugs helped the liner dock at the port***

(b) *(naval)*

◊ **battleship** *(not usually in service in most navies)* very large ship with banks of high calibre guns; ***the battleship is the biggest ship in the navy, apart from the carriers***

◊ **carrier** flat-decked ship designed to carry aircraft; ***even the rough sea didn't stop the planes taking off from the carrier***

◊ **corvette** small ship usually equipped for escorting convoys or for anti-submarine service; ***the corvette hurried around the convoy carefully watching its progress***

◊ **destroyer** larger class of ship capable of carrying missiles or large guns; ***the destroyer lay out of harbour beyond the smaller ships***

◊ **frigate** small fast-moving ship; ***he commanded a frigate during the wars against Napoleon***

◊ **minesweeper** ship designed to carry out mine clearance; ***the minesweeper began its sweep of the area***

◊ **submarine** ship which can travel on or under water; ***soon after the submarine left port it dived and continued under water***

shop

noun place where you can buy things; ***quite a few shops are open on Sunday***

◊ **arcade** covered shopping street with an arched glass roof; ***the short arcade had some lovely little shops***

◊ **baker's** shop where you can buy bread and cakes; ***can you go to the baker's and get a loaf of brown bread?***

◊ **butcher's** shop where you can buy meat; ***can you get me some sausages from the butcher's?***

◊ **chemist's** shop where you can buy medicine, toothpaste, soap, etc.; ***go to the chemist's and get me some cough medicine***

◊ **department store** large shop with many departments; ***Oxford Street has several department stores***

◊ **greengrocer's** shop where you can buy fruit and vegetables; ***can you get me some potatoes from the greengrocer's?***

◊ **kiosk** small shelter for selling goods out of doors; ***she runs the newspaper kiosk next to the station***

◊ **shopping mall** enclosed covered shopping area with shops, restaurants, banks and other facilities; ***most cities now have a shopping mall***

◊ **stall** small moveable stand in a market, where a trader displays and sells goods; ***he has a flower stall in the market***

◊ **store** shop, usually a big shop; ***you can buy shoes in any of the big stores in town***

◊ **supermarket** large store selling mainly food and household goods, where customers serve themselves and pay at a checkout; ***we do all our weekly shopping in the local supermarket***

short

adjective

(a) *(time)* not long, lasting only a little time; ***we had a short holiday in June***; ⇨**brief**

◊ **fleeting** short and quick; ***she only caught a fleeting glimpse of the princess***

◊ **instantaneous** done at once, taking almost no time; ***he gave an instantaneous response to the government announcement***

◊ **momentary** which only lasts for a very short time; ***even a momentary lack of attention can produce a bad accident when driving***

◊ **temporary** which is not meant to last a long time; ***she has a temporary job with a construction company***

◊ **transient** *(formal)* which will not last; ***fame for most pop groups is very transient***

(b) *(size)* not long; ***I need a short piece of electric wire; he wrote a short note thanking the chairman***

shout

verb to make a loud cry, to speak very loudly; ***they stamped on the floor and shouted***

◊ **cheer** to shout praise or encouragement; ***the crowd cheered when the first marathon runners appeared***

◊ **clamour** to shout or demand loudly; ***people were clamouring for tickets***

◊ **roar** to make a loud noise; ***the lion roared and then attacked***

◊ **scream** to make loud cries of fear or distress; ***he screamed with pain when he broke his leg***

◊ **yell** to shout loudly; ***the policeman yelled to her to get out of the way***

show

verb to let someone see something, to point something out to someone; ***he showed me his holiday photos***; ***show me where the accident happened***

◊ **demonstrate** to show how something works; ***the salesman demonstrated the vacuum cleaner***

◊ **display** *or* **exhibit** to put something on show; ***she is displaying her collection of Persian carpets at the antique fair***

◊ **expose** *or* **reveal** to show something that was hidden; ***the plastic coating had rubbed off to expose the metal beneath***

◊ **flaunt** to display in a vulgar way to attract attention; ***she flaunted her engagement ring all around the office***

sign

noun

(a) movement of the hand which means something; ***he made a sign to us to sit down***

◊ **gesture** movement of the hands, etc., to show feeling; ***she made a slight gesture of impatience with her hand***

◊ **signal** sign or movement which tells someone to do something; ***he gave a signal to start the race***

(b) drawing, notice, etc., which advertises something; ***the office has a big sign outside it***; ⇨**indication**

◊ **badge** small sign pinned or sewn to someone's clothes; ***all the staff at the exhibition must wear badges***

◊ **notice** piece of writing giving information, usually in a place where everyone can see it; ***he pinned up a notice about the staff tennis match***

◊ **signpost** post with signs showing directions to places; ***the signpost said it was 20 miles to Bristol***

◊ **token** thing which is used as a sign of something; ***please accept this small gift as a token of our gratitude***

silly

adjective not showing any sense; ***he asked a lot of silly questions***; ⇨**stupid;** ⇨**foolish;** ⇨**idiotic;** ⇨**senseless**

◊ **absurd** *or* **ridiculous** which everyone should laugh at; ***she was wearing an absurd hat***

◊ **frivolous** not meant to be serious; ***he made some frivolous complaint just to be noticed***

◊ **illogical** not sensible, not reasonable; ***it's illogical to increase prices as sales are falling***

◊ **preposterous** *(formal)* absurd; ***she made several preposterous suggestions which were all rejected***

◊ **rash** done without thinking; ***it was rash of him to say he would pay for everyone***

◊ **ridiculous** which everyone should laugh at; ***it's ridiculous to ask everyone to wear suits in the office when it's so hot***

simple

adjective not difficult, not complicated, needing no effort; ***they had a simple meal of bread and soup***; ⇨**easy**

◊ **basic** *or* **elementary** at the simplest level; ***knowledge of basic Spanish is enough for the job***

◊ **convenient** which does not cause any practical problems; ***a bank draft is a convenient way of sending money abroad***

◊ **plain** simple and uncomplicated, easy to understand; ***we made it plain to them that this was our final offer***

simply

adverb in a easy way; ***he described simply how the accident had happened***; ⇨**easily**

◊ **effortlessly** without appearing to use any energy; ***he effortlessly rose through the company to become managing director***

◊ **naturally** in a normal way; ***he reacted quite naturally to the news***

◊ **readily** easily and quickly; ***this product is readily available in most shops***

◊ **smoothly** in a untroubled way; ***the engine is running smoothly***

size

noun measurements of something, how big something is; ***their garage is about the same size as our house***

◊ **area** surface space of something; ***the area of the floor is 4 square metres***

◊ **breadth** *(formal)* measurement of how broad something is; ***the breadth of the plot of land is over 300m***

◊ **capacity** *or* **volume** amount which something can hold; ***this barrel has a larger capacity than that one***

◊ **depth** how deep something is; ***the submarine dived to a depth of 200m***

◊ **dimensions** *or* **measurements** sizes found out when something is measured; ***what are the dimensions of the hall?***

◊ **height** measurement of how high something is; ***the height of the bridge is only 3m***

◊ **length** measurement of how long something is; ***the table is at least 12 feet in length***

◊ **weight** how heavy something is; ***what is the maximum weight of parcel the Post Office will accept?***

◊ **width** measurement of how wide something is; ***I need to know the width of the sofa***

sleep

noun rest, usually at night, with your eyes closed, and when you are not conscious of what is happening; ***I need eight hours sleep a night***

◊ **doze** *or* **nap** *or* **snooze** short, light sleep; ***she had a doze between jobs round the house***

◊ **hibernation** long winter sleep taken by some animals; ***bears go into hibernation for the winter***

◊ **rest** being quiet and peaceful; ***we took a few minutes rest and started running again***

sleep

verb to rest with your eyes closed not knowing what is happening around; ***he slept through the TV news***

◊ **doze** *or* **nap** *or* **snooze** to take a short, light sleep; ***he dozed off for a while after lunch***

◊ **hibernate** *(of animals)* to take a long winter sleep; ***many animals hibernate through the winter***

◊ **rest** to be quiet and peaceful; ***they ran 10 miles and then rested***

slow

adjective not fast, needing a long time to do something; ***the car was going at a slow speed***

◊ **gradual** which changes a little at a time; ***we are forecasting a gradual improvement in the weather***

◊ **hesitant** being slow to act because you are unable to decide; ***he is still hesitant about agreeing to the deal***

◊ **leisurely** *or* **unhurried** without any hurry; ***they had a leisurely holiday sailing along the canals***

◊ **sluggish** lazy, slow-moving; ***the economy is still sluggish***

◊ **tedious** slow and boring; ***filing invoices is a tedious job***

small

adjective not big, not much; ***we have a very small garden***

◊ **compact** small, close together; ***the computer system is very compact***

◊ **dainty** small and delicate; ***the baby has dainty little fingers***

◊ **infinitesimal** tiny, very small indeed; ***they found an infinitesimal amount of bacteria in the drinking water***

◊ **little** *adjective* not big, not much; ***we drink very little milk***

◊ **microscopic** so small as to be visible only through a microscope; ***microscopic forms of life are visible in the oldest rocks***

◊ **miniature** *or* **minute** very small; ***he has a miniature camera***

◊ **petite** *(of a woman)* small and dainty; ***she was petite and took a very small size in clothes***

◊ **tiny** very small; ***can I have just a tiny bit more pudding?***

smell

noun something you sense through your nose; ***I love the smell of fresh coffee***; ⇨**odour** *(formal)*

◊ **aroma** pleasant smell of something you can eat or drink; ***the aroma of fresh coffee***

◊ **fragrance** pleasant smell; ***I love the aroma of flowers in a garden***

◊ **perfume** substance used for the sake of its pleasant smell; ***do you like my new perfume?***

◊ **scent** **(i)** perfume; ***she bought some new scent*** **(ii)** pleasant smell; ***I love the scent of roses*** **(iii)** smell which can be followed; ***the dogs followed the scent of the escaped convicts***

◊ **stench** unpleasant, strong smell; ***the receding flood left a stench of rotting material***

◊ **stink** very nasty smell; ***there's a terrible stink in the kitchen***

soldier

noun person serving in the army; ***the soldiers marched past during the parade***

◊ **conscript** person who is legally obliged to join the armed services; ***the conscripts all had a thorough basic training***

◊ **guerrilla** soldier who is not part of a regular national army; ***the guerrillas fought their way to the capital***

◊ **mercenary** soldier who is paid to fight for a foreign country; ***he was one of a group of mercenaries hired to protect the president***

◊ **regular** professional soldier serving in the army as a career; ***he was a regular for twenty years before leaving the army***

◊ **veteran** soldier, sailor, etc., who has fought in a war; ***the veterans visited war graves on the fiftieth anniversary of the battle***

song

noun words which are sung; ***he was singing a song in the bath***

◊ **anthem** solemn song for a choir; ***the choir sang an anthem at the end of the funeral service***

◊ **aria** solo song in an opera; ***she sang an aria from 'The Marriage of Figaro'***

◊ **ballad** simple romantic song; ***a concert of folk ballads***

◊ **carol** special song sung at Christmas; ***the children are practising Christmas carols***

◊ **hymn** song sung during a Christian religious service; ***the congregation stood for the first hymn***

◊ **lullaby** song sung to help babies go to sleep; ***she sang a lullaby which her mother had taught her***

◊ **lyrics** words of a song; ***he wrote the lyrics for the musical***

◊ **serenade** love song; ***he sang a serenade to her***

sorry

adjective sad about something that has happened; ***everyone was sorry that you were ill***

◊ **apologetic** showing that you are sorry for something; ***she wrote us an apologetic letter***

◊ **contrite** sorry for something you have done; ***he was very contrite about the accident he had caused***

◊ **repentant** *(formal)* full of regret for what you have done; ***when he was told off he didn't look at all repentant***

special

adjective referring to someone or something which is not ordinary but has a particular importance or use; ***this is a special day, it's our 25th wedding anniversary***

◊ **important** which matters a great deal; ***I have to go to London for an important meeting***

◊ **original** new and different; ***the planners have produced some original ideas for the new town centre***

◊ **singular** odd, strange; ***we found ourselves in a really singular position***

◊ **unique** different from everything else, the only one that exists; ***the stamp is unique and so worth a great deal***

speak

verb to say words; ***she spoke to me when the meeting was over***; ⇨**talk**

◊ **harangue** to make a loud speech addressed to crowd; ***the leader harangued his followers at the meeting***

◊ **lecture** to give a talk to students or any other group of people on a particular subject; ***she lectured the group on proper behaviour at meetings***

speech

noun formal talk given to an audience; ***he made some notes before giving his speech***; ⇨**address**

◊ **harangue** loud speech addressed to crowd; ***the leader gave an harangue to his followers***

◊ **lecture** talk to students or any other group of people on a particular subject; ***she gave a lecture on Chinese art***

◊ **monologue** long speech by one actor or other person alone; ***the little boy stood on a chair and recited a monologue***

◊ **sermon** serious talk giving someone advice; ***he gave a sermon about the need to love your neighbour***

◊ **talk** lecture about a subject; ***she gave a short talk about the history of the town***

◊ **tirade** long speech attacking something; ***he was expecting to hear a tirade about the mess in his room***

speed

noun rate at which something moves or is done; ***the coach travelled at a high speed along the motorway***; ⇨**velocity**

◊ **acceleration** the action of going faster; ***our car has wonderful acceleration***

◊ **rate** *or* **tempo** speed and rhythm at which something happens; ***he found it difficult to keep up with the rate of life in the city***

spirit

noun being without a body; ***some people believe they can communicate with the spirits of their ancestors***

◊ **angel** heavenly spirit; ***angels are often considered as messengers from God***

◊ **demon** *or* **devil** evil spirit; ***some people believe demons can hurt real people***

◊ **fairy** little creature who can work magic; ***I believed in fairies when I was little***

◊ **ghost** spirit of a dead person which appears; ***they say the house is haunted by the ghost of its last owner***

◊ **soul** the spirit in a person; ***do you believe your soul lives on when your body dies?***

sponsor

verb to support in return for advertising; ***the company sponsored the local football team***

◊ **endorse** to show approval of; ***I endorse what has just been said***

◊ **help** to make it easier for someone to do something, to give aid or assistance; ***he helped the old lady up the steps***

◊ **promote** to make sure people know about something by advertising it; ***there are posters all over town promoting the new night club***

◊ **support** to provide money to help; ***we hope the banks will support us during the expansion period***

sponsor

noun person who supports something in return for advertising; ***the company is the sponsor of the local team***

◊ **guarantor** person who promises to pay the debts of another person; ***he said he would be guarantor for his brother***

◊ **patron** person who protects or supports someone or something; ***she is a great patron of young artists***

◊ **promoter** person who presents something to the public; ***the boxing promoter put on a championship fight***

◊ **proposer** person who puts someone forward for a position; ***he wanted to be secretary but he couldn't find a proposer***

◊ **supporter** person who encourages a team; ***he is a Leicester City supporter***

sport

noun games or races which people compete in; ***do you like watching sport on TV?***

◊ **athletics** running, jumping and throwing competitions; ***we spent the afternoon watching athletics on TV***

◊ **field sports** outdoor sports such as hunting and fishing; ***field sports are popular with people who like the countryside***

◊ **Games** large organized sports competition; ***the Olympic Games***

◊ **water sports** competitions carried out in or on water; ***water skiing is becoming one of the favourite water sports***

◊ **winter sports** sports which are played in winter, such as skiing, skating, etc.; ***we go to Switzerland every February for the winter sports season***

spy

noun person who is paid to try to find out secret information from within another group or organization; ***he was executed as a spy***; ⇨**secret agent**

◊ **detective** policeman who investigates crimes or someone who is not part of a police force but finds information for a fee; ***detectives have interviewed four suspects***; ***he hired a detective to follow his wife***

◊ **double agent** spy who works for opposite sides at the same time; ***being a double agent is the most dangerous job in the world***

◊ **informer** *or* **grass** *(informal)* person who betrays information to the authorities; ***the police were given the information by an informer***

◊ **private eye** *(informal)* detective who is not a member of a police force, but who finds out information for a fee; ***he hired a private eye to follow his partner***

state

noun independent country; ***you can travel freely from one member state of the European Union to another***; ⇨**country;** ⇨**nation**

steal

verb to take something which belongs to another person; ***someone tried to steal my handbag***; ⇨**pinch** *(informal)*

◊ **burgle** to enter a building and steal things from it; ***their flat was burgled while they were on holiday***

◊ **cheat** to break the rules or act dishonestly in order get what you want or gain an advantage; ***he cheated by taking notes into the exam room with him***

◊ **kidnap** to steal a child or a person and take them away illegally; ***the millionaire was kidnapped and held for two weeks***

◊ **pilfer** to steal small objects or small amounts of money from the place where you work; ***they pilfered stationery from the office where they worked***

◊ **pirate** to copy a book, disk, design, etc., which is copyright; ***the designs for the new dress collection were widely pirated***

◊ **plagiarize** to copy the work of another author and pretend it is your own; ***she was accused of having plagiarized a book by an American author***

◊ **ransack** to cause a lot of damage and mess while searching a place; ***while she was out someone had ransacked her room***

◊ **rob** to attack and steal from someone; ***a gang robbed our local bank***

◊ **shoplift** to steal from shops while pretending to be a customer; ***the sales assistant was sure that the woman was shoplifting***

stop

verb

(a) to make someone or something not do something any more, to prevent someone or something being done; ***the rain stopped the picnic***; ***we stopped the children from buying unwrapped sweets***

◊ **cancel** to stop something that has been planned; ***the trip was cancelled because the weather was too bad***

◊ **control** to keep in order, to direct or restrict; ***the police were out in force to control the crowds***

◊ **counteract** to act against the actions or effects of something; ***the lotion should counteract the irritant effect of the spray***

◊ **hinder** to make it difficult for something to be done or happen; ***the economic situation is hindering any increase in living standards***

◊ **limit** *or* **restrict** not to allow something to go beyond a certain point; ***the government limited the number of new motorways that can be built***

◊ **neutralize** to cancel the effect of something; ***we acted immediately to neutralize the threat from their navy***

◊ **oppose** to try and prevent something from happening; ***several groups oppose the new law***

◊ **prevent** to stop something happening, to stop someone doing something; ***the police prevented anyone from leaving the building***

◊ **prohibit** to say that something must not be done; ***the rules prohibit singing in the dining room***

◊ **regulate** to control by using rules or laws; ***speeds are strictly regulated on all classes of roads***

◊ **restrain** to try and stop someone doing something; ***it took six policemen to restrain the man who became violent***

◊ **suppress** to not allow to continue; ***all opposition newspapers have been suppressed***

(b) to make something come to an end; ***he stopped the meeting by insisting that a vote be taken***; ⇨**complete;** ⇨**finish;** ⇨**halt**

◊ **conclude** to end, to bring to an end; ***he concluded his speech by thanking everyone who had helped***

◊ **discontinue** to stop stocking, selling, making a product; ***we discontinued that line some time ago***

◊ **end** to be finished, to come to an end; ***the fighting ended in disorder***

◊ **finalize** to put the finishing touches to something; ***we hope to finalize the agreement tomorrow so it can be signed***

◊ **pause** to stop doing something for a short time; ***she ran along the road, only pausing to look at her watch***

◊ **terminate** to bring to an end, to finish; ***the bank terminated the offer yesterday so we can't take advantage of it now***

storm

noun high wind and very bad weather; ***several ships got into difficulty in the storm***

◊ **blizzard** *or* **snowstorm** heavy snow with a high wind; ***there were blizzards in the Highlands during the weekend***

◊ **gale** very strong wind; ***several trees were blown down in the gale***

◊ **hurricane** *or* **typhoon** tropical storm with strong winds and rain; ***the hurricane damaged properties all along the coast***

◊ **tornado** violent storm with a column of very high wind; ***a tornado struck the southern coast***

story

noun description of things that did not happen but were made up by someone; ***she writes children's stories about animals***; ⇨**tale**

◊ **allegory** story where the characters are symbols of ideas or other things; ***the story is an allegory of life in a police state***

◊ **fable** moral story, usually about animals, making them seem like human beings; ***in the book 'Animal Farm' Orwell wrote a modern fable***

◊ **legend** story from the past which may not be based on fact; ***the legend of Jason and the Golden Fleece***

◊ **myth** ancient story about gods; ***the myths of Greece and Rome***

◊ **parable** short story with a religious or moral point; ***the story is a parable about an unjust society***

◊ **saga** old story of heroic achievement or adventure, especially in Norway and Iceland; ***the sagas of the ancient kings of Iceland***

strange

adjective not usual, which you have not seen before, where you have never been before; ***the car engine is making a strange noise***; ***I find it difficult getting to sleep in a strange room***; ⇨**peculiar**

◊ **abnormal** not normal, that does not usually happen; ***the animal's behaviour seemed abnormal to me***

◊ **curious** strange and interesting; ***she has a curious high pitched voice***

◊ **exotic** unusual, referring to a strange, foreign, often tropical place; ***spices make the meat taste more exotic***

◊ **extraordinary** marvellous, strange and unusual; ***a peacock's feathers are quite extraordinary***

◊ **fantastic** strange, like a dream; ***his stories are full of fantastic creatures***

◊ **miraculous** wonderful, which cannot be explained; ***she has made a miraculous recovery***

◊ **mysterious** which cannot be explained; ***he died in mysterious circumstances***

◊ **odd** *or* **queer** *(old)* strange and puzzling; ***it's odd that he can never remember how to get to their house***

◊ **outlandish** strange or different from the usual; ***many of the clothes at fashion shows are too outlandish for ordinary people to wear***

◊ **supernatural** which cannot be explained by the laws of nature; ***she believes in supernatural occurrences like ghosts***

◊ **unusual** strange, not normal; ***it is unusual to have rain at this time of year***

stranger

noun person whom you have never met; person in a place where he has never been before; ***children are told not to accept lifts from strangers; I can't tell you how to get to the Post Office, I am a stranger here myself***

◊ **alien** *or* **foreigner** person who is not a citizen of the country; ***aliens are not permitted to travel outside the capital***

◊ **immigrant** person who comes to a country to settle; ***many immigrants came to Britain during the 1930s***

◊ **newcomer** person who has just come to a place; ***the family are newcomers to the village***

◊ **outsider** person who does not belong to a group, community, etc.; ***she has always been a bit of an outsider***

◊ **refugee** person who has left his country because of war, religious persecution, etc.; ***at the beginning of the war thousands of refugees fled over the border***

street

noun road in a town or village, usually with houses on each side; ***her flat is on a noisy London street***

◊ **avenue** wide street in a town, often with trees along the sides; ***a leafy suburban avenue***

◊ **cul-de-sac** small street only open at one end; ***the street is a small cul-de-sac with only six houses***

◊ **dead-end** street or way which leads nowhere; ***we drove into a little street and found it was a dead-end***

◊ **high street** most important street in a town or village; ***all the main shops are on the high street***

◊ **path** narrow track for walking; ***there's a path across the field***

◊ **promenade** walkway in a resort built along the side of the sea; ***our hotel was right on the promenade***

◊ **road** hard pathway used by vehicles to travel along; ***the road to York goes directly north from London***

◊ **side street** small street which leads off a main street; ***there were no shops in the side streets***

strength

noun power of action, having force, being able to resist; ***she hasn't got the strength to lift it***; ⇨**force**; ⇨**might**; ⇨**power**

◊ **energy** force or strength of a person; ***he used up a lot of energy rushing around doing the Christmas shopping***

◊ **stamina** strength to do something over a long period; ***does she have the stamina for the job? - it involves very long hours***

◊ **vitality** great energy; ***his vitality is the key to his success***

strong

adjective which has a lot of force; ***the wind was so strong that it blew tiles off the roof***

◊ **energetic** using force, lively; ***she is an energetic campaigner for animal rights***

◊ **hardy** able to survive in cold conditions; ***Icelanders are a hardy people***

◊ **irresistible** which you cannot help giving in to; ***the tornado was an irresistible force which destroyed everything in its path***

◊ **mighty** *or* **powerful** very strong; ***with one mighty heave he lifted the sack onto the lorry***

◊ **sturdy** strong and reliable; ***don't sit on that chair, it's not very sturdy***

◊ **vigorous** strong and energetic; ***she went for a vigorous run around the park before breakfast***

student

noun person who is studying at a college or university; ***all the science students came to my lecture***

◊ **disciple** follower of a religious leader, famous teacher or thinker; ***he is an enthusiastic disciple of Freud's approach to psychiatry***

◊ **postgraduate** person who has a first degree from a university and is studying for a higher degree; ***he's a postgraduate in the physics department***

◊ **scholar** student at school or university who has a special award to help pay the costs; ***because I was a scholar my parents didn't have to pay any fees***

◊ **schoolboy** *or* **schoolgirl** boy or girl attending a school; ***a group of schoolboys*** *or* ***schoolgirls were waiting at the bus stop***

◊ **schoolchildren** children who go to school; ***the village schoolchildren are collected every morning by bus***

study

verb to examine something carefully to learn more about it; ***we are studying the possibility of setting up an office in New York***; ***he is studying medicine because he wants to be a doctor***

◊ **know** to have learned something, to have information about something; ***do you know how to start the computer?***

◊ **learn** to find out about something, or how to do something; ***he's learning to ride a bicycle***

◊ **memorize** to learn something by heart; ***for homework we all had to memorize a poem***

◊ **research** to study, to try to find out facts; ***research your subject thoroughly before you start writing the article***

◊ **revise** to study a lesson again; ***I'm revising for my history test***

succeed

verb to do well, to achieve something you have been trying to do; ***she succeeded in passing her driving test***

◊ **accomplish** to achieve something successfully; ***what do you hope to accomplish at the meeting?***

◊ **achieve** to succeed in doing something; ***what do you want to achieve by writing to your MP?***

◊ **flourish** to do well; ***the company is flourishing***

◊ **graduate** to get a degree from a university; ***she graduated from Edinburgh University***

◊ **prosper** to succeed, to become rich; ***he worked hard and prospered***

◊ **thrive** to grow well and be strong; ***the company is thriving after making record profits***

◊ **win** to get (a prize, etc.); ***she won first prize in the art competition***

success

noun doing something well, getting what you have been trying for; ***she had great success in finding a job in a library***

◊ **achievement** thing which has been done successfully; ***he is very modest about his achievements***

◊ **fame** being well-known; ***fame hasn't spoilt her at all***

◊ **prosperity** being rich; ***they owe their prosperity to the discovery of oil on their land***

◊ **triumph** great victory, great achievement; ***they scored a triumph in their game against the French***

◊ **victory** winning of a battle, a fight, a game, etc.; ***they won a clear victory in the general election***

successful

adjective who or which does well; ***he is a successful businessman***

◊ **effective** which produces the required result; ***it's a very effective remedy for colds***

◊ **famous** well-known; ***he's a famous footballer***

◊ **fruitful** which produces good results; ***the discussions were serious and fruitful***

◊ **profitable** producing money or results as the result of a deal; ***she signed a profitable deal with a Russian company***

◊ **prosperous** wealthy, rich; ***Salisbury is a prosperous town***

◊ **thriving** growing well and strong; ***Telford is a thriving new town***

◊ **triumphant** victorious, happy because you have won; ***he gave a triumphant wave as he crossed the finishing line***

◊ **victorious** who has won a game or battle; ***the victorious army marched into the town***

suddenly

adverb quickly and giving you a shock; ***suddenly the room went dark***

◊ **abruptly** shortly and not very politely; ***he replied abruptly to the silly question***

◊ **hastily** quickly and carelessly; ***we hastily gathered our picnic things up when the rain came***

◊ **hurriedly** in a rush, too quickly; ***he finished his speech and sat down hurriedly***

◊ **promptly** immediately, at once; ***he replied to my letter very promptly***

◊ **unexpectedly** in a way not that was not expected; ***just as the party was starting his mother walked in unexpectedly***

suffer

verb to feel pain; ***she didn't suffer at all and was conscious until she died***

◊ **despair** not to hope; ***after two months he despaired of being rescued***

◊ **grieve** to be sad, especially because someone has died; ***he is grieving for his son who was recently killed***

◊ **worry** to be anxious because of something; ***I worry when the children stay out late***

suffering

noun feeling pain over a long period of time; ***the doctor gave him an injection to relieve his suffering***

◊ **agony** *or* **torment** extreme pain; ***after the accident, she was in agony for weeks***

◊ **anguish** great mental suffering; ***he caused his parents great anguish***

◊ **depression** mental state where you feel miserable and hopeless; ***she suffers from fits of depression***

◊ **despair** absolute hopelessness; ***when he lost his job he was filled with despair***

◊ **discomfort** lack of comfort; ***we suffered acute physical discomfort on the flight***

◊ **distress** great sorrow or pain; ***I don't want to cause the family any distress***

◊ **grief** crushing sadness; ***she couldn't hide her grief at the funeral***

◊ **misery** great unhappiness; ***there were scenes of appalling human misery in the refugee camps***

◊ **pain** feeling of being hurt; ***if you have a pain in your chest, you ought to see a doctor***

◊ **sadness** *or* **sorrow** feeling of being very unhappy; ***she felt great sadness on the death of her cat***

◊ **torture** making someone suffer pain as a punishment or to make them reveal a secret; ***they accused the police of using torture to get information***

suggest

verb to mention an idea to see what other people think of it; ***the chairman suggested that the next meeting should be in October***; ⇨**propose**

◊ **advise** to suggest what should be done; ***he advised her to put all her money into a deposit account***

◊ **hint** to say something that makes people guess what you mean; ***she hinted that her sister was pregnant***

◊ **imply** to suggest indirectly; ***he implied that he knew where the papers had been hidden***

◊ **prompt** to suggest to someone that he should do something; ***it prompted him to write to the local paper***

◊ **remind** to make someone remember something; ***remind me to book the tickets for New York***

◊ **submit** to put something forward for someone to examine; ***he submitted a claim to the insurers***

◊ **urge** to advise someone strongly to do something; ***I would urge you to vote for the proposal***

◊ **warn** to inform someone in advance of danger or difficulty; ***the weather forecast warned of storms***

suggestion

noun idea that you mention for people to think about; ***we have asked for suggestions from our passengers***

◊ **hint** hidden suggestion, clue; ***he didn't give a hint as to where he was going***

◊ **offer** thing which is proposed; ***he accepted her offer of a job in Paris***

◊ **proposal** plan which has been suggested; ***the committee made a proposal to rebuild the club house***

◊ **proposition** thing which has been suggested; ***the proposition is not very attractive***

◊ **reminder** thing which makes you remember something; ***keep this picture as a reminder of happier days***

◊ **warning** information about a possible danger; ***he shouted a warning to the children***

system

noun way in which things are organized; ***I've got my own system for dealing with invoices***

◊ **arrangement** putting into an order; ***the arrangement of the pictures in a book***

◊ **habit** *or* **routine** regular way of doing something; ***he has the habit of going to bed at 9 o'clock and reading***

◊ **method** way of doing something; ***what is the best method of payment?***

◊ **organization** action of arranging something; ***the organization of the meeting is done by the secretary***

◊ **rule** strict order of the way to behave; ***according to the rules, your tickets must be paid for in advance***

Tt

talk

verb to say things, to speak; ***the guide was talking French to the tourists***; ⇨**speak**

◊ **chat** to talk in a casual and friendly way; ***they were chatting about their holidays when the bus arrived***

◊ **debate** to talk about a serious matter or problem; ***they debated which was the best method of voting***

◊ **gossip** to talk about people saying things that may or may not be true; ***they spent hours gossiping about other people working in the office***

◊ **harangue** to make a loud speech addressed to crowd; ***the leader harangued his followers at the meeting***

◊ **lecture** to give a talk to students or any other group of people on a particular subject; ***she lectured the group on proper behaviour at meetings***

◊ **mention** to refer to something; ***the press has not mentioned the accident***

◊ **mumble** to talk in a low indistinct voice; ***he mumbled an excuse and left the room***

◊ **murmur** to talk very quietly; ***she murmured something and then went to sleep***

◊ **preach** to give a sermon in church; ***he preached to a packed congregation about tolerance***

◊ **rant** to complain or shout loudly; ***she was ranting on about the decision of the planning committee***

◊ **shout** to make a loud cry, to speak very loudly; ***they stamped on the floor and shouted***

◊ **whisper** to talk very quietly; ***he whispered instructions to the other members of the gang***

tax

noun money taken by the government from incomes, sales, etc., to pay for government services; ***the government is planning to introduce a tax on food***

◊ **assessment** calculation of amount to be paid; ***the assessment of costs will take about a week***

◊ **council tax** tax charged by a local council to help pay for its services; ***the council tax is going up substantially next year***

◊ **duty** tax which has to be paid on certain goods; ***you may have to pay customs duty on goods imported from outside the European Union***

◊ **income tax** tax on money earned as wages or salary; ***income tax is deducted from his salary each month***

◊ **levy** tax or other payment demanded and collected; ***I think the import levy on luxury goods is too high***

◊ **taxation** action of imposing taxes; ***money raised by taxation pays for government services***

◊ **toll** payment for using a road, bridge or ferry; ***you have to pay a toll to cross the bridge***

◊ **value added tax (VAT)** tax imposed as a percentage of the sales price of certain goods and services; ***VAT in Britain is currently 17.5%***

teach

verb to give lessons, to show someone how to do something; ***she taught me how to dance***; ⇨**educate**

◊ **coach (i)** to train sportsmen and sportswomen; ***she was coached by a former Olympic gold medallist*** **(ii)** to give private lessons to someone; ***all the actors had to be coached separately***

◊ **enlighten** to make someone understand something; ***will someone please enlighten me on what is happening?***

◊ **instruct** to show someone how to do something; ***the stewardess will instruct you in how to evacuate the aircraft in an emergency***

◊ **lecture** to teach a subject by giving talks to students or any group of people; ***she lectures on history at Birmingham University***

◊ **train** to teach someone or an animal how to do something; ***guide dogs are trained to lead blind people***

teacher

noun person who gives lessons, especially in a school; ***Mr Jones is our maths teacher***

◊ **coach** person who trains sportsmen or sportswomen; ***her coach was an Olympic gold medallist***

◊ **guru** respected teacher, often a religious or spiritual teacher; ***he was the great guru of the civil disobedience movement***

◊ **head teacher** teacher who is in charge of a school; ***the head teacher plans to retire next year***

◊ **instructor** teacher, especially of a sport; ***he works as a ski instructor in Switzerland***; ***the driving instructor told her to take her foot off the brake pedal***

◊ **lecturer** teacher in a university or college; ***she has been a lecturer for five years***

◊ **principal** head, senior administrator (of a school or a college); ***the principal wants to see you in her office***

◊ **professor** most senior teacher in a subject at a university; ***he's professor of English at York University***; ***an economics professor will give us a lecture today***

◊ **tutor** teacher, especially a person who teaches only one student or a small group of students; ***his first job was as a private tutor to some German children***

tell

verb to communicate something to someone by speaking; ***she told me about how she got lost in London***

◊ **advertise** to make sure that people know about something by display or broadcast; ***there are posters all over town advertising the circus***

◊ **advise** to suggest what should be done; ***he advised her to put her money into a deposit account***

◊ **announce** to say officially or in public; ***she announced the results of the competition to the crowd***

◊ **command** *or* **order** to instruct someone to do something; ***he commanded the workmen to move the lorry***

◊ **confess (i)** to admit that you have done something wrong; ***he confessed to committing six burglaries*** **(ii)** to tell your sins to a priest; ***she went to church to confess to the priest***

◊ **confide** to tell someone a secret; ***he has always confided in his mother***

◊ **demand** to make a firm request for something; ***we demanded payment for the work done***

◊ **divulge** to reveal a secret; ***she refused to divulge where the papers were hidden***

◊ **inform** to tell someone officially about something; ***have you informed the police about the theft?***

◊ **instruct** to tell someone officially to do something; ***the inspectors instructed the restaurant to replace its kitchen equipment; the fireman instructed everyone to leave the building***

temporary

adjective which is not meant to last a long time; ***she has a temporary job with a construction company***; ⇨**provisional**

◊ **brief** short; ***he wrote a brief note of thanks***

◊ **ephemeral** which does not last long; ***it was an ephemeral hairstyle, popular for a short time in the 1980s***

◊ **makeshift** used temporarily in place of something else; ***they used a makeshift ladder to get down into the well***

◊ **periodic** repeated after a regular period of time; ***we carry out periodic reviews of the financial position***

◊ **seasonal** which only lasts for a season, usually the holiday season; ***there are lots of seasonal jobs at the resort***

◊ **short-term** for a short period only; ***staying in a hotel is only a short-term solution to accommodation problems***

◊ **transient** *(formal)* which will not last; ***fame for most pop groups is very transient***

theatre

noun building in which plays are shown; ***what is the play at the local theatre this week?***; ⇨**playhouse**

◊ **auditorium** large hall for concerts, ceremonies, etc.; ***the prize-giving will be held in the school auditorium***

◊ **cinema** building where you go to watch films; ***we went to the cinema on Friday night***

◊ **concert hall** large building where programmes of music are played in public; ***the concert hall is in the centre of the city***

◊ **opera house** theatre in which operas are performed; ***Covent Garden Opera House is one of the most famous in the world***

◊ **stadium** large building for sport, with seating arranged around a sports field; ***our sports stadium was packed with spectators***

thief

noun person who takes something which belongs to another person; ***the police think they will catch the thief who stole the painting***; ***a thief tried to steal my handbag***

◊ **burglar** person who enters a building and steals things from it; ***the burglar got into their flat while they were on holiday***

◊ **kidnapper** someone who steals a child or a person and takes them away illegally; ***the kidnapper held the millionaire for two weeks***

◊ **pickpocket** person who steals things from people's pockets; ***'Watch out! Pickpockets are operating in this area'***

◊ **poacher** person who catches wild rabbits, deer, birds, etc., illegally; ***the poacher had two pheasants hidden inside his coat***

◊ **robber** person who attacks and steals from someone; ***a robber stole our neighbour's wallet while he was out walking***

◊ **shoplifter** person who steals from shops while pretending to be a customer; ***the sales assistant was sure that he was a shoplifter***

◊ **swindler** person who gets money from someone by a trick; ***the swindler got into the old lady's house and cheated her out of all her savings***

thin

adjective not fat; ***she's too thin - she should eat more***; ⇨**lean** *(person)*; ⇨**slender**; ⇨**slim**

◊ **bony** thin, with bones that you can see easily; ***he was riding a bony horse***

◊ **gaunt** very thin; ***he looked gaunt and pale after his years in prison***

◊ **willowy** tall and slender; ***the model was a willowy girl nearly six feet tall***

think

verb to use your mind; ***we never think about what other people might say***

◊ **consider** to think carefully about something; ***we have to consider the position of the children after the divorce***

◊ **contemplate** *or* **meditate** *or* **ponder** to think deeply and for a long time; ***he stood contemplating the painting***

◊ **daydream** to let your thoughts wander; ***she was sitting at her desk daydreaming about the holidays***

◊ **imagine** to picture something in your mind; ***imagine yourself sitting on a beach in the hot sun***

◊ **reflect** to think carefully about something; ***he reflected that this was the sixth time he had been arrested for speeding***

throw

verb to send something through the air; ***how far can you throw a cricket ball?***

◊ **fling** to throw wildly; ***he flung the empty bottle into the sea***

◊ **hurl** to throw violently; ***the crowd hurled stones at the police***

◊ **pitch** to throw a ball; ***I pitched him a high ball to see if he could catch it***

◊ **sling** to throw casually; ***she slung her briefcase into the back of the car***

◊ **toss** to throw into the air; ***he tossed me his car keys***

ticket

noun piece of paper or card which allows you to travel, go into a cinema or exhibition, etc.; ***they won't let you get on to Eurostar without a ticket***

◊ **label** piece of card, plastic, etc., attached to something to show price, contents, someone's name and address, etc.; ***the price on the label is £25***; ***make sure all your suitcases have labels***

◊ **pass** *or* **permit** piece of card or plastic which allows you to do something; ***you need a pass to enter the ministry offices***

◊ **token** piece of paper, card, metal, etc., which is used in place of money; ***you can use these tokens to pay for meals***

◊ **voucher** paper which is given instead of money; ***the voucher was worth £25***

tidy

adjective in order; ***I want your room to be tidy before you go out***; ⇨**neat**

◊ **clean** not at all dirty; ***I asked the waiter for a clean glass as the one I had been given had some marks on it***

◊ **fastidious** hard to please, careful about tidiness and cleanliness; ***put the book back in the right place - the librarian is very fastidious about that sort of thing***

◊ **orderly** well arranged; ***the papers were stacked in orderly piles***

time

noun amount of hours, days, weeks, etc.; ***he spent all that time watching TV***

◊ **epoch** major period of time; ***the 1980s and 90s have been one of the most important epochs in European history***

◊ **era** long period of history; ***the Victorian era***

◊ **instant** moment or second; ***for an instant, he stood still and then walked on***

◊ **period** length of time; ***it was an unhappy period in his life***

◊ **season** one of four parts of a year; ***the four seasons are spring, summer, autumn and winter***

◊ **term (i)** official length of time; ***his term as president was marked by a lot of disagreement*** **(ii)** one of the parts of a school or university year; ***cricket is played during the summer term only***

tired

adjective feeling that you need rest; ***we're all tired after a long day at the office***; ⇨**fatigued**

◊ **lazy** not wanting to do any work; ***she's just lazy - that's why the work never gets done on time***

◊ **lethargic** when your movements are tired and slow and you are almost inactive; ***the heat of the sun makes many animals lethargic***

◊ **sleepy** feeling ready to go to sleep; ***sitting in front of the TV late at night made him feel sleepy***

◊ **sluggish** lazy, slow-moving; ***the economy is still sluggish***

tool

noun instrument which you hold in the hand to do certain work, such as a hammer, spade, drill, mixer, etc.; ***a set of tools for mending the car***; ⇨**implement**

◊ **equipment** all the tools, arms, machinery, etc. which are needed; ***do you really need all this fire-fighting equipment on a ship?***

◊ **gadget** useful tool; ***a useful gadget for taking the tops off bottles***

◊ **instrument** piece of equipment; ***the technical staff have instruments which measure the output of electricity***

◊ **machine** which works with a motor; ***we have bought a machine for putting leaflets in envelopes***

top

noun highest place, highest point of something; ***he climbed to the top of the stairs and sat down***

◊ **apex** the top of a triangle or pyramid; ***the rock was shaped like a triangle with its apex 150m above the sea***

◊ **brow** top of a hill; ***having reached the brow of the hill they stopped to look at the view***

◊ **crest** highest point along the length of a mountain ridge, highest point along the length of a wave; ***the crests of some of the waves reached 30 feet***

◊ **peak** *or* **summit** top of a mountain; ***can you see that snow-covered peak in the distance?***

trade

noun business of buying and selling; ***Britain's trade with the rest of Europe is up by 10%***

◊ **business** occupation, trade or commercial organization for making money; ***he's just got a job in an electronics business***

◊ **commerce** the buying and selling of goods and services; ***a trade mission went to South America to boost British commerce in the region***

◊ **industry** manufacturing business (but can include other types of commercial activity); ***the tourist industry brings in a lot of foreign currency***; ***the country's coal industry is in decline***

tradition

noun beliefs, customs and stories which are past from one generation to the next; ***it's a family tradition for the eldest son to take over the business***

◊ **culture** a country's civilization, including music, art, literature, etc.; ***he is taking a course in Russian culture***

◊ **custom** habit, thing which is usually done; ***it's a local custom in this part of the world***

◊ **folklore** traditional stories and beliefs; ***she is making a study of Icelandic folklore***

◊ **habit** regular way of acting; ***he has the habit of going to bed at nine o'clock and reading***

traditional

adjective according to the beliefs, customs and stories which are past from one generation to the next; ***it's traditional in our family for the eldest son to take over the business***

◊ **ancient** very old; ***she's studying ancient history***

◊ **customary** usual, in the way something is usually done; ***it is customary to put money into the collecting box when attending a church service***

◊ **old** not young, having existed for a long time; ***my uncle is an old man - he's 84***; ***this old painting is valuable, it dates from the 17th century***

◊ **old-fashioned** not in fashion, out-of-date; ***she wore old-fashioned clothes***

◊ **venerable** very old and likely to be respected; ***he died at a venerable age***

travel

verb to move from one country or place to another; ***she travels 50 miles by car to go to work every day***

◊ **emigrate** to leave your country to live in another; ***my daughter and her family have emigrated to Australia***

◊ **explore** to travel and discover (especially unknown parts of the world); ***we spent our holidays exploring Holland by canal***; ***it's a part of the jungle which has never been explored***

◊ **go** to leave, to move from one place to another; ***when the play was over it was time to go home***; ***he has gone to work in Washington***

◊ **hitch-hike** to stand by the road and signal to passing motorists showing that you want a free ride to a place; ***hitch-hiking is forbidden on motorways***

◊ **leave** to go away from somewhere; ***Eurostar leaves Waterloo for Brussels every day at 8.25***

◊ **ride** to go on a horse, a bike, etc.; ***he rode his bike down the road to the shops***

◊ **tour** **(i)** to go on holiday, visiting various places; ***they toured the south of France*** **(ii)** to visit various places to perform or speak; ***the opera company toured Eastern Europe last year***

◊ **trek** to make a long hard journey; ***they trekked across the desert***

◊ **walk** to go on foot; ***the baby is just starting to walk***

◊ **wander** to walk around without any particular aim; ***they wandered round the town in the rain***

trick

noun clever action to deceive or confuse someone; ***they got into the house by a trick***

◊ **fraud** making money by making people believe something which is not true; ***she is facing trial for fraud***

trick

verb to deceive or confuse someone; ***he tricked the old lady out of all her savings***

◊ **cheat** to break the rules or act dishonestly in order get what you want or gain an advantage; ***he cheated by taking notes into the exam room with him***

◊ **swindle** to get money from somebody by a trick; ***he swindled the old lady out of her savings***

trouble

noun something that makes you worry, something that causes upset; ***the trouble with old cars is that they sometimes don't start***

◊ **aggravation** when something is made worse; ***the treatment was an aggravation to the illness not a cure***

◊ **calamity** *or* **disaster** great and sudden misfortune or accident; ***we are insured against calamities such as hurricanes and earthquakes***

◊ **crisis** serious situation where decisions have to be taken rapidly; ***an international crisis has developed in the area***

◊ **difficulty** something which makes it hard to do something; ***the difficulty is that no one has a driving licence***

◊ **hardship** difficult conditions, suffering; ***she faced hardship when her husband died and left her in debt***

◊ **hindrance** something which makes it difficult for something else to happen; ***having six children is something of a hindrance when arranging holidays***

◊ **inconvenience** something which causes difficulties; ***losing my car keys was a real inconvenience***

◊ **misfortune** bad luck; ***it was his misfortune to be born in the year when his father was declared bankrupt***

◊ **predicament** trouble or difficult situation; ***she's got herself into an awful predicament***

◊ **problem** something which is a difficult question; ***the police are trying to solve the problem of how the thieves got into the house***

◊ **suffering** feeling pain over a long period of time; ***the doctor gave him an injection to relieve his suffering***

try

verb to make an effort to do something; ***the boy tried to climb up the tree***; ⇨**attempt**

◊ **endeavour** *(formal)* to try hard; ***he endeavoured to contact her by phone and fax***

◊ **strive** to try very hard; ***everyone is striving for a solution to the dispute***

◊ **venture** to risk doing something dangerous; ***they ventured out into the blizzard***

tunnel

noun long passage under the ground; ***the Channel Tunnel links Britain to France***

◊ **burrow** rabbit hole; ***the rabbits all popped down their burrow when we came near***

◊ **mine shaft** hole in the ground leading to a coal mine; ***they had closed off the dangerous old mine shaft***

◊ **sewer** large underground pipe or tunnel which takes waste water and refuse away from buildings; ***the final scene of the film took place in the sewers of Vienna***

◊ **subway** underground passage along which pedestrians can pass (such as under a busy road); ***there's a subway from the bus station to the shopping centre***

◊ **underpass** road which is built under another; ***turn left at the traffic lights when you come out of the underpass***

Uu

ugly

adjective not beautiful, not pleasant to look at; ***what an ugly pattern!***

◊ **ghastly** *or* **horrible** very bad, frightening or unpleasant; ***what ghastly wine, it tastes of soap!***

◊ **gruesome** which makes you shocked; ***the police made a gruesome discovery in the cellar***

◊ **hideous** very ugly indeed; ***where did you get that hideous dress?***

◊ **monstrous** huge and horrible; ***a monstrous sea serpent***

◊ **repellent** which drives people away; ***the yellow colour in the bathroom was really repellent***

◊ **repulsive** unpleasant, which makes you disgusted; ***where did you get that repulsive tie?***

◊ **unsightly** unpleasant to see; ***the council is planning to move the unsightly refuse dump***

understand

verb to know what something means; ***it is difficult to understand how he could have done such a stupid thing***; ⇨**comprehend** *(formal)*

◊ **discern** *(formal)* to see, to find out about something; ***it was simple to discern their plan of campaign***

◊ **know** to have learned something, to have information about something; ***do you know how to start the computer programme?***

◊ **learn** to find out about something, or how to do something; ***he's learning to ride a bicycle***

unhappy

adjective not happy; ***he's unhappy because the holidays have come to an end***; ⇨**dejected;** ⇨**miserable;** ⇨ **sad**

◊ **depressed** *or* **dispirited** feeling miserable and hopeless; ***she was depressed after failing her test***

◊ **disappointed** sad because things did not turn out as expected; ***he was disappointed with his exam results***

◊ **discontented** not satisfied; ***groups of discontented dock workers marched on the offices of the port authority***

◊ **gloomy** sad in mind and outlook; ***he felt gloomy about the future because he had no job***

◊ **grief-stricken** crushed with sadness; ***she was grief-stricken over the death of her father***

uniform

noun special clothes worn by all members of an organization or group; ***the holiday camp staff all wear yellow uniforms***

◊ **costume** set of clothes worn by an actor or actress in a play or film or on TV; ***the costumes for 'Henry V' are magnificent***

◊ **robes** outer clothes worn on formal occasions to signify rank or position; ***the judges all wore their robes in the procession***

◊ **vestments** robes worn at religious ceremonies; ***the priest wore white vestments at the Easter ceremonies***

unpopular

adjective not liked by other people; ***the new manager was very unpopular with the staff***

◊ **disliked** not liked; ***she was disliked because of her bad manners***

◊ **friendless** without friends; ***he found himself friendless in a foreign country***

◊ **lonely** feeling sad because of being alone; ***it's odd how lonely you can be in a big city***

◊ **unwanted** which is not wanted; ***take any unwanted Christmas presents and give them away***

unreliable

adjective which cannot trusted to do what is needed; ***old cars can become very unreliable***

◊ **ambiguous** which has two meanings, which is not clear; ***the letter was ambiguous so we weren't sure what to do***

◊ **fickle** changeable, not steady; ***we can't rely on the fickle April weather for our garden party***

◊ **precarious** not safe, likely to fall; ***the house is in a precarious position on top of the cliff***

◊ **risky** which is dangerous; ***he lost all his money in some risky ventures in South America***

◊ **treacherous** likely to betray you; ***her treacherous behaviour led to the minister's downfall***

◊ **unpredictable** which cannot be predicted or forecast; ***the weather can be quite unpredictable in March***

unusual

adjective strange, not normal; ***it is unusual to have rain at this time of year***; ⇨**peculiar**

◊ **abnormal** not normal, that does not usually happen; ***the animal's behaviour seemed abnormal to me***

◊ **curious** strange and interesting; ***she has a curious high-pitched voice***

◊ **different** not the same; ***living in the town is very different from living in the country***

◊ **exotic** unusual, referring to a strange, foreign, often tropical place; ***spices make the meat taste more exotic***

◊ **extraordinary** marvellous, strange and unusual; ***a peacock's feathers are quite extraordinary***

◊ **fantastic** strange, like a dream; ***his stories are full of fantastic creatures***

◊ **miraculous** wonderful, which cannot be explained; ***she has made a miraculous recovery***

◊ **mysterious** which cannot be explained; ***she died in mysterious circumstances***

◊ **odd** *or* **queer** *(old)* strange and puzzling; ***it's odd that he can never remember how to get to their house***

◊ **outlandish** strange or different from the usual; ***many of the clothes at fashion shows are too outlandish for ordinary people to wear***

◊ **singular** odd, strange; ***we found ourselves in a really singular position***

◊ **special** referring to someone or something which is not ordinary but has a particular importance or use; ***this is a special day - it's our 25th wedding anniversary***

◊ **strange** not usual, which you have not seen before, where you have never been before; ***the car engine is making a strange noise***; ***I find it difficult getting to sleep in a strange room***

◊ **supernatural** which cannot be explained by the laws of nature; ***she believes in supernatural occurrences like ghosts***

urban

adjective referring to towns; ***they enjoy an urban lifestyle***

◊ **cosmopolitan** made up of people from different parts of the world; ***Berlin is a very cosmopolitan city***

◊ **inner city** referring to the central part of a city; ***inner city hotels are most convenient but can be noisy***

◊ **metropolitan** referring to a large capital city; ***she found it difficult to get used to the metropolitan life of London***

◊ **suburban** referring to the outer areas around a city or town; ***many people from suburban London travel by train to work***

useful

adjective who or which can help you do something; ***I find these scissors very useful for opening letters***

◊ **adaptable** able to change, able to deal with a new situation; ***she is very adaptable, I'm sure she will be able to alter her timetable***

◊ **convenient** which does not cause any practical problems; ***a bank draft is a convenient way of sending money abroad***

◊ **effective** which produces the required result; ***it's a very effective remedy against colds***

◊ **functional** useful but not decorative; ***these old black saucepans are very functional***

◊ **handy** practical and useful; ***this small case is handy when travelling***

◊ **helpful** which helps; ***they were very helpful when we moved house***

◊ **utilitarian** used for a practical purpose not decoration; ***there's no decoration in the office - it's all very utilitarian***

useless

adjective which is of no help or has no use; ***these scissors are useless - they won't cut anything***; ⇨**futile**

◊ **impractical** which is not easy to put into practice; ***it is quite impractical to expect three people to move all the furniture in two hours***

◊ **ineffectual** weak, not having any effect; ***he's a nice man but quite ineffectual as a salesman***

◊ **obsolete** no longer used; ***obsolete aircraft are stored before being dismantled***

◊ **pointless** with no sense; ***it's pointless to wait any longer, the last bus must have gone***

◊ **redundant** no longer needed; ***we rented out the redundant office space***; ***redundant workers have been offered retraining***

◊ **superfluous** which is more than is needed; ***we decided that several members of staff were superfluous to our requirements***

Vv

valuable

adjective worth a lot of money; ***the burglars stole everything that was valuable***

◊ **expensive** which costs a lot of money; ***it was an expensive holiday but it was so good it was worth it; fresh vegetables are usually more expensive in winter***

◊ **important** which matters a great deal, who holds a high position; ***it is important to be in time for the meeting***; ***he has an important government job***

◊ **irreplaceable** which cannot be replaced; ***the photographs of 19th century London are irreplaceable***

◊ **priceless** extremely valuable; ***his priceless collection of paintings were destroyed in the fire***

◊ **rare** valued because it is so uncommon; ***the woodland is the home of a rare species of frog***

◊ **superior** of very high quality; ***she gave him a very superior box of chocolates***

◊ **unique** different from everything else, the only one that exists; ***the stamp is unique, and so worth a great deal***

violent

adjective which hurts people; ***her husband was a very violent man***; ***it took six policemen to restrain the man who became violent***

◊ **aggressive** ready to attack; ***why are you so aggressive?***

◊ **brutal** cruel and violent; ***the police said it was a particularly brutal murder***

◊ **cruel** which causes pain, which makes a person or an animal suffer; ***it was cruel of him to make fun of her***

◊ **frenzied** wild and uncontrollable; ***the group launched a frenzied attack on the driver who had caused the accident***

◊ **rough** not gentle; ***don't be rough when you are playing with the puppy***

vote

verb to show by marking a paper, holding up your hand, etc. which one you choose in an election; ***more people voted for the winning candidate than for all the other candidates put together***

◊ **choose** *or* **pick** to select someone or something you like best or that will do the best job; ***they chose the best player as captain of the team***

◊ **elect** to choose by voting; ***the Member of Parliament was elected by a very small majority of votes***

◊ **select** to choose carefully; ***she selected her smartest outfit for the interview***

vote

noun choice made in an election made by marking a paper, holding up your hand, etc.; ***there were more votes for the winning candidate than for all the other candidates put together***

◊ **ballot** way of voting where people mark papers with a cross; ***the ballot produced a clear majority***

◊ **election** choice made by voting; ***the election was won by a very small majority of votes***

◊ **poll** time when people are asked to make a choice by voting or expressing an opinion; ***a poll of the workers showed that over 50% supported the union's demands***

◊ **referendum** vote where all the people of the country are asked to vote on a single question; ***the government announced that it will hold a referendum on the issue***

Ww Xx Yy Zz

wait

verb to stay where you are until something happens or someone comes; ***they waited in the rain until the bus arrived***

◊ **linger** to stay longer than necessary, longer than expected; ***don't linger at the office because we are going out tonight***

◊ **loiter** to stand or wander about doing nothing; ***various suspicious characters were seen loitering near the bank***

◊ **mark time** to stay on one spot, not to move forward; ***sales are marking time, we need to advertise more***

◊ **queue** to stand in a line waiting for something; ***we queued for hours to get the theatre tickets***

walk

verb to go on foot; ***the baby is just starting to walk***

◊ **amble** to walk in a relaxed way without hurrying; ***he was ambling along enjoying the sunshine***

◊ **limp** to walk with an uneven step; ***after the accident she limped badly***

◊ **march** to walk in step; ***the guards marched after the band***

◊ **plod** *or* **trudge** to walk slowly and heavily; ***the camels plodded across the desert***

◊ **prowl** to creep about quietly looking for something; ***the burglar prowled about outside the house waiting for everyone to go to bed***

◊ **saunter** *or* **stroll** to walk slowly for relaxation; ***they sauntered through the park in the sunshine***

◊ **shuffle** to walk, dragging your feet along the ground; ***she shuffled into the room in her slippers***

◊ **stride** to walk with long steps; ***he strode into the room and quickly made the announcement***

◊ **strut** to walk in a proud and self-important way; ***she strutted across the stage to collect her prize***

◊ **swagger** to walk in a proud way, swinging your shoulders; ***he swaggered into the office showing off his new suntan***

◊ **waddle** to walk with short steps swaying from side to side; ***the ducks waddled across the path***

war

noun fighting between countries; ***in 1914 a war broke out in Europe***; ⇨**hostilities**

◊ **battle** important fight between armed forces; ***many soldiers were killed and wounded in the battle***

◊ **campaign** organized military attack; ***Napoleon's Russian campaign of 1812***

◊ **civil war** war between citizens inside a country; ***the English Civil War was fought between supporters of the king and supporters of parliament***

◊ **crusade** *(history)* medieval war fought by Christian kings against the Muslims in the Middle East; ***knights from all over Europe went on the Crusades***

◊ **guerrilla war** war fought by soldiers who are not part of a regular army and who attack in small groups in unexpected places; ***the guerrilla war went on for over twenty years before negotiations began***

◊ **nuclear war** war in which atomic weapons are used; ***it is possible that no one at all would survive a nuclear war***

warm

adjective with comfortable heat; ***the temperature is below freezing outside but it is nice and warm in the office***

◊ **close** hot and airless; ***it's very close in here, can somebody open a window?***

◊ **hot** very warm, with a high temperature; ***if you're too hot, take your coat off***

◊ **lukewarm** not very hot; ***we sent back the coffee because it was lukewarm***

◊ **tepid** slightly warm; ***there was hardly any hot water left so my bath was only tepid***

◊ **tropical** referring to hot countries; ***in tropical countries it is always hot***

waste

verb to use something to no result; to leave something unused; ***you wasted your time learning French - we're going to Greece for our holiday***; ***you made far too many sandwiches, most of them will be wasted***

◊ **dissipate** *or* **fritter away** *or* **squander** to waste money, talent, etc., on unimportant things; ***after winning the lottery he dissipated his winnings on drink and expensive cars***

waste

noun things which are no use and are thrown away; anything left over from a process which needs to be disposed of; ***that broken chair is just waste now***; ***the waste from the chemical factory was taken away by tanker lorries***; ⇨**refuse**; ⇨**rubbish**

◊ **junk** useless articles, rubbish; ***you should clear out all that junk you've collected under your bed***

◊ **litter** rubbish left about in streets or other public places; ***the council tries to keep the main street clear of litter***

◊ **nuclear waste** radioactive waste from a nuclear reactor; ***the disposal of nuclear waste is causing problems worldwide***

◊ **sewage** waste water and other refuse carried away in large pipes or tunnels from buildings; ***the sewage must be treated before being allowed into the river system***

◊ **toxic waste** waste which is poisonous or harmful to people, animals or the environment; ***protesters gathered to complain about toxic waste being dumped at sea***

way

noun means of doing something; ***my mother showed me the way to make marmalade***

◊ **approach** way of dealing with a situation; ***his approach to the problem was different from hers***

◊ **manner** way of behaving; ***she has a very unpleasant manner***

◊ **method** *or* **technique** way of doing something; ***we used the most up-to-date manufacturing methods***

◊ **procedure** way in which something ought to be carried out; ***to obtain permission to build a new house you need to follow the correct procedure***

◊ **tactics** way of doing something so as to get an advantage; ***the manager's tactics were to defend until a clear opportunity came and then attack very quickly***

weak

adjective not strong; ***after his illness he is still very weak***; ⇨**feeble**

◊ **decrepit** old, feeble and falling to pieces; ***the house will be sold cheaply because of its decrepit state***

◊ **frail** weak and thin; ***she's getting very frail, and may soon have to go into a nursing home***

◊ **helpless** not able to do anything; ***he was almost helpless without his secretary***

◊ **infirm** *(formal)* old and weak; ***most of the residents in the home are elderly and infirm***

wealth

noun large amount of money; ***his wealth was inherited from his grandfather***; ⇨**affluence;** ⇨**fortune**

◊ **capital** money which is invested; ***a company with £100,000 capital***

◊ **luxury** great and expensive comfort; ***he lived a life of great luxury***

◊ **money** coins or notes which are used for buying things; ***how much money have you got in your wallet?***

◊ **opulence** great luxury or wealth; ***the film shows the opulence of the Titanic's first-class accommodation***

◊ **prosperity** being rich; ***they owe their present prosperity to the discovery of oil on their land***

weapon

noun object used for fighting; ***the crowd used iron bars as weapons***

◊ **ammunition** bullets, shells, etc., fired from a gun; ***they fought all day until their ammunition began to run low***

◊ **bomb** explosive weapon, dropped from an aircraft or placed by hand; ***enemy aircraft dropped bombs on the army base***

◊ **chemical weapons** weapons which use poisonous gas, bacteria, etc.; ***the stores of chemical weapons were destroyed as a result of the international agreement***

◊ **club** large heavy stick; ***she was knocked to the ground by a blow from the club***

◊ **conventional weapons** ordinary weapons such as guns, bombs, etc., not nuclear or chemical weapons; ***only conventional weapons were used in the war***

◊ **gun** weapon which shoots bullets or shells; ***he kept a gun in the house but it didn't make him feel any safer***

◊ **grenade** small bomb, usually thrown by hand; ***he threw a tear gas grenade into the crowd***

◊ **knife** metal blade fitted with a handle; ***the gang of youths regularly carried knives***

◊ **missile** explosive rocket which can be guided to its target; ***they think the plane was brought down by an enemy missile***

◊ **nuclear weapons** weapons which cause an atomic explosion; ***nuclear weapons are for mass destruction***

weather

noun conditions outside, i.e. if it is raining, hot, cold, windy, sunny, etc.; ***what's the weather going to be like today?***

◊ **climate** general weather conditions in a certain place; ***the climate in the south of the country is warmer than in the north***

◊ **season** one of four parts of a year; ***the four seasons are spring, summer, autumn and winter***

◊ **temperature** heat measured in degrees; ***the temperature in winter is quite low***

◊ **weather forecast** description of the sort of weather which is going to come in the next few hours or days; ***the weather forecast for the week is good***

well-behaved

adjective good, having good manners; ***she's never naughty, always so well-behaved***; ⇨ **good**

◊ **courteous** *or* **polite** *or* **respectful** showing good manners and respect; ***I found the hotel staff very courteous***

◊ **disciplined** trained and well controlled; ***a highly disciplined police force***

◊ **docile** quiet, not aggressive; ***some breeds of dogs are docile and easy to train***

◊ **dutiful** who does what should be done; ***he is a very dutiful son, he always checks to see if his mother needs anything***

◊ **obedient** doing what you are told to do; ***our old dog is very obedient - he always comes when you call him***

◊ **obliging** willing to help; ***it was very obliging of you to wait for me***

◊ **trustworthy** who can be depended upon; ***you are lucky to have such trustworthy staff***

wet

adjective which has a lot of water or other liquid on it; ***she forgot her umbrella and got wet coming back from the shops***

◊ **damp** rather wet; ***the cellar has cold damp walls***

◊ **drenched** *or* **soaked** very wet; ***they came home drenched after the heavy rain storm***

◊ **moist** slightly wet; ***he cleaned the table top with a moist cloth***

◊ **saturated** as full of a liquid as can be absorbed; ***the ground is saturated so we can't start ploughing yet***

◊ **sodden** wet through; ***we needed to get the children out of their sodden clothes and into a warm bath***

◊ **waterlogged** flooded, full of water; ***after so much rain the waterlogged golf course had to be closed***

winner

noun person who comes first in a race, beats someone in a game, gets a prize, etc.; ***the winner of the race gets a silver cup***

◊ **champion** best in a particular competition; ***he's the world champion in the 100m***

◊ **record-holder** person who holds the record in a sport; ***he's the world record-holder in the 200m***

◊ **victor** person who wins a fight, game, battle; ***the victor ran round the track waving a flag***

woman

noun adult female human being; ***that tall woman is my sister***; ***a woman stopped us and asked to see our tickets***; ⇨**lady**

◊ **aunt** sister of your father or mother, wife of your father's or mother's sister; ***Aunt Emma is coming to stay with us***

◊ **godmother** woman who sponsors a child at baptism; ***she was godmother to four children***

◊ **grandmother** mother of your mother or father; ***my grandmother always gives me money for my birthday***

◊ **mother** woman who has a son or daughter; ***her mother is a well-known writer***

◊ **sister** girl or woman who has the same mother and father as someone else; ***my sister Jane is three years older than me***

◊ **spinster** woman who is not married; ***she never married and was a spinster all her life***

◊ **wife** woman to whom a man is married; ***his wife runs an employment agency***

work

noun job done regularly to earn money; ***her work involves a lot of travelling***

◊ **assignment** job of work; ***he was given the assignment of reporting on the war***

◊ **business** occupation, trade or commercial organization for making money; ***he's just got a job in a electronics business***

◊ **calling** *or* **vocation** work you feel you have been called to do or for which you have a special talent; ***for her, nursing is a calling***

◊ **chore** piece of routine work, especially housework; ***it's a real chore, having to save our computer files every day***

◊ **employment** *or* **job** *or* **occupation** regular work which you get paid for; ***she found full-time employment in a supermarket***

◊ **profession** work which needs special training, skill or knowledge; ***members of the legal profession protested against the new regulations***; ***they are negotiating a new pay structure for the teaching profession***

◊ **task** job of work which has to be done; ***there are many tasks which need to be done in the garden***

◊ **trade** job which requires learning particular skills; ***he is a plumber by trade***

worried

adjective in an anxious state; ***I'm worried that we might run out of petrol***; **⇨anxious; ⇨concerned**

◊ **agitated** very nervous, worried or upset, not able to keep still; ***the relatives of the miners trapped in the mine were very agitated***

◊ **dismayed** shocked and upset; ***crowds of dismayed depositors rushed to the bank***

◊ **distressed** very sad and worried; ***when she came out of the hospital ward she was very distressed***

◊ **uneasy** nervous and worried; ***I'm rather uneasy about lending her so much money***

worry

noun something which makes you anxious; ***go on holiday and try to forget your worries***; ⇨**anxiety;** ⇨**concern**

◊ **agitation** nervous worry, upset, not being able to keep still; ***she came to see me in a state of considerable agitation***

◊ **dismay** shock and upset; ***the dismay of the depositors when the bank failed***

◊ **distress** great sorrow or pain; ***I don't want to cause the family any more distress***; ***when she came out of the hospital she was in great distress***

◊ **trouble** something that makes you worry, something that causes upset; ***the trouble with old cars is that they don't always start***

◊ **unease** feeling uncomfortable and worried; ***he couldn't hide his unease when asked to talk in front of the other delegates***

worship

noun praise and respect to God; ***prayer is the most important part of worship***

◊ **devotions** *(formal)* prayers; ***she is at her devotions***

◊ **hymn** song sung during a Christian religious service; ***the congregation stood for the first hymn***

◊ **meditation** silent, calm state, as part of religious practice; ***she's deep in meditation***

◊ **petition** prayer asking God for something; ***she offered many petitions in church***

◊ **prayer** speaking to God; ***she says her prayers every night before going to bed***

write

verb to put words or numbers on paper, etc., with a pen, word processor, etc.; ***she wrote the address on the back of an envelope***

◊ **inscribe (i)** to write, especially to write a note inside a book when giving it to someone; ***the book is inscribed "With best wishes, from the author"*** **(ii)** to write permanently, as on stone; ***the names of the dead soldiers are inscribed on the walls of the cemetery***

◊ **jot** to make quick notes about something; ***he jotted down her phone number***

◊ **print** to write capital letters or letters not joined together; ***print your name in the space below***

◊ **scrawl** *or* **scribble** to write badly or carelessly; ***she scrawled a few notes on a bit of paper***

writer

noun person who writes for publication; ***he's a writer of books on gardening***; ⇨**author**

◊ **biographer** person who writes the story of someone's life; ***he is the biographer of Charles Dickens***

◊ **columnist** journalist who writes a regular piece for a newspaper; ***he's a columnist who writes a regular gardening feature each week***

◊ **correspondent** journalist who writes articles for newspapers or reports for TV or radio on a particular subject; ***a report from our sports correspondent***

◊ **critic** person who writes comments on new plays, literature, films, etc.; ***she is the TV critic of the Times***

◊ **diarist** person who writes a diary; ***Samuel Pepys, the famous 17th century diarist***

◊ **hack** *(slang)* journalist; ***he's a hack writing for one of the tabloids***

◊ **historian** person who studies or writes about history; ***the book was written by a French historian***

◊ **journalist** person who writes for newspapers or periodicals; ***the film stars were interviewed by journalists at the première of the new film***

◊ **novelist** person who writes books of fiction; ***Jane Austen is one of the most important English novelists***

◊ **poet** person who writes poems; ***Lord Byron, the famous English poet***

wrong

adjective not correct; ***he gave three wrong answers and failed the test***; ⇨**mistaken**

◊ **false** *or* **untrue** not true; ***she gave a false name to the police***

◊ **inaccurate** not accurate, not exact; ***his calculations were wildly inaccurate***

◊ **misleading** quite wrong, likely to cause a mistake; ***she gave misleading information to the press***

young

adjective not old; ***she's very young, she's only six***; ⇨**youthful**

◊ **adolescent** referring to the period between childhood and adulthood; ***he teaches a class of adolescent boys***

◊ **immature** not adult; ***two immature swans followed their parents across the lake***

◊ **juvenile** referring to young people; ***young offenders are tried before a juvenile court***

◊ **teenage** referring to young people aged between 13 and 19; ***the teenage market for their music is enormous***

zoo

noun place where wild animals are kept, and where people can go to see them; ***we went to the zoo to see the pandas and penguins***; ⇨**zoological gardens** *(formal)*

◊ **game reserve** large natural area where wild animals are preserved; ***animals are free but safe in a game reserve***

◊ **menagerie** collection of wild animals in cages exhibited to people; ***he had a private menagerie which he liked to show to his friends***

◊ **safari park** park where large wild animals are free to roam and visitors drive through in their cars to look at them; ***safari parks are a popular day out with many families***

INDEX

abandon *leave*
abbey *church*
abide by *accept*
ability *power*
able *clever, good*
abnormal *strange, unusual*
abruptly *suddenly*
abscond *escape, leave*
absolve *release*
abstain (from) *avoid*
abstract *painting*
absurd *funny, silly*
abundance *plenty*
abundant *many*
academy *college, school*
accelerate *hurry*
acceleration *speed*
accept *agree*
accessible *open*
accompanist *performer*
accomplice *partner*
accomplish *succeed*
accounts *records*
accumulate *collect*
accuse *blame*
ache *pain*
achieve *succeed*
achievement *success*
acknowledge *answer, accept*
acknowledgement *answer*
acquaintance *friend*
acquiesce *agree*
acquire *get, obtain, receive*
acquit *release*
acrobat *performer*
act *perform*
active *busy*
actor *performer*
actress *performer*
actual *real*
adaptable *useful*
address *speech*
adequate *enough*
adjacent *near*
adjoining *near*
adjust *change*
adjutant *assistant*
administer *manage, control, govern, organize*
administration *government*
administrator *manager*
admiration *respect*
admire *respect, like*
admit *accept*
adolescent *young*
adopt *choose*
adore *like, love*
advance *loan*
advertise *tell*
advice *information*
advise *guide, help, suggest, tell*
adviser *guide*
affection *love, friendship*
afflict *hurt*
affluence *wealth*
affluent *rich*
affray *fight*
afresh *again*
afternoon *day*
again and again *again*
aggravate *annoy, offend*
aggravation *problem, trouble*
aggressive *violent*
aghast *afraid*
agitate *disturb*
agitated *worried*
agitation *worry*
agnosticism *doubt*
agony *pain, suffering*
agree *accept*
agreeable *nice*
agribusiness *farm*
aid *help*
aide *assistant*
ailing *ill*
ailment *illness*
aim *purpose*
airforce *armed forces*
airgun *gun*
airmail *mail*
ajar *open*
alarm *fear*
alarmed *afraid*
album *book*
alert *ready*
alien *foreign, stranger*
allegiance *duty*
allegory *story*
alleviate *cure*
allotment *garden*
ally *friend, partner*
alone *lonely*
alter *change*
amalgamate *mix*
amass *collect, save*
ambassador *diplomat*
ambiguous *doubtful, unreliable*
ambition *hope*
amble *walk*
ambush *capture*
amend *fix, repair*
amicable *friendly*

ammunition *weapon*
amphibian *animal*
ample *big, enough, many*
amputate *cut*
amuse *entertain, please*
amusement park *park*
amusing *funny, nice*
anchorage *port*
ancient *old, traditional*
anew *again*
angel *spirit*
anguish *sadness, suffering*
announce *advertise, tell*
annoy *hurt*
annoyed *angry*
anonymous *secret*
anorak *coat*
antagonize *offend*
anthem *song*
anthology *book*
anti aircraft gun *gun*
anti tank gun *gun*
anticipate *hope, plan, prepare*
anticipation *hope*
anticlimax *failure*
antidote *cure, medicine*
antiquated *old*
antique *old*
antiquity *past*
anxiety *worry*
anxious *worried, afraid*
apart *separately*
apartment *house*
apex *top*
apologetic *sorry*
appeal *ask*
appliance *machine*
appreciate *like, love, respect*
apprehend *capture*
apprehensive *afraid*
approach *way*
appropriate *obtain*
approve *agree*
aptitude *qualification*
aqueduct *bridge*
arbitrate *judge*
arcade *shop*
archives *museum, records*
arduous *difficult*
area *size*
argument *discussion*
aria *song*
armchair *seat*
armistice *peace*
army *armed forces*
aroma *smell*
arrange *organize, manage*
arrangement *music, system*
arrest *capture*
arrogance *pride*
arrogant *proud*
art gallery *museum*
artillery *gun*
ascertain *learn*
aspiration *hope*
aspire *hope*
assassinate *kill*
assassination *murder*
assemble *join, meet*
assembly *meeting*
assent *agree*
assessment *tax*
assign *appoint*
assignment *job, profession, work*
assimilate *learn*
assist *help*
assistance *help*
assistant *partner, servant*
associate *member, partner*
assume *accept, guess*
assumption *guess*
assurance *promise*
astute *clever*
asylum *shelter*
athletics *sport*
atlas *book, map*
atoll *island*
attach *join*
attack *fight*
attempt *try*
attic *room*
attractive *beautiful, nice*
auction *sell*
audit *check*
auditorium *theatre*
aunt *woman*
authentic *real*
author *writer*
authoritative *official*
authority *power*
authorization *licence*
automobile *car*
auxiliary *nurse*
avant-garde *modern, new*
avarice *greed*
avaricious *greedy, selfish*
avenue *street*
average *middle, normal, ordinary*
avoid *escape*
await *hope*
award *give, pay*
away *absent*

awful *bad*
awkward *difficult*
B & B *hotel*
bachelor *man*
backer *partner*
backing group *band*
badge *sign*
bail *insurance*
bailiff *official*
bake *cook*
baker's *shop*
balanced *sensible*
ball *celebration*
ballad *song*
ballet *performance*
ballot *vote*
bankrupt *poor*
banner *flag*
banquet *celebration, meal*
bar *restaurant*
barbecue *cook , meal*
bargain *agreement*
basic *simple*
bathroom *room*
batter *hit*
battle *fight, war*
battleship *boat, ship*
be in debt *owe*
be in power *govern*
be in the red *owe*
beach *coast*
beat *hit*
bedridden *ill*
bedroom *room*
befriend *like*
beg *ask*
belief *hope, opinion, religion*
believe *hope*
belt *region*
bench *seat*
beneficial *good*
benevolence *kindness*
benevolent *friendly, good, kind*
benign *friendly*
bequeath *give*
beseech *ask*
best *favourite*
bestow *give*
bid (for) *buy*
bid *offer*
big business *business*
biographer *writer*
biography *book*
birthplace *place*
bit *part, share*
bitter *angry*
bizarre *funny*
blackmailer *criminal, thief*
blame *complain*
blameless *good*
blaze *fire*
blend *mix, join*
bliss *happiness*
blissful *happy*
blizzard *storm*
blockbuster *book*
bloke *man*
blues *music*
blunder *mistake*
board *enter*
boastful *proud*
boat *ship*
bobby *police*
bodyguard *guard, servant*
boil *cook*
bold *brave*
bolt *close*
bomb *weapon*
bond *promise*
bonfire *fire*
bonus *gift*
bony *thin*
booklet *book, magazine*
borough *city*
borrow *hire, owe*
boss *leader*
bother *disturb*
bottle *container*
boundary *border*
box *container, fight*
boycott *avoid, separate*
brain *mind*
brainwave *idea*
brainy *clever*
brand-new *modern, new*
brass band *band*
brasserie *restaurant*
breadth *size*
break in *enter*
break open *open*
break *damage*
breakfast *meal*
bribe *buy*
brief *short, temporary*
briefcase *bag*
bright *clever, light*
brightness *light*
brilliant *clever, light*
bring *carry*
broadcast *advertise, publish, send*
brochure *magazine*
broke *poor*

bronze age *past*
brook *river*
brother *man*
brow *top*
browse *read*
brutal *violent*
buffoon *fool*
bug *listen*
build *make*
building society *bank*
bulky *big*
bulletin *news*
bully *frighten, hurt*
bungalow *house*
bungler *fool*
buoyant *light*
bureau *office*
bureaucrat *official*
burglar *thief*
burgle *steal*
burrow *dig, hole, tunnel*
business *trade, work*
busk *perform*
bustling *busy*
butcher *kill*
butcher's *shop*
buxom *fat*
buy *order, own*
by-law *law*
by-pass *road*
C.I.D (Criminal Investigation Department) *police*
cabaret *performance*
café *restaurant*
calamity *trouble, disaster*
calculate *measure*
call *enter*
calling *job, profession, work*
calm *quiet, peace, quiet*
calmly *quietly*
camouflage *hide*
campaign *war*
cancel *prevent, stop*
cannon *gun*
canoe *boat*
canon *law*
canteen *restaurant*
capability *qualification*
capable *able, clever, good, sensible*
capacity *size*
capital offence *crime, offence*
capital punishment *punishment*
capital *city, money, wealth*
captive *prisoner*
car park *park*
careful *reliable*
caricature *picture*
carol *song*
carrier bag *bag*
carrier *boat, ship*
carry *move*
carton *container*
cartoon *picture*
cartoonist *artist*
carve *cut*
carver *artist*
cascade *fall*
case study *records*
case *container*
cash flow *money*
cash *money*
castle *house*
casual *informal*
cataclysm *disaster*
catastrophe *disaster*
catch *capture*
category *kind*
cathedral *church*
cause *reason*
cautious *careful*
cave *hole*
cavern *hole*
cavity *hole*
celebrated *famous*
celebrated *popular*
cell *prison*
cellar *room*
censor *judge*
censor *judge*
censure *blame*
central *middle*
ceremonial *formal*
chair *seat*
chalet *house*
chamber music *music*
chamber orchestra *orchestra*
champion *winner*
chance *opportunity*
chancellor *principal*
chap *man*
chapel *church*
charge (for) *price*
chargé d'affaires *diplomat*
charge *run*
charity *kindness, pity*
charming *nice*
chart *map*
charter *hire, law*
chase *follow, run*
chastise *punish*
chastisement *punishment*
chat *talk*

cheat *liar, steal, thief*
check *search*
checklist *list*
cheer up *please*
cheer *shout*
cheerful *happy*
chemical weapons *weapon*
chemist's *shop*
cherish *love*
chic *fashionable*
chief *leader*
child *person*
chilled *cold*
chilly *cold*
choose *vote*
chop down *cut*
chop up *cut*
choral music *music*
chore *job, work*
chosen *favourite*
chubby *fat*
chuckle *laugh*
cinema *theatre*
cipher *secret*
circulate *publish*
citadel *castle*
citation *prize*
civil servant *official, servant*
civil war *war*
clamour *shout*
clan *people*
clandestine *secret*
clarification *proof*
clarify *explain, prove*
classic *book*
classical music *music*
classy *fashionable*
clause *part*
clean *tidy*
cleanse *clean*
clemency *pity*
clever *sensible, able*
climate *weather*
cloak *coat*
close *finish, warm*
closure *finish*
cloudburst *rain*
clown *performer*
club *weapon*
cluster *group*
coach *teach, teacher*
coaster *boat, ship*
coastline *coast*
cocky *proud*
code *law, secret*
coerce *make*
coexistence *peace*
collaborator *assistant*
collapse *fall*
colleague *assistant, friend, partner*
collect *carry, meet, receive*
college *school*
colossal *big*
columnist *writer*
combat *fight*
combine *join*
come *arrive*
comedian *performer*
comedy *play*
comfort *help, nurse, please*
comfortable *nice*
comic *magazine*
comical *funny*
command *law, order, order, manage, tell*
commander *leader*
commander-in-chief *leader*
commandment *law*
commemorate *remember*
commence *begin*
commendable *good*
commerce *business, trade*
commission *income, pay, profit*
commitment *promise*
common knowledge *information*
common law *law*
common *normal, ordinary*
commonplace *ordinary*
communication *message*
communique *news*
communism *government*
community *people*
compact *agreement, little, promise, small*
companion *friend*
compassion *pity*
compel *make*
compensate *pay*
compensation *income, pay*
competent *able, good*
competition *game*
complaint *illness*
complete *close, finish, full, stop*
completion *finish*
complimentary *free*
comply *agree*
comply *obey*
compose *make*
composed *calm*
composition *music*
comprehend *know, understand*
comprehensive *school*
comrade *friend, partner*
con *cheat*

conceal *hide*
concealed *secret*
concede *accept*
conceit *pride*
conceited *proud*
concentrate *listen*
concept *idea*
concern *worry*
concerned *worried*
concert hall *theatre*
concert *music, performance*
conclave *meeting*
conclude *close, finish, stop*
conclusion *finish, result*
conclusive proof *proof*
concur *agree*
condemn *judge*
condemn *punish*
condolences *pity*
conductor *performer*
confederate *partner*
confer *give*
conference *meeting*
confess *tell*
confide *tell*
confidence trickster *criminal*
confirm *agree*
conflagration *fire*
conform *obey*
congregate *meet*
conjecture *guess*
conjecture *guess*
conjuring *magic*
con-man *liar*
connect *join*
consciousness *mind, reason*
conscript *hire, soldier*
consecutive *next*
consensus *agreement*
consent *agreement, agree*
consequence *result*
conserve *save*
consider *think*
considerable *big, many*
considerate *good*
consolation prize *prize*
conspiracy *secret*
constantly *always*
constitution *law*
construct *build, make*
consultant *guide*
consume *drink, eat*
container ship *boat, ship*
contemplate *think*
contemplation *prayer*
contemporary *modern, new*
contempt *pride*
contemptuous *proud*
contented *happy*
continually *always*
contract *agreement, promise, promise*
contrite *sorry*
control *prevent, stop*
controlled *calm*
controller *manager*
convene *meet*
convenient *simple, useful*
convention *meeting*
conventional weapons *weapon*
conventional *ordinary*
converge *meet*
conversation *discussion*
convert *change*
convertible *car*
convey *carry*
convict *prisoner*
conviction *hope, opinion*
cool *cold*
co-opt *choose*
copper *police*
copy *repeat, draw*
cordial *friendly*
coroner *judge*
corporal punishment *punishment*
corpulent *fat*
correct *accurate, fix, official, repair*
correspondence *mail*
correspondent *writer*
corroborate *prove*
corvette *boat, ship*
cosmopolitan *urban*
cost (of) *price*
costly *expensive*
costume *uniform*
cottage industry *business*
cottage *house*
council tax *tax*
council *meeting*
counsel *advise, guide, help*
counsellor *guide*
count *measure*
counteract *prevent, stop*
counterfeit *artificial*
country *region, state*
coupe *car*
couple *join*
courageous *brave*
court order *order*
courteous *well-behaved*
courtesy *respect*
couturier *artist*
covetous *greedy*

cowardice *fear*
cower *fear*
co-worker *assistant, partner*
crackpot *fool*
craftsman *artist*
cram *fill*
crate *container*
crater *hole*
craving *feeling*
craze *fashion*
crazy *mad*
create *build, make*
creation *product*
credit broker *bank*
credit card *cheque*
credit union *bank*
credit *loan*
crest *top*
crime *offence*
criminal *bad*
crisis *problem, trouble*
critic *writer*
criticize *blame*
criticize *complain*
croft *farm*
cross *angry*
cross-country *race*
crowd *group*
crucial *important, serious*
cruel *violent*
cruise liner *boat, ship*
crusade *war*
crushing *heavy*
cul-de-sac *street*
cult *religion*
cultivate *farm, grow*
culture *tradition*
cumbersome *heavy*
cup *prize*
cure *improve, nurse*
curious *strange, unusual*
currency *money*
custom *tradition*
customary *traditional*
cylinder *container*
daily *magazine, often*
dainty *little, small*
damaging *bad*
damp *wet*
dance band *band*
dance *perform*
dancer *performer*
dangerous *serious*
daring *brave*
dash *run*
data *information*
daub *painting*
dawn *day*
daybreak *day*
daydream *think*
daylight *light*
dazzling *light*
dead-end *street*
deadly *bad*
deafening *loud*
dear *expensive, good*
debate *discussion, talk*
debt *loan*
deceased *dead*
deceive *cheat, pretend*
decency *honour*
decimate *kill*
decisive *important*
decline *fall, refuse*
decoration *prize*
decree *law, order, order*
decrepit *weak*
defence *protection*
deference *respect*
defraud *cheat*
defunct *dead*
degree *qualification*
deity *god*
dejected *sad, unhappy*
dejection *sadness*
delicious *good*
delight *entertain, happiness*
delighted *happy*
delightful *nice*
delirious *mad*
deluge *rain*
demand *ask, order, order, tell*
demanding *difficult*
demented *mad*
democracy *government, politics*
demolish *damage*
demon *spirit*
demonstrate *show*
dentist *doctor*
depart *go*
department store *shop*
dependable *good, reliable*
deplore *blame*
deport *move, send*
deposit *insurance, save*
depressed *sad, unhappy*
depression *sadness, suffering*
depth *size*
deranged *mad*
descend *fall*
design *draw*
designate *appoint*

designation *name*
designer *artist*
desire *feeling*
desolate *lonely*
despair *sadness, suffer, suffering*
despise *dislike*
destitute *poor*
destroy *damage*
destroyer *boat, ship*
destructive *bad*
detached house *house*
detain *keep*
detainee *prisoner*
detect *find*
detective *spy*
detention centre *prison*
detest *dislike*
detrimental *bad*
develop *grow, improve*
devil *spirit*
devoted *friendly*
devotion *love, friendship*
devotions *prayer, worship*
devour *eat*
diarist *writer*
diary *book*
dictate *make*
dictator *ruler*
dictatorship *government*
dictionary *book*
die out *finish*
diesel engine *engine*
diet *food*
different *unusual*
differentiate *separate*
difficulty *problem, trouble*
dim *dark*
dimensions *size*
dine *eat*
diner *restaurant*
dinghy *boat*
dining room *room*
dinner *meal*
diploma *qualification*
diptych *painting*
dire *bad*
direct *order, manage, organize, control*
directive *order*
director *leader, manager*
disable *damage*
disappointed *sad, unhappy*
disapprove *blame*
disaster *trouble*
disbelief *doubt*
discern *look, see, understand*
discerning *clever, sensible*
disciple *student*
discipline *punish*
disciplined *well-behaved*
discomfort *pain, suffering*
discontented *sad, unhappy*
discontinue *stop*
discover *find*
discriminate *separate*
disease *illness*
disguise *change, hide*
disgust *offend*
disliked *unpopular*
dismay *fear, worry*
dismayed *worried*
disorder *illness*
dispatch *send, news*
dispirited *sad, unhappy*
displace *move*
display *show*
displease *offend*
displeased *angry*
disqualify *dismiss*
dissipate *waste*
distinct *separate*
distinguish *look, see*
distinguished *famous*
distort *change*
distress *hurt, pain, suffering, worry*
distressed *worried*
district *place, region*
ditch *hole*
ditto *again*
divert *entertain*
divide *separate*
dividend *profit*
divine *holy*
divinity *god*
divorce *separate*
divulge *tell*
do *perform*
docile *well-behaved*
dock *arrive, port*
documentation *records*
donate *give*
donation *gift*
doodle *draw*
dormitory *room*
dossier *records*
double agent *spy*
doubt *question*
downpour *rain*
doze *sleep, sleep*
drama *play*
dramatic *interesting*
drawing *picture*
drawn-out *long*

dread *fear*
dreadful *bad*
dream *hope*
drenched *wet*
driveway *road*
drizzle *rain, rain*
drop in *enter*
drug *medicine*
dry-clean *clean*
dual carriageway *road*
dubious *doubtful*
dud *failure*
duel *fight*
dull *dark*
duplicate *copy, repeat*
durable *permanent*
dust *clean*
dusty *dirty*
dutiful *good, well-behaved*
duty *tax*
dwelling *house*
dwindle *fall*
earn *get, obtain*
earnings *income, pay, profit*
easily *simply*
easy *simple*
eavesdrop *listen*
echo *answer*
economical *cheap*
ecstasy *happiness*
educate *teach*
effect *result*
effective *good, successful, useful*
efficient *able, good*
effortlessly *simply*
egotistical *selfish*
eject *move, send*
elated *happy*
elderly *old*
elect *choose, vote*
election *vote*
electric motor *engine*
elegant *beautiful*
elementary *simple*
elevated *high*
elope *escape*
elucidate *explain*
elude *avoid, escape*
e-mail *message*
emancipate *release, save*
emancipated *free*
emigrate *leave, travel*
eminent *famous, high*
emissary *diplomat*
emotion *feeling*
emperor *ruler*
employ *hire*
employment *work, job, profession*
empress *ruler*
empty *free*
encounter *meet*
encounter *meeting*
encyclopaedia *book*
end product *product, result*
end *finish, stop*
endeavour *try*
endlessly *always*
endorse *accept, sponsor*
enduring *permanent*
energetic *strong*
energy *strength*
engage *appoint, hire*
engaged *busy*
engine *machine*
engraver *artist*
engraving *picture*
engrossed *busy*
enhance *improve*
enigma *secret*
enjoyable *nice*
enjoyment *happiness*
enlighten *advise, teach*
enlightened *sensible*
enlist *appoint, hire*
enormous *big*
enquiry *question*
enrage *offend*
ensemble *orchestra*
ensign *flag*
ensue *follow*
ensuing *next*
enterprise *adventure, business*
entertain *perform*
entertainer *performer*
entire *full*
entreat *ask*
envious *greedy*
envoy *diplomat*
ephemeral *temporary*
epic *long*
epoch *time*
equipment *tool*
era *time*
erect *build, make*
erode *damage*
errand *job*
error *mistake*
escape *avoid, go*
eschew *avoid*
escort *guard, guard, protect*
establish *begin, prove*
estate car *car*

esteem *respect*
estimate *opinion, price*
eternal *long*
eternally *always*
ethical *good*
ethnic group *people*
euphoria *happiness*
euthanasia *murder*
evacuate *leave*
evade *escape*
even *flat*
evening *day*
event *game*
everyday *normal, ordinary*
evict *move, send*
evidence *proof*
evil *bad*
exact *accurate*
exalted *high*
examination *question*
examine *check, search*
exasperate *annoy*
excavate *dig*
excavation *hole*
excellent *good*
excerpt *part, share*
exchange *replace*
exclude *dismiss*
exclusive *good*
execute *kill, punish*
execution *murder, punishment*
executive *manager*
exempt *free*
exhibit *show*
exhibition *museum*
existence *life*
exorbitant *expensive*
exotic *foreign, strange, unusual*
expand *increase*
expect *hope*
expectation *hope*
expedite *hurry*
expel *dismiss, move, send*
expense *price*
expensive *good, valuable*
experience *qualification*
expert *able, clever, guide, professional*
expire *finish*
explanation *answer*
exploration *adventure*
explore *travel*
expose *show*
exquisite *beautiful, good*
extensive *big*
extinct *dead*
extortionate *expensive*
extract *part*
extraordinary *strange, unusual*
fable *story*
fabulous *good*
facetious *funny*
facsimile *copy*
factory ship *boat, ship*
facts *information*
factual *official, real*
fad *fashion*
faintly *quietly*
fair *reliable*
fairy *spirit*
faith healer *doctor*
faith *religion*
faithful *friendly*
fake *artificial*
fallacy *mistake*
false *wrong*
falsehood *lie*
fame *success*
familiar *ordinary*
famished *hungry*
famous *popular, successful*
fantasize *pretend*
fantastic *strange, unusual*
faraway *distant*
farce *humour, play*
farcical *funny*
fare *price*
farm *grow*
fascinating *interesting*
fashionable *popular*
fast *quick*
fastidious *tidy*
fat *big*
father *man*
fatigued *tired*
faulty *bad*
favourable *good*
fearful *afraid*
fearless *brave*
feast *celebration, holiday, meal*
federation *government*
fee *price*
feeble *weak*
feed *eat*
feeling *opinion*
fellow *member*
felony *crime, offence*
fence *criminal*
ferret out *find*
ferry terminal *port*
ferry *boat, carry, ship*
festival *celebration, holiday*
feud *fight*

feverish *ill*
fiasco *failure*
fickle *unreliable*
fiddle *cheat*
field gun *gun*
field sports *sport*
file *records*
fill in *fill*
fill up *fill*
film star *performer*
filthy *dirty*
finale *finish*
finalize *close, finish, stop*
finance house *bank*
finance *money*
find out *find*
finish *close, stop*
fire *dismiss*
firm *hard*
first aider *nurse*
first class *good*
first-rate *good*
fish farm *farm*
fit *healthy*
fix *repair*
flame *fire*
flash *light*
flat *house, level*
flaunt *show*
flawed *bad*
flawless *good*
flee *escape, go, run*
fleeting *short*
fling *throw*
flock *group*
flog *sell, hit*
flop *failure*
flourish *succeed*
flush (with) *flat*
fly-over *bridge*
folk *people*
folklore *tradition*
following *next*
fondness *friendship*
fondness *love*
foolish *silly*
footbridge *bridge*
footpath *road*
force *make, strength, power*
foreigner *stranger*
forename *name*
forge *copy*
forger *criminal*
formidable *difficult*
fort *castle*
fortress *castle*
fortunate *good*
fortune *wealth*
foul *bad, dirty*
fraction *part, share*
fragment *part, share*
fragrance *smell*
frail *weak*
fraud *liar*
freezing *cold*
frenzied *mad, violent*
frequently *often*
fresco *picture*
fresh *new*
friendless *lonely, unpopular*
friendly *kind*
friendship *love*
frigate *boat, ship*
fright *fear*
frightened *afraid*
fritter away *waste*
frivolous *silly*
frontier *border*
frozen *cold, hard*
fruitful *successful*
fry *cook*
functional *useful*
fundamental *important*
funds *money*
furious *angry*
fuse *join*
futile *useless*
gadget *machine, tool*
gag *joke*
gain *get, obtain, increase*
gale *storm*
gallant *brave*
gallery *museum*
gallop *hurry*
game reserve *zoo*
games *sport*
gang *group*
gaping *open*
gash *cut*
gatecrash *enter*
gather *collect*
gathering *meeting*
gauge *measure*
gaunt *thin*
gaze *look*
gear *equipment*
generate *make*
generosity *kindness*
generous *kind*
gentleman *man*
genuine *real*
gesture *sign*

get *obtain, receive*
ghastly *bad, ugly*
ghost *spirit*
gifted *able, clever*
gigantic *big*
giggle *laugh*
give notice *dismiss*
glad *happy*
glare *light, look*
glimmer *light*
glimpse *look, see*
glitter *light*
glittering *light*
gloom *sadness*
gloomy *sad, unhappy*
gluttony *greed*
go *move, travel, leave*
gobble *eat*
godfather *man*
god-forsaken *lonely*
godmother *woman*
good *well-behaved, kind*
good-looking *beautiful*
goodness *honour*
goodwill *kindness*
gorge *eat*
gorgeous *beautiful*
gospel *Bible*
gossip *information, news, talk*
govern *control*
government *politics, power*
governmental *official*
GP (General Practitioner) *doctor*
GPO *mail*
gradual *slow*
graduate *succeed*
grammar school *school*
grandfather *man*
grandmother *woman*
grant *gift, give*
grasp *know*
gratify *please*
gratis *free*
gratuity *gift, income, pay*
grave *hole*
grave *important, serious*
grazing land *field*
great *good*
greedy *selfish*
Green Belt *field*
greengrocer's *shop*
grenade *weapon*
grief *sadness, suffering*
grief-stricken *sad, unhappy*
grieve *suffer*
grill *cook*
grimy *dirty*
grin *laugh*
gripping *interesting*
group *band*
grow up *grow*
grow *farm, increase*
gruesome *ugly*
grumble *complain*
guarantee *promise, insurance*
guarantor *sponsor*
guard *protect*
guardian *guard*
guerrilla war *war*
guerrilla *soldier*
guerrillas *armed forces*
gulp *drink*
gun *weapon*
guru *teacher*
guy *man*
habit *system, tradition*
hack *cut, writer*
halfwit *fool*
halt *stop*
hamlet *city*
hammer *hit*
hand gun *gun*
handbag *bag*
handbook *book*
handiwork *product*
handsome *beautiful*
handy *useful*
harangue *speech, talk*
harass *disturb*
harbour *port*
hard up *poor*
hard *difficult*
hardship *trouble*
hardy *strong*
harm *damage, hurt*
harmony *agreement, music*
harvest *farm, product*
hastily *quickly, suddenly*
hasty *fast, quick*
hatchback *car*
hate *dislike*
have no objection *agree*
have *own*
haven *shelter*
haversack *bag*
hazardous *dangerous*
head of state *ruler*
head teacher *principal, teacher*
head *leader*
headache *pain*
heal *cure, nurse*
hear *listen*

hearsay *information, news*
hearse *car*
height *size*
help *kindness, sponsor*
helper *assistant, partner, servant*
helpful *kind, useful*
helpless *weak*
herb garden *garden*
herd *group*
heroic *brave*
hesitant *doubtful, slow*
hesitation *doubt*
hibernate *sleep*
hibernation *sleep*
hidden *secret*
hideous *ugly*
High Commissioner *diplomat*
high street *street*
high-chair *seat*
highlands *mountain*
high-priced *expensive*
highway *road*
hilarious *funny*
hill *mountain*
hinder *prevent, stop*
hindrance *problem, trouble*
hint *advise, information, suggest, suggestion*
hire purchase *loan*
hire *appoint, buy*
historian *writer*
history *past*
hitch-hike *travel*
hoard *save*
hold office *govern*
hold *keep*
holdall *bag*
hollow *hole*
homicide *murder*
honest *reliable*
honour *respect, respect*
honourable *good*
hop *jump*
horizontal *level*
horrible *bad, ugly*
horror *fear*
hospitable *kind*
hospital doctor *doctor*
hostage *prisoner*
hostel *hotel*
hostilities *war*
hot *warm*
house breaker *criminal*
House of Commons *politics*
House of Lords *politics*
housekeeper *servant*
huge *big*
humane *kind*
humanity *people*
humorous *funny*
hunt *search*
hurl *throw*
hurricane *storm*
hurried *fast, quick*
hurriedly *quickly, suddenly*
hurt *angry, damage*
husband *man, partner*
hush *peace, quiet*
hushed *quiet*
hygienic *clean, healthy*
hymn *music, song*
hypocrite *liar*
hysterical *mad*
icon *picture*
icy *cold*
idea *opinion*
idiot *fool*
idiotic *silly*
idle *lazy*
idolize *like, love*
illogical *silly*
illusion *magic*
illusionist *performer*
illustrate *draw*
illustration *picture*
illustrator *artist*
imagine *guess, pretend, think*
imitate *copy, pretend*
imitation *artificial*
immaculate *clean*
immature *young*
immemorial *permanent*
immigrant *stranger*
immune *safe*
immunity *protection, safety*
immunize *protect*
impair *damage*
impasse *problem*
impeccable *good*
imperfect *bad*
imperial *royal*
imperturbable *calm*
implement *tool*
implore *ask*
imply *suggest*
important *valuable, serious, special*
imported *foreign*
impossibility *problem*
impostor *liar*
impoverished *poor*
impractical *useless*
impregnable *safe*

impression *idea, opinion*
inaccessible *distant*
inaccurate *wrong*
inanimate *dead*
inaugurate *begin*
incensed *angry*
incentive *reason*
incessantly *always*
income *pay, profit*
income tax *tax*
inconvenience *problem, trouble*
independent *free*
index *list*
indication *sign*
indignant *angry*
indisposed *ill*
individual *separate, person*
indolent *lazy*
indomitable *brave*
industry *business, trade*
ineffectual *useless*
inexpensive *cheap*
infamous *famous*
infant school *school*
infiltrate *enter*
infinite *big*
infinitesimal *little, small*
infirm *weak*
infirmity *illness*
influence *manage, power*
inform *tell*
information *knowledge, news*
informer *spy*
infrequent *few*
inherit *receive*
inheritance *income, pay*
inhibit *prevent*
initial *first*
initiate *begin*
injunction *order*
injure *hurt, damage*
injury *offence*
inn *hotel*
inner city *urban*
innumerable *many*
inquire *ask, search*
inquiry *question*
insane *mad*
inscribe *write*
insect *animal*
insecure *dangerous*
insist *make*
insolvent *poor*
inspect *check, look*
instalment *part*
instant *time*
instantaneous *short*
instinct *feeling, guess*
institute *begin*
instruct *order, teach, tell*
instructions *information*
instructor *teacher*
instrument *tool*
insular *separate*
insult *offence, offend*
insurance *protection*
integrity *honour*
intellect *mind, reason*
intelligence *information, reason*
intelligent *clever, sensible*
intend *hope*
intent *purpose*
intention *purpose, hope*
intercession *prayer*
interfere *disturb*
intermediate *middle*
Internet (the net) *network*
interpret *explain*
interrogation *question*
intersperse *mix*
interview *question*
intimidate *frighten*
intrepid *brave*
intrude *enter*
intuition *feeling, guess, reason*
invade *enter*
invariably *always*
invent *make*
inventory *list*
invest *save*
investigate *check*
investigation *question*
invite *ask*
invulnerable *safe*
IOU *cheque, loan*
irate *angry*
iron age *past*
irreplaceable *valuable*
irresistible *strong*
irritate *annoy*
isle *island*
isolated *lonely, separate*
jail *prison*
jalopy *car*
jazz band *band*
jazz *music*
jet engine *engine*
job *work, profession*
jog *run*
joke *humour*
jot *write*
journal *magazine*

journalism *press*
journalist *writer*
joy *happiness*
joyful *happy*
juggler *performer*
jumble *mix*
junior school *school*
junk *waste*
just *sensible*
Justice of the Peace *judge*
justify *prove*
juvenile *young*
keep *have, own, save*
key *important, serious*
kidnap *steal*
kidnapper *criminal, thief*
kill *punish*
killing *murder*
kin *family*
kind *good*
king *ruler*
king-size *big*
kiosk *shop*
kirk *church*
kit *equipment*
kitchen garden *garden*
kitchen *room*
knife *weapon*
knock *hit*
know *understand, learn, study*
label *ticket*
laborious *difficult*
lady *woman*
land *arrive*
landscape *painting*
large *big*
lasting *permanent*
laughing stock *fool*
launch *boat*
law *politics, order*
lazy *tired*
lead *guide*
leader *manager, principal*
lean *thin*
leap *jump*
learn *study, understand*
learning *knowledge*
lease *hire*
leave *go, holiday, move, travel*
lecture *speech, talk, teach*
lecturer *teacher*
legend *story*
leisure time *holiday*
leisurely *slow*
lend *hire*
length *size*
lengthy *long*
let *hire*
lethargic *tired*
letter *mail, message*
level *flat*
level-headed *sensible*
levy *tax*
liability *duty*
liberate *release, save, separate*
library *museum*
lie *mistake, pretend*
lifeguard *guard*
lifeless *dead*
lightweight *light*
like *love*
liking *friendship, love*
limit *border, control, prevent, stop*
limitless *big*
limousine *car*
limp *walk*
liner *boat, ship*
linger *wait*
link *join*
litany *prayer*
litter *waste*
little *small*
lively *fast, quick*
livestock *animal*
living room *room*
loan *hire*
loathe *dislike*
loathsome *bad*
local *near*
locality *place*
locality *region*
locate *find*
location *place*
lock *close*
locker *container*
lodge *house*
lodger *guest*
log *book*
loiter *wait*
lonely *separate, unpopular*
longstanding *long, permanent*
long-term *long*
look *see*
lounge *room*
love *friendship, like*
lovely *beautiful*
lover *partner*
loyalty *duty*
ludicrous *funny*
lukewarm *warm*
lull *quiet*
lullaby *song*

luminous *light*
lunatic *mad*
lunch *meal*
luxurious *good*
luxury *wealth*
lyrics *song*
mac *coat*
machine *tool*
machinery *machine*
macintosh *coat*
magician *performer*
magistrate *judge, official*
maiden *first*
mail *send*
main road *road*
maisonette *house*
make believe *pretend*
makeshift *temporary*
mammal *animal*
mammoth *big*
man *person*
manage *control, organize*
manager *leader*
mandatory *official*
manic *mad*
manipulate *organize*
mankind *people*
manner *way*
manor *house*
mansion *house*
manslaughter *murder*
manual *book*
manufacture *make*
marathon *race*
march *walk*
marina *port*
marines *armed forces*
mark time *wait*
market garden *farm, garden*
market *sell*
mask *hide*
massacre *kill, murder*
massive *heavy, big*
match *game*
mate *friend*
mature *grow, ready*
meadow *field*
mean *middle*
measurements *size*
mechanism *machine*
medal *prize*
media *press*
median *middle*
medication *medicine*
medicine *cure*
medieval *old*
meditate *think*
meditation *prayer, worship*
Meeting House *church*
melody *music*
memorize *remember, study*
menacing *dangerous*
menagerie *zoo*
mend *fix, repair*
mentality *mind*
mention *talk*
mentor *guide*
mercenaries *armed forces*
mercenary *soldier*
merchant bank *bank*
merciful *kind*
mercy *kindness, pity*
merge *join, mix*
merry *happy*
messy *dirty*
method *system, way*
meticulous *careful*
metropolitan *urban*
microscopic *little, small*
mid- *middle*
midday *day*
midnight *day*
might *strength, power*
mighty *strong*
migraine *pain*
military police *police*
militia *armed forces*
mime *perform*
mind *reason*
mine shaft *tunnel*
mine *dig, hole*
minesweeper *boat, ship*
mingle *mix*
miniature *little, small*
minster *church*
minute *little, small*
minutes *records*
miraculous *strange, unusual*
miscalculation *mistake*
mischievous *bad*
misdemeanour *crime, offence*
miserable *sad, unhappy*
miserly *greedy*
misery *sadness, suffering*
misfortune *trouble*
misjudgement *mistake*
misleading *wrong*
missile *weapon*
missing *absent*
mistaken *wrong*
mistress *partner*
misunderstanding *mistake*

modern *new*
modernize *improve*
modify *change*
moist *wet*
momentary *short*
monarch *ruler*
monarchy *government*
money order *cheque*
money *wealth*
moneylender *bank*
monograph *book*
monologue *speech*
monsoon *rain*
monstrous *ugly*
monthly *magazine, often*
monumental *big*
moonlight *light*
morning *day*
mortgage *loan*
mosaic *picture*
mosque *church*
motel *hotel*
mother *woman*
motive *reason*
motorway *road*
move *go, carry, send*
movie star *performer*
MP (Member of Parliament) *politics*
muddy *dirty*
mugger *criminal*
multiply *increase*
mumble *talk*
mural *picture*
murder *kill*
murderer *criminal*
murky *dark*
murmur *talk*
musical *play*
musician *performer*
muster *meet*
muted *quiet*
mysterious *strange, unusual*
mystery *secret*
mystical *holy*
myth *story*
nanny *servant*
nap *sleep, sleep*
nasty *bad*
nation *state, people*
natural *normal, ordinary*
naturally *simply*
nature reserve *park*
naughty *bad*
navy *armed forces*
near *next*
neat *tidy*
necessitate *make*
needy *poor*
neglect *forget*
negotiation *discussion*
neighbour *friend*
neighbouring *near*
nervous *afraid*
neurotic *mad*
neutrality *peace*
neutralize *prevent, stop*
never-ending *long*
New Testament *Bible*
new *modern*
newcomer *stranger*
newfangled *modern, new*
news *information, press*
newspaper *magazine, press*
next *near*
nibble *eat*
niche *hole*
nickname *name*
night *day*
nil *nothing*
nobody *nothing*
noiseless *quiet*
noiselessly *quietly*
noisy *loud*
nominate *choose*
none *nothing*
noon *day*
normal *ordinary*
notable *famous*
note *message*
noted *famous*
notice *look, see, sign*
notify *advise*
notion *idea*
notorious *famous*
nourishment *food*
novel *book, new*
novelist *writer*
nuclear war *war*
nuclear waste *waste*
nuclear weapons *weapon*
numerous *many*
nuncio *diplomat*
nursery school *school*
nursery *farm*
nutrition *food*
oath *promise*
obedient *reliable, well-behaved*
obese *fat*
objective *purpose, real*
obligation *duty*
oblige *make, help*
obliging *good, well-behaved*

obnoxious *bad*
observe *look, obey, see*
obsolete *useless*
obtain *get*
occupant *guest*
occupation *work*
occupied *busy*
occupy *have*
odd *funny, unusual, strange*
odour *smell*
off *bad*
offence *crime*
offer *suggestion*
official *leader, manager, formal*
oil painting *painting*
old master *painting*
Old Testament *Bible*
old *traditional*
olden days *past*
old-fashioned *old, traditional*
omit *forget*
onerous *heavy*
opaque *dark*
open prison *prison*
open *release*
opening *opportunity*
opera house *theatre*
opera *performance*
operate *perform*
operetta *performance*
opinion *guess*
oppose *prevent, stop*
optimistic *happy*
opulence *wealth*
opulent *rich*
orchard *field*
orchestrate *manage, organize*
order *ask, law, tell*
orderly *tidy*
ordinary *normal*
organization *system*
organize *manage, plan, prepare*
original *first, new, painting, special*
originate *begin*
ornamental garden *garden*
ornamental *beautiful*
ostentation *pride*
ostentatious *proud*
outlandish *strange, unusual*
outline *plan, prepare*
output *product*
outsider *stranger*
outsize *big*
overcast *dark*
overcoat *coat*
overdraft *loan*
overhear *listen*
overloaded *heavy*
overlook *forget*
over-priced *expensive*
oversight *mistake*
overture *offer*
overweight *fat*
own *have*
pacifism *peace*
pack *group*
pact *agreement*
paddock *field*
pagoda *church*
pain *suffering*
painkiller *medicine*
painstaking *careful*
painter *artist*
painting *picture*
palace *house*
palliative *cure*
pamphlet *book, magazine*
panic *fear, fear*
pantomime *performance, play*
paperback *book*
parable *story*
paramedic *nurse*
paramilitaries *armed forces*
paranoid *mad*
park *field*
parliament *politics*
parole *release*
part *share*
partner *assistant, member*
party politics *politics*
party *celebration, meeting*
pass *ticket*
passion *feeling, love*
past its sell-by date *bad*
pastiche *painting*
pastime *game*
pasture *field*
path *road, street*
patrol *guard, protect*
patron *guard, friend, sponsor*
pause *stop*
pawnbroker *bank*
pay *income*
pay attention *listen*
peace *quiet*
peaceful *quiet*
peacefully *quietly*
peacefulness *peace, quiet*
peak *mountain, top*
peckish *hungry*
peculiar *funny, strange, unusual*
peddle *sell*

penitentiary *prison*
pennant *flag*
penniless *poor*
pension *income, pay*
perceive *see*
percentage *part, share*
perception *reason*
perfume *smell*
period *time*
periodic *temporary*
periodical *magazine*
perjury *lie*
permanently *always*
permission *licence*
permit *licence, ticket*
pernicious *bad*
perpetual *long, permanent*
persecute *punish*
persecution *punishment*
persuade *ask*
pester *disturb*
pet *animal*
petite *little, small*
petition *prayer, worship*
petrol engine *engine*
pew *seat*
phobia *fear*
photocopy *copy, picture*
photograph *picture*
physician *doctor*
pick *choose, vote*
pickpocket *criminal, thief*
picnic *meal*
picturesque *beautiful*
piece *part, share*
piecemeal *separately*
piercing *loud*
pilfer *steal*
pilgrimage *adventure*
pinch *steal*
pioneer *begin*
pirate *steal*
pistol *gun*
piston *engine*
pit *hole*
pitch *throw*
place *region*
placid *calm*
plagiarize *steal*
plain *simple*
plan *purpose, prepare*
plateau *mountain*
play *performance*
playground *park*
playhouse *theatre*
playing field *park*
plead *ask*
pleasant *nice*
pleased *happy*
pleasure *happiness*
pledge *promise*
plod *walk*
plot *garden, secret*
plough *dig*
plummet *fall*
plump *fat*
plush *rich*
poacher *thief*
pocket money *money*
poet *writer*
pointless *useless*
poised *ready*
police *guard, protect*
polish *clean*
polished *clean*
polite *well-behaved*
political party *politics*
politics *power*
poll *vote*
polluted *dirty*
pomposity *pride*
pompous *proud*
ponder *think*
ponderous *heavy*
pop group *band*
pop music *music*
pop star *performer*
popularize *explain*
population *people*
port *city*
portable *light*
portion *part, share*
portly *fat*
portrait *painting*
posh *fashionable*
possess *have, own*
possibility *opportunity*
post *job, mail, send, send*
postal order *cheque*
postcard *message*
postgraduate *student*
pothole *hole*
pour *rain*
power *strength*
powerful *able, strong*
practical joke *joke*
practise *prepare*
prayer *worship*
preach *talk*
prearrange *organize, plan, prepare*
precarious *dangerous, unreliable*
precise *accurate*

predicament *problem, trouble*
preferable *favourite*
prehistoric *old*
prehistory *past*
premises *office*
prep school (preparatory school) *school*
prepare *organize, plan*
prepared *ready*
preposterous *funny, silly*
prescription *cure*
present *gift, give*
preservation *protection*
preserve *keep, save*
preside *manage, organize*
president *ruler*
press agent *press*
press release *news*
pretence *lie*
pretentious *proud*
pretty *beautiful*
prevent *stop*
priceless *valuable*
primary *important*
prime *prepare*
principal *manager, teacher*
print *picture, publish, write*
prise open *open*
prize money *prize*
probe *search*
problem *trouble*
problematic *doubtful*
procedure *way*
proceeds *profit*
procure *get, obtain*
produce *make*
product *result*
profession *job, work*
professor *teacher*
proficient *professional*
profit margin *profit*
profitable *good, successful*
profusion *plenty*
prohibit *control, prevent, stop*
prohibitive *expensive*
prolific *many*
promenade *street*
promote *sponsor*
promoter *sponsor*
prompt *fast, quick, suggest*
promptly *suddenly*
proper *formal*
propitious *good*
proposal *offer, suggestion*
propose *suggest, plan*
proposer *sponsor*
proposition *suggestion*
prospect *search*
prosper *succeed*
prosperity *success, wealth*
prosperous *rich, successful*
protect *guard*
protected *safe*
protection *help, insurance, safety*
protest *complain*
proud *selfish*
provide *give*
providential *holy*
provisional *temporary*
provisions *equipment, food*
prowl *walk*
prudent *careful*
pry *look, search*
psychiatric nurse *nurse*
psychiatrist *doctor*
psychologist *doctor*
pub *hotel*
public *people*
public gardens *park*
public school *school*
public servant *official, servant*
publication *magazine*
publicize *advertise*
pull *move*
pun *joke*
punch *hit*
purchase *buy*
purify *clean*
pursue *follow*
push *move*
put a deposit on *order*
put off *avoid*
put right *repair, fix*
putrid *bad*
qualified *able, professional*
quarry *hole*
quartet *orchestra*
quay *port*
queen *ruler*
queer *strange, unusual*
query *question*
quest *adventure*
questionable *doubtful*
questionnaire *question*
queue *wait*
quick *fast*
quicken *hurry*
quiet *peace*
quintet *orchestra*
quit *leave*
quotation *part, price*
quote *repeat*
race meeting *race*

race *people*
racecourse *race*
racing car *car*
radiant *beautiful, light*
raincoat *coat*
raise *grow*
rally *game, meet, meeting*
ranch *farm*
rancid *bad*
range *mountain*
ransack *search, steal*
ransom *buy*
rant *talk*
rapid *fast, quick*
rapidly *quickly*
rare *valuable*
rash *silly*
rate *price, speed*
ratify *agree*
rations *equipment*
ravenous *hungry*
raw *cold*
readily *simply*
reality *life*
realize *know*
reap *farm*
rear *farm*
reason *mind*
reasonable *sensible*
rebuff *refuse*
rebuke *blame*
rebut *answer*
recall *remember*
recapitulate *repeat*
receive *get, obtain*
recent *modern, new*
recognize *know*
recollect *remember*
recommend *advise, guide*
reconnoitre *search, see*
recreation ground *park*
recruit *appoint, hire*
rectify *fix, repair*
rector *principal*
redirect *send*
redundant *useless*
reef *island*
referee *judge, judge*
referendum *vote*
refine *improve*
reflect *think*
reform *improve*
refrain *avoid*
refreshing *nice*
refreshments *food, meal*
refuge *shelter*
refugee *stranger*
refund *pay*
refuse *waste*
regal *royal*
region *place*
register *list*
regular *soldier*
regularly *often*
regulate *control, manage, organize, prevent, stop*
regulation *order, law, order*
rehabilitate *fix, repair*
reign *govern*
reigning *royal*
reimburse *pay*
reinforce *help*
reinforcement *help*
reject *refuse*
rejuvenate *repair, fix*
relation *family*
relative *family*
relaxed *informal*
relay *carry, race*
reliability *honour*
reliable *good*
relief *help*
religious *holy*
remand centre *prison*
remedy *cure, fix, medicine, repair*
remind *remember, suggest*
reminder *message, suggestion*
reminisce *remember*
remote *distant*
renovate *fix, repair*
renowned *famous*
rent *price*
rental *price*
repair *fix*
repay *pay*
repeatedly *again, often*
repel *offend*
repellent *ugly*
repentant *sorry*
replenish *fill*
replica *copy*
reply *answer, answer*
report *information, news*
reprimand *punish, punishment*
reproduce *copy, repeat*
reproduction *copy, picture*
reptile *animal*
republic *government*
repulsive *ugly*
reputable *good*
request *ask*
require *ask*

requisition *order, order*
rescue *help, save*
research *learn, study*
resent *dislike*
reserve *choose, order*
resist *fight*
respect *like*
respectful *well-behaved*
respond *answer*
response *answer*
responsibility *duty*
responsible *reliable*
rest *peace, quiet, sleep, sleep*
restful *nice*
restore *fix, repair*
restrain *control, prevent, stop*
restrict *control, prevent, stop*
result *product*
retail price *price*
retail *sell*
retain *keep, have, own*
retell *repeat*
retire *leave*
retort *answer, answer*
retribution *punishment*
return *profit*
reunion *meeting*
reveal *show*
revenge *punishment*
revere *respect*
reverence *respect*
review *magazine*
revise *learn, study*
revive *fix, repair, cure*
revolting *bad*
revolutionary *modern, new*
revolver *gun*
revue *play*
reward *gift, give, income, pay*
rhythm and blues *music*
riddle *question*
ride *travel*
ridiculous *funny, silly*
rifle *gun*
righteous *good*
rigid *hard*
rinse *clean*
ripe *ready*
ripen *grow*
riposte *answer*
risky *dangerous, unreliable*
road map *map*
road *street*
roar *shout*
roast *cook*
rob *steal*
robber *criminal, thief*
robes *uniform*
robust *healthy*
rock music *music*
rocket motor *engine*
rocking chair *seat*
rodent *animal*
rotten *bad*
rough *violent*
route *road*
routine *system*
row *fight*
rowing boat *boat*
rubbish *waste*
rucksack *bag*
ruinous *bad*
rule *govern, law, order, system*
rummage *search*
rumour *news*
rush *hurry, run*
rushed *fast, quick*
sabbatical *holiday*
sack *dismiss, bag*
sacred *holy*
sad *unhappy*
sadness *suffering*
safari park *zoo*
safe *container*
safeguard *guard, protect*
safety *protection*
saga *story*
salary *income, pay*
saloon *car*
sample *share*
sanctuary *shelter*
sarcasm *humour*
satchel *bag*
satire *humour*
satisfaction *happiness*
satisfied *happy*
satisfy *please*
satisfying *nice*
saturate *fill*
saturated *wet*
saunter *walk*
scamper *run*
scan *look, read, search, see*
scandalize *offend*
scandalous *bad*
scanty *few*
scarce *few*
scare *frighten*
scared *afraid*
scent *smell*
sceptical *doubtful*
schizophrenic *mad*

scholar *student*
scholarship *knowledge*
school *college*
schoolboy *student*
schoolgirl *student*
scour *search*
scrawl *write*
scream *shout*
scribble *write*
scrub *clean*
scrupulous *careful, honest*
scrutinize *check*
scuffle *fight*
sculptor *artist*
scurry *run*
seaboard *coast*
seal *close*
seashore *coast*
season *time, weather*
seasonal *temporary*
secluded *lonely, secret*
secondary school *school*
secret agent *spy*
secrete *hide*
section *part, share*
secure institution *prison*
secure *close, keep, safe*
security *protection, safety*
sedate *calm*
seek *search*
segment *part, share*
segregate *separate*
seize *capture*
select *choose, good, vote*
selfish *greedy, proud*
selfishness *greed*
semi-detached house *house*
seminary *college*
send *move*
senile *old*
sensational *interesting*
senseless *silly*
sensible *good, reliable*
sentence *punish, punishment*
sentry *guard*
serenade *song*
serene *calm*
serialize *publish*
serious *important*
sermon *speech*
service *help*
settee *seat*
sever *cut*
several *many*
sewage *waste*
sewer *tunnel*
shack *house*
shadow *follow*
shaft *hole*
share *part*
shatter *damage*
shelter *protect, safety*
sheltered *safe*
shield *protect*
shift *carry, move, send*
shiny *clean*
ship *boat, carry, send*
shock *offend*
shoddy *bad*
shop-lift *steal*
shoplifter *thief*
shopping mall *shop*
short-term *temporary*
shotgun *gun*
shout *talk*
show *performance, play*
shower *rain*
shrewd *clever, sensible*
shuffle *mix, walk*
shun *avoid*
sick *ill*
sicken *offend*
sickening *bad*
sickness *illness*
side arm *gun*
side street *street*
sight *see*
signal *sign*
signpost *sign*
silence *quiet*
silent *quiet*
silently *quietly*
simplify *explain*
sin *offence*
sincere *honest*
sincerity *honour*
sing *perform*
singer *performer*
singly *separately*
singular *special, unusual*
sink *fall*
sip *drink*
sister *woman*
site *place*
sixth form college *school*
sketch *draw, picture*
skilful *good, able, clever*
skim *read*
skirmish *fight*
slam *close*
slap *hit*
slash *cut*

slaughter *kill, murder*
slave *servant*
slay *kill*
sleepy *tired*
slender *thin*
slice *cut*
slim *thin*
sling *throw*
slip *mistake*
slit *cut*
slothful *lazy*
sluggish *slow, tired*
slump *fall*
smack *hit*
small *little*
smallholding *farm*
smart *clever, fashionable*
smash *damage*
smile *laugh, laugh*
smooth *flat*
smoothly *simply*
snack *meal*
snack bar *restaurant*
snare *capture*
snicker *laugh*
snigger *laugh*
snobbery *pride*
snobbish *proud*
snooze *sleep, sleep*
snowstorm *storm*
soaked *wet*
soaring *high*
society *people*
sodden *wet*
sofa *seat*
solemn *serious*
solitary *lonely, lonely*
soloist *performer*
solution *answer*
sombre *dark*
somebody *person*
someone *person*
song *music*
sorcery *magic*
sorrow *sadness, suffering*
sort *kind*
soul *spirit*
sound *healthy*
sow *farm*
spacious *big*
spar *fight*
sparkling *light*
sparse *few*
spasm *pain*
speak *talk*
Special Branch *police*
special *police, unusual*
specialist *professional*
specialized *professional*
speculate *guess*
speed *hurry*
speedy *fast, quick*
spinster *woman*
spiritual *holy*
sport *game*
sports car *car*
spot *see*
spotless *clean*
spread *increase, meal*
spring-clean *clean*
sprint *race, run*
spy *look, search, see*
squalid *dirty*
squander *waste*
stadium *theatre*
staff college *college*
stage fright *fear*
stale *bad*
stall *shop*
stamina *strength*
stampede *fear*
standard *flag, ordinary*
star *perform, performer*
stare *look, see*
startle *frighten*
starving *hungry*
station wagon *car*
statistics *information*
statute *law*
stealthily *quietly*
steam engine *engine*
steep *high*
stench *smell*
sterile *clean*
stew *cook*
still life *painting*
still *quiet*
stillness *quiet*
stimulant *medicine*
stimulus *reason*
stink *smell*
stir-fry *cook*
stone age *past*
stool *seat*
stop *prevent*
stop press *press*
store *keep, save, shop*
stout *fat*
strange *funny, unusual*
stream *river*
street *road*
strength *power*

stride *walk*
strident *loud*
strike *hit*
strive *try*
stroll *walk*
strong *healthy*
stronghold *castle, shelter*
struggle *fight*
strut *walk*
study *learn, room*
stuff *fill*
stupid *silly*
sturdy *strong*
style *fashion*
stylish *beautiful, fashionable*
subconscious *mind*
subdivide *separate*
sublet *hire*
sublime *high*
submarine *boat*
submarine *ship*
submit *suggest*
subpoena *order*
subsequent *next*
subside *fall*
subsidize *give*
substandard *bad*
substantiate *prove*
substitute *replace*
suburb *city*
suburban *urban*
subway *tunnel*
succeed *follow*
successive *next*
suck *drink*
suffering *pain, trouble*
sufficient *enough*
suggest *advise*
suicide *murder*
suitability *qualification*
suitable *good*
suitcase *bag*
summit *mountain, top*
summons *order*
sunlight *light*
sunshine *light*
super *good*
superfluous *useless*
superior *leader, principal, valuable*
supermarket *shop*
supernatural *strange, unusual*
superstition *magic*
supervise *control, manage, organize*
supervisor *manager*
supper *meal*
supplement *price*
supplies *food*
support *help, help, sponsor*
supporter *partner, sponsor*
suppose *guess*
supposition *guess*
suppress *control, hide, prevent, stop*
supreme being *god*
supremo *leader*
surcharge *price*
surface mail *mail*
surgeon *doctor*
surname *name*
survey *measure*
suspect *guess*
suspicion *guess*
swagger *walk*
swear *promise*
sweep *clean*
swell *increase*
swift *fast, quick*
swiftly *quickly*
swig *drink*
swindle *cheat*
swindler *criminal, liar, thief*
swing *music*
sympathetic *friendly, kind*
sympathize *like*
sympathizer *member, partner*
sympathy *kindness, pity*
symphony orchestra *orchestra*
synthetic *artificial*
system *network*
table *list*
tactics *way*
tail *follow*
take flight *fear*
take revenge *punish*
take *receive*
takings *profit*
tale *story*
talented *able, clever*
talk *speech*
tall *high*
tangible *real*
tank *container*
tanker *boat, ship*
tap *hit, listen*
tapestry *picture*
target *purpose*
tariff *price*
tarnished *dirty*
task *job, work*
taste *eat*
tasteful *fashionable*
taxation *tax*
tax-free *free*

taxi *car*
tea *meal*
teach *explain*
teacher *guide*
team *group*
teashop *restaurant*
technique *way*
tedious *slow*
teem *rain*
teenage *young*
teletext *news*
televise *publish*
tell *order*
temperature *weather*
temple *church*
tempo *speed*
temporary *short*
tend *nurse*
tender *offer*
tepid *warm*
term *time*
terminal *ill*
terminate *close, finish, stop*
terraced house *house*
terrified *afraid*
terrify *frighten*
territory *place, region*
terror *fear*
terrorize *frighten*
text book *book*
the legal profession *profession*
the medical profession *profession*
the teaching profession *profession*
theme park *park*
theological college *college*
theory *guess*
therapy *cure*
thesaurus *book*
thief *criminal*
thought *idea*
thrash *hit*
threaten *frighten*
threatening *dangerous*
thrill *happiness*
thrilling *interesting*
thrive *succeed*
thriving *successful*
throne *seat*
thunderous *loud*
thunderstorm *rain*
tidy *clean*
timeless *good*
timetable *list*
tiny *little, small*
tip *gift, pay*
tirade *speech*
tiring *difficult*
title *name*
titled *royal*
to give your word *promise*
to keep your word *promise*
toast *drink*
toilet *room*
token *sign, ticket*
tolerant *good, kind, sensible*
toll bridge *bridge*
toll *tax*
tome *book*
tonic *medicine*
top secret *secret*
torment *frighten, hurt, pain, suffering*
tornado *storm*
torture *pain, punish, punishment, suffering*
toss *throw*
total *full*
touch down *arrive*
tour *travel*
tourer *car*
tournament *game*
towering *high*
town *city*
toxic waste *waste*
trace *copy*
track *road*
trade *work*
traditional *old*
traffic police *police*
tragedy *disaster, play*
trail *follow*
train *prepare, teach*
tranquil *quiet*
tranquillity *peace, quiet*
transcendental *holy*
transcribe *copy*
transfer *carry, move, send*
transform *change*
transgression *offence*
transient *short, temporary*
transmit *send*
transport *carry, move, send*
trap *capture*
travel *go*
travelers' check *check, cheque*
travellers' cheque *check, cheque*
trawler *boat, ship*
treacherous *dangerous, unreliable*
treasure *love*
treat *cure, nurse*
treatise *book*
treatment *cure*
trek *travel*
trench *hole*

trend *fashion*
trespass *enter*
tribe *people*
tributary *river*
trio *orchestra*
triptych *painting*
triumph *success*
triumphant *successful*
troops *armed forces*
tropical *warm*
trouble *disturb, problem, worry*
troublesome *difficult*
truce *peace*
trudge *walk*
true *level*
trunk *container*
trustworthy *honest, good, reliable, well-behaved*
truthful *honest*
try *judge*
tug *boat, ship*
tumble *fall*
tune *music*
tunnel *dig, hole*
turbine engine *engine*
turnover *profit*
tutor *teacher*
twilight *light*
twinge *pain*
type *kind*
typhoon *storm*
typical *normal, ordinary*
tyrant *ruler*
ultimatum *order*
umpire *judge, judge*
unassailable *safe*
unattached *separate*
unbearable *heavy*
unbridled *free*
unceasingly *always*
uncertain *doubtful*
uncertainty *doubt*
unchecked *free*
uncle *man*
unconventional *informal*
uncork *open*
uncover *open*
undercover *secret*
undercut *sell*
underpass *tunnel*
understand *learn, know*
understanding *agreement, reason*
understatement *lie*
undertaking *promise*
underwrite *promise*
unearth *find*
unease *worry*
uneasy *worried*
unexpectedly *suddenly*
unfasten *open*
unfenced *open*
unhappy *sad*
unhurried *slow*
uniformed officer *police*
unique *special, valuable*
unison *agreement*
unite *join*
universal *full*
university college *college*
university *college*
unjust *bad*
unlock *open*
unoccupied *free*
unpopular *lonely*
unprecedented *first, new*
unpredictable *unreliable*
unrestrained *free*
unruffled *calm*
unsafe *dangerous*
unsightly *ugly*
unstable *dangerous*
untrue *wrong*
unusual *strange*
unwanted *unpopular*
upland *mountain*
upright *good*
upset *annoy, disturb, offend*
upshot *result*
up-to-date *modern, new*
urge *advise, guide, suggest*
useless *bad*
utilitarian *useful*
vacant *free*
vacation *holiday*
vain *proud, selfish*
valiant *brave*
value added tax (VAT) *tax*
value *like, love, respect*
vanity *pride*
variety *kind*
vast *big*
vault *jump*
velocity *speed*
venerable *old*
venerable *traditional*
venerate *respect*
venture *try*
veracity *honour*
verification *proof*
verify *prove*
vermin *animal*
vestments *uniform*

vet *doctor*
veteran *soldier*
vex *annoy*
viaduct *bridge*
vicarage *house*
vicious *bad*
victimization *punishment*
victimize *punish*
victor *winner*
victorious *successful*
victory *success*
view *opinion*
viewpoint *opinion*
vigilant *ready*
vigorous *healthy, strong*
vile *bad*
village *city*
villainous *bad*
vindicate *prove*
vineyard *farm*
virtuous *good*
vision *hope*
visit *enter*
visitor *guest*
visualize *see*
vital *important, serious*
vitality *strength*
vocation *job*
vocation *profession, work*
vogue *fashion*
voice mail *message*
volume *book, size*
vote for *choose*
vouch for *promise*
voucher *ticket*
vow *promise, promise*
waddle *walk*
wage war *fight*
wages *income, pay*
walk *travel*
wander *travel*
war *fight*
warden *guard*
warm up *prepare*
warn *advise, guide, suggest*
warning *information, suggestion*
warrant *licence*
warranty *insurance*
wary *careful*
wash *clean*
watch *look, see*
watchdog *guard*
water sports *sport*
watercolour, watercolor *painting*
watercourse *river*
waterlogged *wet*
waterway *river*
way *road*
weaken *damage*
wealth *money, plenty, rich*
weather forecast *weather*
web *network*
weekly *magazine, often*
weight *size*
weightless *light*
weighty *heavy*
weld *join*
well *healthy*
well-dressed *fashionable*
whimsy *humour*
whine *complain*
whip *hit*
whisper *talk*
white lie *lie*
who-dunnit? *book*
whole *full*
wholehearted *honest*
wholesale price *price*
wholesome *good*
wicked *bad*
width *size*
wife *partner, woman*
willowy *thin*
win *get, obtain, succeed*
winnings *profit*
wintry *cold*
wisdom *knowledge*
wise *clever, sensible*
wish *hope*
witchcraft *magic*
withhold *keep*
witty *funny*
woman *person*
wood cut *picture*
word *promise*
work *perform*
workable *good*
workplace *office*
work-shy *lazy*
world wide web *network*
worried *afraid*
worry *suffer*
worship *like, love, prayer, religion*
WWW (world wide web) *network*
yacht *boat*
yawning *open*
yell *shout*
yield *product*
youthful *young*
zero *nothing*
zone *place, region*
zoological gardens *zoo*